A Cinema of Contradiction

For Nicholas McDowell

A Cinema of Contradiction
Spanish Film in the 1960s

Sally Faulkner

Edinburgh University Press

© Sally Faulkner, 2006

Edinburgh University Press Ltd
22 George Square, Edinburgh

Typeset in 11/13pt Ehrhardt MT
by Servis Filmsetting Ltd, Manchester, and
printed and bound in Great Britain by
Antony Rowe Ltd, Chippenham, Wilts

A CIP record for this book is available from the British Library

ISBN 0 7486 2160 1 (hardback)

The right of Sally Faulkner
to be identified as author of this work
has been asserted in accordance with
the Copyright, Designs and Patents Act 1988.

#63399160

Contents

Acknowledgements

This book could not have been written without grants from the British Academy and the School of Modern Languages, University of Exeter, which enabled me to carry out research in Spain, and sabbatical leave, jointly funded by the Arts and Humanities Research Council and the University of Exeter, which gave me time to complete the project. A grant from the University of Exeter's Keith Whinnom Memorial Fund enabled me to attend the 41st International Festival of Cinema, Gijón, Spain.

Much of this work was presented as seminar and conference papers at the School of Modern Languages and Centre for Research in Film Studies Research Seminar, University of Exeter; the 50th Anniversary Programme Research Seminars, Department of Hispanic, Portuguese and Latin-American Studies, University of Bristol; the Annual Conference of the Association of Hispanists of Great Britain and Ireland, University of Cambridge; the 'Hispanic Cinemas: The Local and the Global' Conference, University of London, and the Hispanic Research Seminar, University of Leeds. I would like to thank the organisers and those who attended for their views. Earlier versions of Chapters 4, 5 and 6 appeared in *Modern Language Review* ('A Cinema of Contradiction: *La tía Tula* [Picazo 1964] and the *Nuevo Cine Español*', 99, 3 [2004]); *Bulletin of Spanish Studies* ('Identity and Nationality in Basilio Martín Patino's *Nueve cartas a Berta* [1965]', 83, 3 [2006]); and *Modern Language Notes* ('Ageing and Coming of Age in Carlos Saura's *La caza* [*The Hunt* 1965]', 120, 2 [2005]).

This book is in part a record of discussion and debate with many colleagues and friends over a number of years. Peter Evans, Susan Hayward, Chris Perriam, Tim Rees, Alison Sinclair and Paul Julian Smith read parts of the manuscript at different stages, and I would like to thank them for their comments. John Hopewell, Duncan Petrie, Núria Triana-Toribio, Kathleen Vernon and Gareth Walters also provided encouragement at different moments as the project developed. Elizabeth Matthews and Andrew Ginger offered advice on questions of art, as did Anthony Faulkner on music, Derek Gagen and Mike Thompson on theatre and Tom Caldin on translations. Helena López and Rob Stone kindly sent me copies of their work. Marga Lobo, Trinidad del Río (Screenings), Javier Herrera

(Library) and their colleagues of the Filmoteca Española, Madrid have always provided me with great support and encouragement. Thanks also to Maruja Rincón Tapias for her generosity and advice. I am grateful to the directors Mario Camus, Julio Diamante, Antxón Eceiza, Basilio Martín Patino and the poet Guillermo Carnero for answering my questions about their work.

Thanks, as always, to my parents, Anthony and Helen Faulkner, who took me to Spain in 1975, and brother, David Faulkner, with whom I began to learn Spanish. Without doubt my greatest debt is to Nicholas McDowell; I dedicate the book to him.

List of Illustrations and Figures

Every reasonable effort has been made to trace those holding rights to the images reproduced and to acquire the relevant permissions.

Textual Note

I have used the original Spanish titles of films in the text, but have given English translations in brackets on first mention and in the index. I have given the International English Title according to the International Movie Database, http://www.imdb.com; for those films that do not have one, I have consulted D'Lugo (1997) and Triana-Toribio (2003), or offered my own translations.

I have translated quotations into English, unless they are very short, in which case English only is given. These translations are my own, unless otherwise indicated.

For information on the filmographies of directors, actors and technical teams I have consulted the International Movie Database.

I have used two abbreviations in the text: NCE, to refer to the 'Nuevo Cine Español' (New Spanish Cinema); and VCE, 'Viejo Cine Español' (Old, or Popular, Spanish Cinema).

Introduction: Contexts

A key decade in world cinema, the 1960s was also a crucial era of change in Spain. This book analyses six films that reflect and interpret some of the political, social, economic and cultural transformations of this period. The coexistence of traditional and modern values following rapid industrialisation and urbanisation, and the timid acceptance of limited change by Franco's authoritarian regime, are symptoms of the uneven modernity that scholars argue characterises Spain of the modern era.[1] Contradiction – the unavoidable effect of that unevenness – is the conceptual terrain explored by the six filmmakers discussed here, whose work ranges across experiences of family and gender roles, rural and urban life, provincial and cosmopolitan mentalities, religious belief and ceremony, and youth and ageing.

The 1960s is also an important decade in the history of Spanish cinema because, as in other Western film industries, this was a period of transition. While television ownership eroded cinema audiences towards the end of the decade onwards, commercial domestic films could still attract massive attendance in the 1960s, with audiences occasionally exceeding four million. Promoters and producers of art film appealed to a more select demographic, in particular the growing number of university students and graduates, in anticipation of this future competition from television.[2] In response to these twin phenomena of a still robust commercial industry and a developing art alternative, I devote Part I of this study to the *Viejo Cine Español* (VCE) (the old, commercial, or popular, Spanish cinema), which was so called to highlight its differences from the *Nuevo Cine Español* (NCE) (the new, art, or auteurist, Spanish cinema), which is the subject of Part II.[3]

The examples of the VCE I analyse in Part I represent the two key tendencies of the commercial industry in the period. Pedro Lazaga's *La ciudad no es para mí* (*The City's Not For Me* 1965) (Chapter 2) was a blockbuster, attracting almost 4,300,000 spectators, and, according to a recent calculation,[4] taking the equivalent of 440,348 euros at the box office, which made it one of the most widely seen and commercially successful films of the decade. Conversely, Fernando Palacios's *La gran familia* (*The Great Family* 1962) (Chapter 1) had the lowest figures for audience attendance of all the films studied in this book, with just over 20,000 spectators.[5] It made a profit (25,000 euros), however, not through success at the box office, but rather through the government subsidies it was awarded when it was given the classification 'National Interest'. In Part II, I analyse four different examples of Spain's contemporary art cinema, the NCE. Mario Camus's *Los farsantes* (*Frauds* 1963) (Chapter 3) is typical of the movement as a whole in its failure to attract audiences (it had 62,000 spectators and made just 5,000 euros), though it is interesting to note that this was three times the attendance figure for *La gran familia*. Miguel Picazo's *La tía Tula* (*Aunt Tula* 1964) and Basilio Martín Patino's *Nueve cartas a Berta* (*Nine Letters to Berta* 1965) (Chapters 4 and 5) are exceptional cases of success,[6] with 408,000 and 417,000 spectators and 67,000 and 60,000 euros profit respectively, while Carlos Saura's *La caza* (*The Hunt* 1965) (Chapter 6) attracted only 341,000 viewers and took just 56,000 euros. Thus, while certain NCE films had the wide appeal that some of the movement's supporters anticipated, it became clear that its natural audiences were the university-educated demographic to which the directors themselves belonged.[7] Notwithstanding the exceptional cases of success, the NCE was financially viable thanks only to government subsidies. In 1964 the propagandist classification 'National Interest', won by VCE films like *La gran familia*, was replaced by 'Special Interest'. This award was for films deemed to be of artistic merit, which meant the NCE. Thus even this brief analysis of production contexts reveals an overlap between the subsidised popular cinema and the NCE in their shared dependence on state protection.

Close readings of the six films suggest further similarities. In Part I, I analyse the ways *La gran familia* and *La ciudad* construct conservative representations that appealed to the government awards committee (Chapter 1), or to mass audiences (Chapter 2), but also suggest that they sustain counter-readings owing to the contributions of certain members of their technical crews and cast. Often working at great speed with scripts and personnel imposed by the producer, commissioned directors of the popular cinema exercised limited creative control. The plural nature of authorship in the popular cinema, therefore, allowed other contributors to express revealing inconsistencies in the films' otherwise conservative messages. Conversely, political opposition was the intent of the auteurist directors of the NCE. In Chapters 3–6, I accept the notion of the director as source of artistic control in these films, but none the less argue for a revised auteurist approach that reveals the roles played by collaboration, and occasional conflict, with other creative personnel. In this regard, each film discussed is very different, and they range from Camus's experience with pre-selected creative and technical personnel in *Los farsantes*, to Saura's work with the sympathetic teams of his like-minded producer in *La caza*. This revised approach liberates us from both an excessive reverence of the auteur, and the expectation that films directly project the vision of their directors. *A Cinema of Contradiction* does not go so far as to invert all expectations: while the two examples analysed in Part I reveal the potential for dissent in the commercial cinema, I do not suggest in Part II that art films, despite their intended opposition, were in fact conservative. I show, however, that the expression of dissent in the NCE was far from straightforward, for these directors, in collaboration with more or less sympathetic creative and technical teams, attacked a government on which they were paradoxically dependent for their work to exist. This contradiction, which lies at the heart of 'possibilism',[8] often made their oppositional work both clever and awkward.

By refusing to isolate art and popular forms, *A Cinema of Contradiction*, therefore, has three aims. In common with recent revisionist histories of Spanish cinema, I show the complexity and possible contestatory value of the widely dismissed commercial cinema under Franco, which often revealed the very contradictions the films intended to conceal. I suggest also that the production contexts of art cinema of the 1960s invite us to reassess these films as products of contradictory contexts, which are no less rich, and may be all the more rich, for their compromising genesis. Finally, this book demonstrates that cross-fertilisation took place between the VCE and the NCE on financial, technical and artistic levels and argues that we should see them as complementary rather than opposing areas of cinematic activity in Spain.[9]

Spain of the *apertura*

Already present in the previous decade, the contradictions inherent in trying to reconcile tradition and modernity characterised 1960s Spain. In the political sphere, these contradictions were triggered by the Franco regime's efforts to harmonise the two mutually undermining objectives of retaining the repressive dictatorship and at the same time opening Spain up to gradual liberalisation, a process termed the *apertura*. In the social arena, Spaniards experienced the conflicting ideologies of Francoist traditionalism, with its reactionary exaltation of Catholic, patriarchal and Nationalist values, and global capitalism, with its cults of the acquisition of wealth, material possessions and the free circulation of goods beyond national borders.

In the early dictatorship years Franco successfully unified disparate elements of his ruling party in the FET y de las JONS, or Movimiento

Nacional, to govern a country split by the Civil War.[10] By the 1960s, fissures in his government were again apparent. These tensions were now triggered less by the co-existence of disparate ideologies such as Falangism and Carlism than by differing responses to the socio-economic changes consequent on the abandonment of autarky and the process of industrialisation that was formalised and given impetus by the Opus Dei technocrats' Stabilisation Plan of 1959.[11] The *apertura*, a period that dates from Manuel Fraga Iribarne's appointment as Minister of Tourism and Communications in 1962 to his dismissal as a result of the cabinet reshuffle of 1969, can be seen as an attempt to counter the so-called *desfase*, which Paul Preston has identified as a characteristic of modern Spanish history. Such a 'lack of synchronisation . . . between the social reality and the political power structure ruling over it (Preston 1996: 10) potentially describes the situation of 1960s Spain, a developing consumer society ruled by an anachronistic dictatorship. The *apertura* was an attempt to realign 'social reality' and the 'political power structure'. It resulted in a contradictory compromise between traditionalist and liberalist tendencies within Francoism, an equivocal exercise in limited social reform by an authoritarian regime, which ultimately ended in failure with the return of hardliners at the end of the decade.

Franco apologists stress that *aperturista* measures, such as the establishment of a Tribunal of Public Order (1963), which meant that political subversion was dealt with by civil as well as military courts, and Fraga's press law (1966), which gave limited freedom to the press, were a liberal response to calls for change. Thus an uninterrupted line of progress is drawn between the economic 'miracle', the *apertura* and political change the following decade in the 1970s. 'By this sleight of hand,' Helen Graham argues, 'political democracy and cultural plurality become the legacy of a benevolent dictator' (1995b: 244). However, the continued exercise of repression to quell political dissent, such as the execution of Joaquín Delgado, Francisco Granados and Julián Grimau in 1963 (despite international protest over the latter, which Fraga energetically supported [Gubern 1981: 224]) and the abolition of the official student union (Sindicato de Estudiantes Universitarios [SEU]) in 1965, the return of political prosecution to military courts in 1968 and the suspension of civil liberties during the State of Exception of 1969, reveals a regime governed by expediency, willing to adopt liberal and repressive measures alike to safeguard one key aim: its own survival.

If the changes in the political arena were ultimately cosmetic, it is difficult to overemphasise the long-term consequences of the economic boom and social transformation of Spain in the period. Even if uneven in distribution, industrialisation caused average incomes to soar, in one historian's calculations, from US$290 per capita in 1955, to $497 in 1965 and $2,486 in 1975 (Schubert 1990: 258). But the shift towards a more liberal economy was both rapid and patchy, triggering the contradictions that characterise uneven development. No cultural text is a neutral illustration of its historical context, and the six films analysed here both camouflage and magnify the tensions and inconsistencies of this contradictory age. These tensions are clustered around four areas of change: the shift from rural to urban life; gender; religion; and generational conflict.

If political and social transformation is a consequence of urbanisation, then immigration from the country to the city is the most fundamental change of twentieth-century Spain. Franco certainly recognised this when he tried to halt the march of progress by exalting country life during the 1940s. The policy of autarky interrupted the processes of industrialisation and urbanisation begun in Spain in the nineteenth century, but the failure of autarkic policy led to a return to this urban development. By the 1960s the conflicts between the previous glorification of rural life and current encouragement of migration to urban centres became acute. In 1940, 44.6 per cent of the Spanish population were employed in agriculture, a figure that rose to 50.3 per cent by 1945 as Spain re-ruralised under autarky (Grugel and Rees 1997: 125 n.18). Figures dropped from 1950, to 42 per cent by 1960, and 20 per cent by 1976, as in the period 1955–75, six million Spaniards – a fifth of the population – moved province: two million to Madrid, 1,800,000 to Barcelona, 1,500,000 to work abroad, and most of the rest to other provincial urban centres (Riquer i Permanyer 1995: 262–3). Spanish cinema recorded and interpreted these far-reaching changes: the village life left behind is an implicit and explicit source of nostalgia in *La gran familia* and *La ciudad*, while *Los farsantes* and *La caza* condemn rural depopulation and deprivation. The lure of the comparative freedoms of the contemporary Spanish capital are explored in *Nueve cartas a Berta* and implied in *La tía Tula*, as the films expose and condemn the sham modernity of provincial Salamanca and Guadalajara.

While women's working rights were formally recognised by the 'Law of Political, Professional, and Labour Rights of Women' (1961), and their participation in the workforce actively encouraged by the inclusion of women's work in the 1963 Development Plan, conservative Catholicism remained the primary source of guidance in personal conduct. Gender roles, particularly in the domestic sphere, were therefore a focus of interest and concern in commercial and art cinemas. For instance, both Palacios's *La gran familia* and Picazo's *La tía Tula* address the clash of tradition and modernity. Both films run through a series of family events – a first communion, a holiday, childhood illness – but while Palacios's film seeks to naturalise pronatalism in a modern capitalist context, Picazo's scrutinises the excessive consequences of a literal interpretation of outdated Catholic gender ideology.

Conflict and change were also the hallmarks of religious life in 1960s Spain. While divisions in the Church became apparent in the period 1953–62, from 1962 to 1971 these widened into splits between arch-conservative groups like Opus Dei and those who, inspired by reforms introduced by the Second Vatican Council (Vatican II),[12] sought a break with the regime (Cooper 1976: 48). But the history of the Church in this period is more than one of a change of allegiance; it is one of gradual abandonment. Stanley Payne reports that, following the 1950s boom, in the mid-1960s, resignations of priests soared, while the registration of clergy decreased ten-fold (1984: 199): 'Although it was not clear to many at the time, the urban, industrial and consumer-orientated society of the 1950s was inaugurating a new phase of secularization' (1984: 187). On the one hand, popular film of the period reflects this process. *La gran familia*, for instance, may begin with a first communion photograph, but the film depicts this event as an opportunity for light-hearted consumerist fun, like buying the children new outfits, rather than sober religious reflection. Similarly, the village priest of *La ciudad* is a target of affectionate ridicule rather than a source of serious authority. If the VCE laughs off the anachronistic presence of religion in a modern context, the NCE earnestly addresses this contradiction. In its anti-clerical assault on hypocrisy and empty ceremony, *Los farsantes* portrays religion in 1960s Spain as if Vatican II were not taking place; *La tía Tula* likewise ignores the contemporary modernisation of the Catholic Church to explore the impact on personal behaviour of conservative doctrine. Conversely, the protagonist of *Nueve cartas a Berta* reflects on Pope John XXIII's reforms, though he ultimately embraces the conservatism represented by the reactionary views of the two priests of his childhood.

Similarly, generational conflict is played in the different keys of conservative comedy and earnest realism in Spanish cinema of the 1960s. A problem that is as old as mankind, generational conflict became a particular focus in early twentieth-century pschoanalysis. 1960s Spanish cinema examines the classic Oedipal scenario of antagonism between middle-aged fathers and adolescent sons (for instance, in *Nueve cartas a Berta*), but the experiences of older relatives, like grandparents, and younger children become a new concern in the period. As Marsha Kinder has shown, Oedipality enabled filmmakers to explore political issues through personal narratives of family relations (1993: 13), but the focus on the very old and the very young in the

1960s encoded a new critique of the longevity of the regime on the one hand, and the inability of the young to succeed it on the other. In a climate of censorship, the Spanish families depicted became hugely over-determined: not only did the young represent the future, but their ages specifically raised the question of what would happen to Spain post-Franco; and the old were often aligned with the increasingly frail dictator, whose mortality became ever clearer as the decade wore on.[13] The films studied in this book are peopled by rebellious and docile children (*La gran familia* and *La tía Tula*) confused adolescents (*La ciudad*, *Nueve cartas a Berta*, *La caza*) and both comically absurd (*La gran familia*, *La ciudad*) and dangerously self-obsessed (*La caza*) old men, who project the contradictions of an age preoccupied by youth, but still ruled by an out-of-touch old man.

The *Viejo Cine Español*

If Spanish intellectuals are traditionally dismissive of their national cinema, this is especially so in the case of popular film. The commercial cinema of the dictatorship is a particular target, as, like all popular culture of the period, it is assumed to be ideologically homogeneous and complicit with the regime.[14] The veteran cultural commentator Eduardo Haro Tecglen is a typical case. A 'child of the Republic',[15] he is well known in Spain as a former member of the anti-Franco intellectual elite, and his present activity writing a daily column and reviews for *El País*, Spain's leading daily, assigns him continued authority as a cultural gatekeeper. In a recent column entitled 'Viejo Cine Español' he recalls that, under Franco, 'Los que mirábamos la cartelera para ir al cine decíamos: ' "No, a ésa no, que es española", sin indagar más' (Those of us who looked at the billboard to see what was on at the cinema would say: 'No, not that one, it's Spanish', without investigating further). The aims of those films were:

> nada que preocupe, no plantear temas, que no cunda el pesimismo; retorcer la comicidad hasta deformar el físico del actor; cambiar la sonrisa por la carcajada de cuerpo, no de cabeza; gastar lo menos posible, que es una de las maneras más conocidas de destruir cualquier producto. (Que conste: hablo en todo caso de generalidad.) (nothing troubling, not to propose themes or spread pessimism; to twist comicalness to the point of deforming an actor's physique; to exchange smiles for guffaws that shook the body, but didn't challenge the mind; to spend as little money as possible, which is a recipe for destroying any product. [Please note: I'm talking about the majority, in any case.]) (Haro Tecglen 2004)

Despite his parenthetical disclaimer, Haro Tecglen dismisses popular cinema for its saccharine optimism, facile humour and low production values. His lament that it fails to be 'troubling . . . propose themes or spread pessimism' is a useful summary of the Marxist orthodoxy of Spanish film criticism, whose most famous proponent was Juan Antonio Bardem (uncle of the acting star, Javier). A member of the illegal Spanish Communist Party during the dictatorship, Bardem was the author and co-author of the first acclaimed dissident films in the 1950s, *Esa pareja feliz* (*That Happy Couple* 1951), *¡Bienvenido Mister Marshall!* (*Welcome Mr. Marshall!* 1952) and *Calle Mayor* (*High Street* 1956). Two statements by this director would influence practitioners and supporters of Spanish art cinema for a generation. Quoted and republished countless times, Bardem declared at the Conversations of Salamanca film conference organised by Patino in 1955 that Spanish popular cinema was '1. politically futile; 2. socially false; 3. intellectually worthless; 4. aesthetically valueless; 5. industrially paralytic' (Hopewell 1986: 57). In another widely disseminated work, '¿Para qué sirve un film?' (What's a film for?), first published in *Cinema universitario* in 1956, he declared that Spanish film should instead 'mostrar en términos de luz, de imágenes y de sonidos la realidad de nuestro contorno, aquí y hoy. Ser testimonio del momento humano. Pues, a mi parecer, el cine será ante todo testimonio o no será nada' (show through light, images and sounds the reality of our environment here and now. Be a witness to its human moment. Because it seems to me that cinema will be above all a witness or it won't be anything) (Fontenla 1966a: 192). The work of a small but vocal group of directors, and the criticism of the majority of critics and historians of Spanish cinema, have acted like an echo chamber for Bardem's rallying cries, in particular the creators and supporters of the NCE, the subject of Part II of this book.

The casualty of the Bardemian orthodoxy was popular film, an area of cinematic activity that merits our attention on at least two counts. First, the decision of Haro Tecglen and his companions to avoid Spanish films was not one shared by millions of their compatriots. The 1960s was the last decade when the domestic national cinema could still consistently attract massive audiences (although the domestic blockbuster has made a recent reappearance in Spain [Lázaro Reboll and Willis 2004a: 14–15]). Casimiro Torreiro reports that audience figures for Spanish cinema in the domestic market in the 1960s (which now in the new millenium hovers around 10 per cent), seem the stuff of fairy tales: 22 per cent in 1966, more than 27 per cent a year later and almost 30 per cent in 1968 (Torreiro 2000: 156). Yet despite the inclusion of these figures Torreiro devotes his attention to the NCE and its Catalan successor, the Barcelona School. In another chapter published in a survey of the same year, the critic does include a section on commercial cinema, but this constitutes only a fraction of the study (1995b: 331–5).

In 1984, Santiago Pozo Arenas argued that, with a 30 per cent market share in 1968, 'El verdadero cine español, el que merece este nombre, el que consiguió mejorar su situación en el mercado fue: . . . *La ciudad no es para mí* [etc.]' (The real Spanish cinema, the one that deserves this name, the one that managed to improve its market situation was . . . *La ciudad no es para mí* [etc.]) (1984: 199–200), and collections of articles on specific films, rather than historical surveys, have included work on both art and popular cinemas, like Augusto Torres's *El cine español en 119 películas* and Julio Pérez Perucha's edited volume *Antología crítica del cine español* (both published in 1997). However, over the past decade, critics have defended a second reason for focusing on popular film. Scholars influenced by cultural studies, like Helen Graham and Jo Labanyi, have argued against a Frankfurt School-influenced view of popular culture as a tool of control to manipulate a passive public (1995a: 3) and used Antonio Gramsci's concept of 'counter-hegemonic cultural tactics' (1995a: 4) to invite us to adjust our focus to the reception of culture, and away from the intention of its author or the government that financed it. This approach invests audiences with agency, raises the possibility of resistant, or 'counter-hegemonic', readings, and provides scholars with an intellectual framework in which to take popular culture seriously. Drawing on both these insights and work on other European popular cinemas (e.g. Dyer and Vincendeau 1992), there followed a book-length critique of the tendency to privilege art, or 'quality', cinema, over popular genres in definitions of Spanish 'national' cinema, Núria Triana-Toribio's *Spanish National Cinema* (2003), then an edited collection that focused exclusively on popular film, *Spanish Popular Cinema* (Lázaro Reboll and Willis 2004b).[16] Part I of *A Cinema of Contradiction* seeks to add to this work by arguing that fault-lines occasionally disrupt the smooth surfaces of the VCE in the 1960s. These fault-lines, which relate to the roles of stars, the use of editing and the construction of space and *mise en scène*, can undermine the edifice of conservatism otherwise constructed by the films, giving rise to resistant or counter-hegemonic readings.

One consequence of the corrective focus on popular film in recent publications is the tendency to divorce this work from art manifestations. However, by adopting the same approach in Parts I and II – an analysis of production contexts combined with close textual readings – this book also aims to show overlaps between the two cinemas. Triana-Toribio has suggested that there is a similarity between *Nueve cartas a Berta* and the VCE film *Marisol, rumbo a Río* (*Marisol Bound for Río*, Palacios 1963) in terms of the question of Spanishness (2003: 92–5). While I analyse a number of conceptual areas, *A Cinema of Contradiction* aims to respond to her observation that:

> Analysis of Spanish film of the 1960s has for too long given undue attention to the Nuevo Cine Español at the expense of the Viejo Cine Español. . . . It is much more profitable an exercise to compare and contrast the different versions of Spanishness projected by these competing cinemas. And while there are obviously stark differences, it is striking how many of their concerns in fact coincide. (2003: 92)

Besides overlaps in terms of concept, which arise from the fact that both cinemas responded to the same contradictions of the time, *A Cinema of Contradiction* also shows that there were practical links between the VCE and the NCE through the presence and participation of the same personnel in each. It is obvious that, in a relatively small industry such as Spain's, art directors would be forced to use some of the same cast, technical crews, sets, laboratories and even producers as their commercial counterparts, but this is the first study to scrutinise the extent and meaning of these overlaps.

The greatest difference between the VCE and NCE is in the area of direction. In the commercial industry, directors often had no formal training, learning their craft as apprentices on set. Fernando Palacios, for instance, worked as an assistant on nineteen films before his directorial début, as did Lazaga, who gained experience as both an assistant director and a scriptwriter (for instance, he wrote the script of Carlos Serrano de Osma's Unamuno adaptation *Abel Sánchez* [1946]). Conversely, NCE directors studied both theory and practice at the state's Official Film School (which opened in 1947 and closed in 1976), and their first experience of a feature film was often as its director[17] – apparently producers would frequently employ trusted assistant directors to work with them in order to mitigate any problems arising from their inexperience (Méndez-Leite 1969: 100). Classes were given by members of the industry, so the NCE directors' instruction by VCE personnel is a potential area of overlap (indeed the Director of the School over the period of the NCE directors' training was José Luis Saénz de Heredia, author of the propagandist pictures *Raza* [*Race* 1941] and *Franco, ese hombre* [*Franco, That Man* 1964]). Directors' memories of the efficacy of the classes and their levels of attendance differ considerably, but all the accounts I have consulted mention that the School was a forum for sharing ideas, swapping banned books and watching films that were otherwise unavailable (Núñez 1964: 7; Monleón and Egea 1965: 10; Torres 1992: 25; García de Dueñas 2003: 82–4; 98–100). The privileged club feel of the School, which was particularly dominated by the banned Communist Party

(Torres 1992: 24; Alberich 2002: 27), was self-perpetuating, for its graduates would subsequently gain teaching posts – as did all the directors studied
in this book apart from Camus. In the late 1950s, one former student was
particularly influential: Carlos Saura. Slightly older than the other NCE
directors, the author of the much-admired *Los golfos* (*Hooligans* 1959)
became the unofficial leader of the NCE 'movement' (Oms 1981: 32), a role
acknowledged in his cameo appearance at the Madrid café in *Nueve cartas a
Berta*, when he is hailed as 'maestro'.[18]

Commissioned directors do not choose their genres, and in the 1960s,
Pedro Masó, the producer of *La gran familia*, *La ciudad* and many of the
key VCE films of the decade, put his money in comedy. The Film School
auteurs may have enjoyed generic freedom, but their work also adhered to
a set of conventions. As I argue in Chapter 3, the NCE's sacred cow was a
loose, and consequently much debated, notion of realism.[19] This is because
the movement was the fruit of the three major sources of cultural influence
on Spanish intelligentsia in the 1950s. First, the NCE drew on a patchy
knowledge of Marxism (Torres 1992: 35), the sources of which included
the outlawed Communist Party delegates Ricardo Muñoz Suay and Jorge
Semprún's 'Operation Realism' in Spanish universities (Labanyi 1995a:
295), the limited availability of banned texts and the sketchy theoretical
coverage offered by journals like *Nuestro Cine* (Monterde 2003: 109–10).
Second, Italian Neorealism, which had penetrated Spain via the two film
weeks organised by the Italian Institute of Culture in 1951 and 1953, continued to cast what Carlos Heredero calls its 'long shadow' (1993: 287) over
1960s Spanish film, though directors had access to only a limited number
of films (Torreiro 2000: 157). Third, the NCE repeated in film what the
1950s Spanish Social Novel had explored in literature, notably Marxist
political concerns, working-class subject matter and a social-realist style.
The film *Llegar a más* (*Getting on in the World* 1963), made by the Social
Novel writer Jesús Fernández Santos (who himself studied at the Film
School), and Camus's adaptations of two other writers, Daniel Sueiro and
Ignacio Aldecoa, are specific examples of the general traffic of influence
between the 1950s novel and 1960s film. If the NCE 'movement' existed
owing to the directors' coincidence at the Film School (Fontenla 1986: 181;
Sánchez Noriega 2003: 257), its only collective characteristic is this tendency towards realism, though, as the examples in this study attest, this
was the loosest of alliances. While Camus's *Los farsantes* emulated the techniques and aims of Italian Neorealism, other NCE films combined realism
with a catholic range of influences, which came from watching films in
national theatres, the Film School and at foreign film festivals: Picazo's *La
tía Tula* drew on melodrama and the gothic; Patino's *Nueve cartas a Berta*,

the formal experimentation of the French New Wave; and Saura's *La caza*, buddy and war film genres as well as documentary.

Despite their different training, some NCE directors would none the less work with the same producers and in similar production conditions as the VCE. This was because of state protection. Just as commercial producers made films with the intention of winning the 'National Interest' subsidy, like *La gran familia*, so they also backed the work of NCE directors in order to win the 'Special Interest' subsidy. For this reason the quintessential VCE producer Ignacio Iquino backed Camus's first two features, *Los farsantes* and *Young Sánchez*. In my discussion of this first film in Chapter 3, I assess the extent to which the director's control was eroded by this production context, and argue that *Los farsantes* also reveals fruitful collaboration between Camus and Iquino's creative and technical teams. Other NCE directors offer more extreme examples: José Luis Borau's directorial début, for instance, was a commissioned spaghetti western, *Brandy* (1963).

Even for those working with the new, sympathetic producers like Elías Querejeta, NCE directors still needed to work with actors and technical crews of the VCE. The migration of actors between popular and art cinemas is a source of major overlap between the two. In his work on film comedy, Steven Marsh has argued that the presence of the same actors in different Spanish genres undoes the critically constructed boundaries between them, and cites the example of José Luis López Vázquez, who plays the same repressed middle-aged character in both comedy films, like Luis García Berlanga's *Plácido* (1961), and realist work, like Saura's *Peppermint frappé* (1967) (2002: 38). I suggest that the migration of actors not only questions genre boundaries, but also upsets the sacred division between Spain's popular and art cinemas. Like López Vázquez, José Isbert, for instance, plays a similarly disruptive role in Berlanga's dissident masterpieces *¡Bienvenido Mister Marshall!* (1952) and *El verdugo* (*The Executioner* 1963), and Palacios's consensual comedy *La gran familia*. Likewise, Aurora Bautista and Alfredo Mayo's bombastic roles in the epic cinema of the 1940s are evoked with critical effect in the NCE's *La tía Tula* and *La caza*. This process of exchange goes both ways: the star image of troubled youth acquired by Emilio Gutiérrez Caba in his roles in *Nueve cartas a Berta* and *La caza* is replayed with comic effect alongside Alfredo Landa in Lazaga's *Los guardiamarinas* (*The Midshipmen* 1967).

Similarly, members of technical crews migrate between the VCE and the NCE, troubling the boundaries between them and acting as agents of cross-fertilisation. To take the key areas of editing and cinematography, the examples of the six films in this book suggest that the VCE and NCE were entwined.[20] The editor Pedro del Rey, for instance, worked on both *La gran familia* and *La tía Tula*; Alfonso Santacana worked on both *La ciudad* and *El verdugo*; and the cinematographer Juan Julio Baena, who created the gothic look of *La tía Tula*, gathered experience in both art cinema (notably *Los golfos*) and popular film. In an interview with Baena published in 1989, Francesc Llinàs notes with surprise that you are 'el primer operador moderno, por decirlo de una forma, que se incorpora a un cierto cine industrial, al tiempo que eres casi el director de fotografía del NCE' (the first modern cameraman, if I can put it that way, who is part of a certain kind of industrial cinema, while at the same time you are almost the director of photography of the NCE), to which Baena responds, 'la experiencia con Lazaga fue magnífica' (the experience with Lazaga was magnificent) (1989b: 218–19). If the blurring of boundaries is upsetting for the critic, we should note that the various experiences are enriching for the professional.

One crucial consequence of the migration of technical crew between the two cinemas is that knowledge of technological advances was shared between them. As Baena notes, new developments such as light-weight cameras, lights and sensitive film stock made the technical innovations of the NCE possible (Llinàs 1989b: 215). While formal experimentation with this new technology was more sustained in the NCE (for instance, in *Nueve cartas a Berta* or *La caza*), it was not absent from the VCE. As I show in Chapter 2, in the prologue of Lazaga's *La ciudad*, the editor Santacana and cinematographer Juan Mariné (who never actually worked in the NCE) draw on new techniques to offer a portrait of Madrid that would not be out of place in an NCE film, and is on a par with the depictions of Paris or London of the contemporary New Cinemas outside Spain.

The *Nuevo Cine Español*

For all this blurring, the difference between the VCE and the NCE is nowhere more apparent than in the amount of critical attention that has been addressed to each. While the VCE was ignored, dismissed or simply mentioned as statistical background data until recently in critical accounts, conversely, scholars have lavished their attention on the NCE. The history of the NCE is a history of extremes. Because it is entwined with both the history of Francoism and the history of Spanish cinema, it attracts either fierce attack or extravagant support. On the one hand, it has been identified with the dictatorship, thus denouncing the NCE means denouncing the regime that protected and promoted it. On the other, it has been linked to democracy, and so supporting the NCE means stressing an oppositional film tradition in Spain under Franco (to match the one that has been championed at home and abroad post-Franco). By restoring the movement to the context of the 1960s, *A Cinema of Contradiction* aims to avoid these extremes, for one of the key contradictions of the NCE is that it is both these things: it was supported by Francoism, yet the films also looked forward to the regime's end.

From the outset the NCE divided critics between supporters and detractors. In the early 1960s, specialist journals were a soap box on which supporters stood and defended both the films and the state's policies that protected them. Conversely, the Francoist press was downright hostile, and later in the decade, journals became critical too.[21] Once the compromises of protectionism became clear, and directors either failed to make a second feature or made second films that did not fulfil the promise of their first (for instance, Picazo's *Oscuros sueños de agosto* [*Obscure August Dreams* 1967] or Patino's *De amor y otras soledades* [*On Love and Other Solitudes* 1969], compared to their *La tía Tula* and *Nueve cartas a Berta*), the NCE's supporters found common cause with its detractors. The movement was condemned by specialist journals, the directors themselves, their successors at the Film School at the Sitges film festival of 1967 and by the Barcelona School.[22]

Hostility towards the NCE continued in different accounts for differing reasons in the following decades. Film commentators who cut their critical teeth on the film journals of the 1960s would continue to condemn the contradictions of protectionism in book-length accounts published in later decades. For instance, Vicente Molina-Foix, writing it should be noted before 1977 and hence before the abolition of censorship in Spain, decries José María García Escudero's policies for giving 'fictitious liberty', summarising his legislation as 'hopelessly inadequate' (1977: 17); similarly, Román Gubern calls the movement one of equivocal 'oposición controlada' (controlled opposition) (1981: 211). In accounts published in 1973, Augusto Torres would condemn the NCE as a 'caricature' (1973: 20) of contemporary European New Cinemas, and blame government protection for the unpaid debt of 230 million pesetas to producers by 1970 (1973: 43), and the Barcelona School director Joaquín Jordá, who worked in collaboration with NCE directors in the early years, would state, 'el cine español es nada' (Spanish cinema is nothing) (Torres 1973: 56). Similarly, in their unambiguously subtitled volume on Spanish cinema, 'algunos materiales por derribo' (materials to destroy it), Carlos and David Pérez Merinero demolished the policy of protectionism. They fiercely attacked those like Querejeta who had benefited from it, whom they accuse of being a mere instrument of the regime (1973: 19 n. 15 *bis*), and Bardem, who is for them 'la institucionalización del cine "crítico"' (the institutionalisation of 'critical' cinema) (1973: 21), and defended directors ignored by it, like Edgar Neville, Marco Ferreri and Fernando Fernán Gómez (1973: 21), summarising the movement as nothing more than propaganda to represent the regime's *apertura* abroad (1973: 25).

These views are echoed in accounts written from the 1980s on, but the distance afforded by time tempers the virulence of earlier critiques. John Hopewell, for instance, criticises the financial flaws of García Escudero's protectionist measures (1986: 65) and the failure of the films to appeal to contemporary audiences (1986: 71), and notes that the preferential treatment given to the young graduates of the Film School stifled alternative creative currents, like the work of Fernán Gómez (1986: 251 n. 39), but salutes the quality of some of the films made (1986: 66–76), in particular the work of Saura (1986: 71–6). Casimiro Torreiro's chapter (1995b) in the standard reference work to the national cinema in Spanish[23] likewise strikes a balance between criticising the movement as a propaganda stunt to improve Spain's image at foreign film festivals (1995b: 306), which ignored older oppositional directors (1995b: 326–31) and failed to connect with Spanish audiences (1995b: 335), and admitting that García Escudero's measures enabled the production of films of 'quality and interest' and provided a platform from which some of Spain's best directors entered the industry (1995b: 340).

From the 1980s, an alternative tendency emerged that celebrated these films as the politically dissident work of a group of auteurs. At a time when Spain's first Socialist government after the return of democracy was introducing a series of protectionist measures that were similar to the 1960s model (the Miró decrees of 1983),[24] a narrative of Spanish film history was told in critical accounts that connected past and present: following Berlanga and Bardem's first dissident films of the 1950s, and the demands of the latter at the Conversations of Salamanca in 1955, the Director-General of Cinema García Escudero introduced protectionist measures that facilitated the production of further oppositional films, which in turn looked forward to the work carried out by filmmakers under democracy (Rodero 1981; Caparrós Lera 1983; García Fernández 1985). This account continues to persuade critics (Higginbotham 1988; Schwartz 1986, 1991; D'Lugo 1997; Kinder 1997b), some of whom have taken it in important new directions to include analyses of national cinemas (Kinder 1993; Stone 2002), and close readings of both canonical and lesser-known films (Heredero and Monterde 2003: 385–454).[25] As we have seen, this narrative privileges the NCE at the expense of popular cinema. By focusing on both the links with the VCE and the contradictory contexts from which these films arise, *A Cinema of*

Contradiction aims to show that the NCE was a more complex and interest-ing phenomenon than hitherto supposed. Like its commercial counterpart, it responded to the tensions of the *apertura*, but was also itself the contra-dictory result of that same *apertura*. First, it was a film movement spon-sored by a dictatorship that its directors ideologically opposed. Second, as Teresa Vilarós has pointed out with respect to the leftist intelligentsia of 1960s Spain in general, it benefited from the tentative political liberalisa-tion that was a corollary of, or at least an adjunct to, economic capitalism, another system that its directors ideologically opposed (1998: 75).

These contradictions characterised the legislation that enabled the films to be made, as well as the films themselves. Fraga appointed García Escudero as Director-General of Cinema in 1962, a post he held until the closure of the department in 1967. With a degree in political science and doctorate in law, this journalist, writer (his books cover studies of journal-ism, politics, law, religion and culture, as well as cinema) and former deputy colonel of Franco's air force (Riambau and Torreiro 1999: 49–50) was a Falangist and devout Catholic, but owing to his desire for reform, 'In the context of the time, both [he and] Fraga . . . passed for liberals' (Vernon 2002: 261). García Escudero's background in film is revealing of the new direction that the regime wanted Spanish cinema to take. He had held the Director-Generalship from 1951, but was sacked the following year for awarding the 'National Interest' prize to José Antonio Nieves Condes's *Surcos* (*Furrows* 1951) in preference to Juan de Orduña's turgid CIFESA[26] biopic of Christopher Columbus, *Alba de América* (*Dawn in America* 1951). *Surcos* tells us a great deal about the minister who cham-pioned it: though progressive in its adoption of the techniques and some of the concerns of Italian Neorealism (an influence denied by the director [Vernon 2002: 256]), it none the less reinforced reactionary Francoist morals in its vilification of the city, and as such is a contradictory hybrid that Kinder describes as 'Falangist Neorealism' (1993: 40). *Surcos* thus projected the limits of García Escudero's own position: he called for a pro-gressive, intellectual cinema, but one contained within the confines of the dictatorship. This *aperturista* belief in progress within limits is confirmed in García Escudero's interventions in the Salamanca conference of 1955, and his 1962 publication *Cine español* – a book Fraga read before offering him the Director-Generalship (Hopewell 1986: 65).

The progress with limits that is expounded in theory in *Cine español* was put into practice in García Escudero's 1960s legislation. In line with the principle stated in his book that Spanish cinema would improve if its prac-titioners were better educated (García Escudero 1962: Chapter 4), the Director-General's first change in 1962 was to reorganise the state Film

School, the Instituto de Investigaciones y Experiencias Cinematográficas (School of Cinematographic Experience and Research) and rename it the Escuela Oficial de Cine (Official Film School). In response to the demands of the Conversations of Salamanca, in 1963 censorship rules were published which, up to this point, had been unknown, and in 1964 García Escudero replaced the propagandist classification 'National Interest', which had proved so controversial in the *Surcos* case, with 'Special Interest', meaning 'quality' or 'art' cinema.[27] This was part of a fourth change, the establishment of a new system of government subsidies dependent on the classification of a film according to censors' analysis of the script (all Spanish films automatically received 15 per cent of box office takings, but a 'Special Interest' film could be awarded up to 50 per cent of its projected production costs).[28] Finally, art cinemas, 'Salas de Arte y Ensayo', were established for subtitled foreign cinema and 'Special Interest' films, which led the Director-General to be dubbed the 'director de cine-clubs' (director of film clubs) (García Escudero 1967: 111). Official statistics suggest that these measures led to the emergence of 46 new directors, whose work amounted to eighty-six films (Rodero 1981: 68), though Torreiro estimates there were only thirty NCE films (2000: 157).

The major contradiction of this legislation was that dissent from the state was supported by that same state. Thus while the previous generation of oppositional cineastes were the *bêtes noires* of Francoism – consider the scandal unleashed by Buñuel's *Viridiana* in Cannes in 1961 – the NCE directors were championed by the regime. Though Berlanga was part of the former group, his description of this contradiction is both crude and to the point:

> tuvimos la buena-mala suerte de que el Director General de Cine . . . fuese un enam-orado de todos nosotros. . . . Toda la legislación que hizo este hombre, que venía del franquismo, hizo que acabásemos desembarcando en un cine nacido del Ministerio, que es lo que ha jodido todo. (we had the good-bad luck that the Director-General of Cinema . . . thought we were all wonderful. . . . All his legislation, which was Francoist, meant that we ended up making films born of the Ministry, which is what's screwed everything up.) (quoted in Angulo 2003b: 45)

García Escudero's legislation was typically *aperturista*: new freedoms were presented as liberalisation, but were in fact a means of control. It was an adoption by the state of the policy of keeping your friends close and your enemies closer. New work by the Film School graduates was simultaneously encouraged and restricted. Production was aided through investment in the School and generous subsidies, and international distribution was encouraged by the preference shown for selecting NCE films for foreign film festivals. However, production was simultaneously hampered through censorship, and national distribution and exhibition restricted by a screen quota system that favoured dubbed Hollywood films.

The place of the NCE within national and international contexts was therefore a particular source of anxiety, as I argue in Chapter 5. The NCE was condemned by the Francoist press for being 'extranjerizante' (foreignified), compared to the 'authentic Spanishness' of the VCE consensual comedies (Triana-Toribio 2003: 78), but no film exists in a national vacuum, impermeable to transnational influences. So while the NCE drew on foreign art movements like Italian Neorealism and the French New Wave, the VCE too was influenced by American and Italian comedy (Barbachano 1966; Palá 1966; Marsh 2002: 16; Marsh 2003: 134), and in fact both cinemas were fertilised by all-pervasive Hollywood film. What made the NCE different from the VCE in terms of nationality was that while the VCE was a domestic cinema, the state sponsors of the NCE wanted the films to enter 'en los mercados nacionales y sobre todo los mercados internacionales' (national markets, and above all foreign markets) (Fraga, quoted in Riambau and Torreiro 1999: 52).

A snapshot of foreign reception of the NCE at film festivals indicates foreign critics' differing responses to the movement. In Britain, *Sight and Sound* gave a thoughtful overview of 'The Young Turks of Spain', singled out the work of Saura, Antxón Eceiza and Francisco Regueiro for particular praise (Clouzot 1966: 69), and saluted *Nueve cartas a Berta* as the forerunner of 'a rebirth of the cinema in Spain' (Wilson 1966: 173). The US trade journal *Variety* also hailed the 'considerable screen expertise' in evidence in *La caza*, though its view of *La tía Tula* was mixed, and it considered *Nueve cartas a Berta* naïve. France's *Cahiers du cinéma*, meanwhile, praised *La tía Tula* as one of the best works of the NCE, criticised *La caza* as over-schematic and described *Nueve cartas a Berta* as 'interesting'.[29] NCE directors and sympathetic critics in Spain played up the negative views, however, and vented their frustration at being misunderstood. They bemoaned the failure of foreign audiences to take into consideration the difficult circumstances of filmmaking in Spain (e.g. the reception of *Plácido* at Cannes [Erice 1962: 23]), their occasional incomprehension of the films (e.g. the condemnation of *El verdugo* as fascist [Fontenla 1966b: 7], or misunderstanding of *Los golfos* [Saura 2003: 457–8]), and their back-handed praise – 'la sobrevaloración paternalista adoptada ante cualquier creación de un país subdesarrollado' (paternalistic over-praising of any creation from an underdeveloped country) (Monleón 1966: 8). As the decade wore on, there was a realisation that foreign audiences saw through the NCE as propagandist window-dressing (e.g. Llinàs and

Marías 1969: 66–7; Torres and Molina-Foix 2003: 16), and directors despaired to see that the political was placed above the cinematographic in consideration of their films. For instance, when *La caza* was awarded the Silver Bear at Berlin in 1966 it was reportedly 'por la valentía e indignación con que presenta una situación característica de su patria y de su tiempo' (for the bravery and indignation with which it presents a situation characteristic of its country and time), reasons that Saura rejected as 'se desvían de lo que es genuinamente cinematográfico, para chocar y caer en el partidismo político' (a diversion away from the genuinely cinematographic in order to shock, and succumb to political partisanship) (Gómez Mesa 1966: 395). This, then, was one more cruel contradiction of the NCE, which I discuss in detail in Chapter 5. Determined to remain in their home country rather than work in exile (Clouzot 1966: 103), NCE directors were criticised for being too foreign in Spain, yet too Spanish abroad.

The corrective critical gesture that disputes foreign consideration of Spanish cinema as different (to paraphrase Fraga) is understandable. And there are many points of comparison between the NCE and contemporary New Cinemas, especially in the area of production. Like the Oberhausen Manifesto (1962) that gave rise to the Young German Cinema of the 1960s, the NCE had a manifesto of sorts in the conclusions of the Conversations of Salamanca (1955) (Kinder 1997b: 597), which similarly enshrined a Romantic notion of individual authorship and implied the need for state protection (Kaes 1997: 614). If the German directors were often self-taught (Kaes 1997: 616), Spain, like France, Italy and a number of Eastern European countries (Torreiro 2000: 158), had an official Film School that became a forum to forge bonds. Closely aligned with the Film School, Spain had specialist journals too, where students would address through the word what they would later explore through the image. Left-leaning *Nuevo Cine*, which replaced *Objetivo* (closed down in 1955 owing to the controversy of the Conversations of Salamanca) and *Cinema universitario* (which lasted till March 1963), was broadly aligned with *Positif* and *Cinema nuovo*, while the admiration of Hollywood genre film in *Film Ideal* made it comparable, if only very loosely, with *Cahiers du cinéma* (Monterde 2003: 105). Both *Nuestro Cine* and *Film Ideal* displayed their kinship with their European counterparts by frequently including translations of their articles into Spanish. Government protection through subsidy is a further key similarity between the NCE and contemporary New Cinemas, which all shared a production context that Casimiro Torreiro summarises as 'El estado asistencial' (The Welfare State) (1995a).[30] Resourceful independent producers, like Querejeta in Spain, or Anatole Dauman and Pierre Braunberger in France, or Franco Cristaldi in Italy (Nowell-Smith 1997a: 570), worked the system of protection to their own advantage and thus backed many of the key films of the period. But in all cases, state money came with strings attached: just as the NCE was to offer a liberal image of *aperturista* Spain abroad, so the French New Wave, for instance, was to showcase to the world an energetic and youthful France that had recovered from the Second World War (Benayoun 1968: 157). Finally, all these New Cinemas were dependent on new technology in order to shake up the conventions of representation that characterised their indigenous popular cinemas (this Oedipal scenario of generational conflict is particularly clear in the French case, where the New Wave directors dismissed the work that preceded them as 'le cinéma de papa' [Daddy's cinema]).[31]

Given these similarities, Heredero argues against the thesis of Spanish exceptionality to suggest that the NCE be considered not as 'una flor de invernadero crecida en el aislamiento de la dictadura franquista, sino un reflejo nacional (todo lo encanijado que se quiera) de una esfervescencia europea' (a hothouse flower grown in the isolation of the Francoist dictatorship, but a national refection [call it as weak as you want] of European effervescence) (1993: 376). Forty years on, it seems churlish to caution against the argument that the NCE was the equivalent of European New Cinemas on the grounds that this repeats the *aperturista* propaganda that Spain was as liberal as its democratic neighbours. However, the tendency to stress the NCE's similarities with Europe leads to a distorted view of the movement that overlooks its particular contexts, like its connections with its domestic popular cinema. Comparisons play an important role in the history of national cinemas, but they must always be grounded in a thorough investigation of each particular case. By arguing that the NCE is inseparable from, though not reducible to, its particular contexts, *A Cinema of Contradiction* aims to offer such an analysis of Spain.

Notes

1. For example, Sieburth (1994: 41–4, 231–44); other scholars refer to 'uneven development' (Graham and Sánchez 1995: 407).
2. Student numbers almost doubled from 69,377 in 1962–3 to 134,945 in 1968–9 in Spain (Riambau and Torreiro 1999: 31). The failure of the NCE to reach a wide audience has been the source of much acrimony: some blame the government for restricting distribution and exhibition, others its directors for their aestheticism. We may move beyond the critical impasse of apportioning blame if we accept that the movement, like the 1950s Social Novel that preceded it, appealed to a select demographic.

3. Joan Francesc de Lasa is credited with naming the movement, giving this title to the Molins del Rei Film Festival of 1963 which he directed, though the phrase is used by the editors of *Film Ideal* in 1960 ('Nuevo Cine Español' 1960). Other epithets include 'la nueva ola española' (Spanish New Wave), 'el joven cine español' (Young Spanish Cinema), 'el Cabo de Buena Esperanza' (Cape of Good Hope) (the latter phrase coined by José Luis Saénz de Heredia [García de Dueñas 2003: 79]) and in the foreign press 'The Young Turks of Spain' (Clouzot 1966). With the less complementary 'cine mesetario', the directors of the Barcelona School condemned the NCE's excessive focus on Castile (whose central plain, evoked in the work of the Generation of 1898, is the 'meseta'), and the two phrases 'cine de funcionarios' (Cinema of Bureaucrats) (Llinás and Marías 1969: 66) and 'los chicos de García Escudero' (García Escudero's Boys) (Triana-Toribio 2003: 66) highlighted the movement's dependency on the government. The literary critic José María Castellet also used the term 'nueva ola' in 1963 to refer to the Spanish novel of the previous twenty years (Schwartz 1976: 7). Marta Hernández and Manolo Revuelta coined the term 'Viejo Cine Español' in 1976 (Triana-Toribio 2003: 75).

4. These and the following statistics on audience attendance and takings are those published on Spain's Ministry of Culture official web-page, http://www. mcu.es/cine/index.jsp, on the link to 'Bases de datos de películas', as at 15 February 2005 and refer to Spain only. It should be noted, however, that official box office control did not begin in Spain until 1 January 1965.

5. Reliable or not, in the interview included on the DVD version of the film released as part of the *El País* 'Un País de Cine' collection in April 2003, Pedro Masó claims that *La gran familia* played to packed houses in the afternoon showings, but, as it attracted fewer audiences in the evening, it spent only two weeks at a top cinema, but then lasted forty-seven weeks at a secondary one.

6. A third exception was *Del rosa . . . al amarillo* (*From Pink to Yellow*, Summers 1963).

7. *Cine Asesor*, a volume that records trade and press information, noted of Saura's *La caza*, for instance, that it would attract a select audience interested in 'el cine de los nuevos valores españoles' (films about new Spanish values). Ángel Fernández Santos's survey (1967) of audiences at the Molins del Rei Festival, 1967, further confirms the NCE's appeal to a narrow demographic, as does José Luis García Escudero's decision to establish separate art cinemas for foreign and NCE films the same year.

8. The playwrights Antonio Buero Vallejo and Alfonso Sastre began a dispute over 'posibilismo' and 'imposibilismo' in 1960, which defined responses to censorship in the coming decades. On the side of 'possibilism', Buero argued that the artist was beholden to work with censorship in order to reach an audience, while Sastre condemned this as an unacceptable compromise, maintaining that the artist should behave as if restrictions did not exist, even if this meant his or her work never reached the public.

9. In this last aim, I have been guided by Núria Triana-Toribio's identification of overlaps between these two areas in her study of Spanish national cinema (2003: 71); Stephanie Sieburth's questioning of the divisions between 'high' and 'low' in her work on Spanish literature (2002: 14); and Colin Crisp's revisionist history of the French New Wave (1993), which reveals its interconnections with the classic French cinema it apparently opposed. I would like to thank Susan Hayward for drawing my attention to Crisp's study.

10. The Falange Española Tradicionalista y de las Juntas de Ofensiva Nacional Sindicalista, created in April 1937, was also known as the Movimiento Nacional (National Movement).

11. Brought in to solve an escalating currency crisis, this encouraged deregulation, introduced deflationary measures and opened Spain up to foreign investment.

12. Vatican II (1962–5) is credited with liberalising the Catholic Church in the modern era. Its reforms included replacing the obligatory Latin mass with vernacular liturgies, increasing power to the laity and approving ecumenicism. It also condemned dictatorship, but Franco denied this was a reference to Spain (Preston 1993: 725).

13. Quoting Payne (1987: 494), Paul Preston entitles the chapter covering the period 1960–3 in his biography of the dictator 'Intimations of Mortality' (1993: 685–713). In 1960, rumours that Franco had suffered a heart attack had to be officially denied (Preston 1993: 685); during 1961, Parkinson's disease was diagnosed (Payne 1987: 495); and a serious hunting accident on Christmas Eve 1961, which seriously injured his left hand, caused particular concern (Preston 1993: 697–8). Tatjana Pavlović, whose work covers an area similar to my discussion of the ageing body in Chapter 6, argues that 'Franco's slow and interminable dying and agony . . . deeply marked the [1960s]' (2003: 70).

14. See Labanyi (1999) on the reception of Spanish popular culture in Spain, where she notes that José Ortega y Gasset's Modernist disdain for 'low' culture is especially influential (1999: 100).

15. 'Eduardo Haro Tecglen: El niño republicano', http://www.eduardoharo tecglen.net/blog/. Consulted 31 May 2005.

16. These revisionist accounts also drew on the work of other Hispanic scholars like Paul Julian Smith (1994; 1998), Peter Evans (2000) and Steven Marsh (2002). For an overview of the role of cultural studies approaches in British Hispanism, see Chris Perriam's edited issue of *Paragraph*, 1999.

17. There were exceptions to this, like Antxón Eceiza's experience on VCE sets where he was employed to teach Francisco Rabal French (Angulo 2003a: 272–3).

18. Some critics name *Los golfos* as the first film of the NCE (Molina-Foix 1977: 19; Kinder 1993: 99), which may be justified because of its thematic concerns and aesthetic influences, but I define the movement as the films funded by García Escudero's legislation, for without this protection they would not have existed. See Zunzunegui (2002b: 103–5) for further discussion of the problem of defining the limits of the NCE.

19. Realism was the pet subject of *Nuestro Cine* through its entire run (1961–71), the yardstick by which it judged VCE, NCE and foreign cinemas alike. For articles devoted to defining the term and its import, see García Hortelano (1961); Ezcurra et al. (1961); San Miguel (1962a; 1962b); Gubern (1963).

20. A further area of overlap is dubbing: American, VCE and NCE films in the period were acoustically linked through the voices of the same dubbing actors.

21. On early support of the movement, see issue 15, *Nuestro Cine* and issue 61, *Film Ideal*. In this period, support is also found in books written by *Nuestro Cine* journalists like Fontenla (1966a) and Gubern et al. (1965). Republican critic Manuel Villegas López also wrote on the movement (1967; 1991), as did García Escudero, the minister responsible for its existence (1967). (García Escudero would continue to defend his role in the NCE and the Barcelona School in numerous subsequent publications: 1970; 1978; 1995). On hostile accounts, see Martínez Tomás (1967); Triana-Toribio (2003: 78); Julián (2002: 83). See Redondo (1964) for an example of criticism of the movement in a specialist journal.

22. For criticism by the journals, see Molina-Foix (2003); Llinás and Marías (1969); by directors, see Patino, quoted in Molina-Foix (1977: 19); by their successors, see Zunzunegui (2002b: 104–5).

23. Torreiro also contributes the chapter on this period to Monterde and Riambau (1995) and Gubern (2000).

24. Full discussion of the reasons for this similarity falls outside the scope of this book. José Enrique Monterde has called post-Franco film of 1973–92 'Un cine bajo la paradoja' (A Cinema of Paradox) (1993), because, just when the country broke free from Francoist protection, world, and particularly European, cinema became dependent on such protection (1993: 17), hence Spain had to return to this policy in order to compete. However, Monterde's argument that Spanish cinema was dependent on the state while world cinema was autonomous (1993: 16–17) is not the case in the 1960s, when other New Cinemas were as reliant on government subsidy as the NCE (Torreiro 1995a).

25. Added to this, there has been a recent tendency to lionise the NCE in Spain. On the one hand, events like retrospectives (such as the one launched at the Gijón International Film Festival, November 2003) and re-releases (such as Suevia Films' new collection of Patino's filmography) are to be celebrated as they mean the work of the NCE may reach a wider audience. On the other, the hagiographic documentary *De Salamanca a ninguna parte* (*From Salamanca to Nowhere*, Peña 2002), and sycophantic volumes on directors like Picazo (Iznaola Gómez 2004b), are monuments to Spain's current cult of nostalgia, which has celebrated in particular oppositional figures from the dictatorship.

26. First a film distributor, CIFESA (Compañía Industrial del Film Español S.A.) was a production company associated with Francoist values under the dictatorship.

27. Pierre Bourdieu's insights (1999) are pertinent to interpreting García Escudero's attempt to define 'art' cinema, as Triana-Toribio has noted in her reading of his 'Judgements of Taste' (2003: 65–9). According to Hopewell, the 'Special Interest' award dates from 1963 (1986: 64).

28. All critics give this figure (except Kathleen Vernon [2002: 261] who quotes up to 70 per cent) but it is common knowledge that production costs were inflated so that the 50 per cent subsidy would entirely finance the film.

29. For *Variety* reviews, see 'Review of *La Caza*' 1983; 'Review of *La tía Tula*' 1983; 'Review of *Nueve cartas a Berta*' 1983; for *Cahiers du cinéma*, 'San Sebastián' 1964; 'Festival de San Sebastián' 1967.

30. Spanish legislation in the 1960s was based on the protectionist model of *avance sur recettes* and special subsidies for films awarded the 'Special Quality' prize instigated by André Malraux in Gaullist France (Torreiro 1995a: 51–5).

31. A further area of comparison is that between 1960s Spain and Eastern Europe, where filmmakers benefited from similarly equivocal new freedoms, and also developed a metaphorical film language to overcome censorship.

PART I

SPANISH POPULAR CINEMA

CHAPTER 1

Franco's Great Family: *La gran familia* (*The Great Family*, Palacios 1962)

One of the last films to be awarded the 'National Interest' prize before José María García Escudero replaced the category in 1964, Fernando Palacios's consensual comedy *La gran familia* seemed to contain everything that the promoters of the *Nuevo Cine Español* considered wrong with the *Viejo Cine Español*. The film is an example of the commercial Spanish industry despised by the young generation of art directors and their sympathisers.[1] It was commissioned by Pedro Masó, a scriptwriter and sometime director (he worked on sixty-nine scripts over his long career, including those of *La gran familia* and *La ciudad no es para mí* [Chapter 2]), who became one of the most financially successful producers of the 1950s–1970s, working for both Asturias Films and his own company. Its director, Palacios, made only ten films before his premature death in 1965, including the sequel to *La gran familia*, *La familia y uno más* (*The Family Plus One* 1965) (Masó made the third part of the trilogy, *La familia, bien, gracias* [*The Family's Fine, Thanks* 1979]) and two Marisol films, after gaining solid training as an assistant director for his uncle, Florián Rey, and Ladislao Vajda, director of the runaway success of 1954, *Marcelino, pan y vino* (*Marcelino, Bread and Wine*) (Heredero 1993: 247). *La gran familia* was a popular film in terms of its production contexts, but not in terms of audience attendance: according to the figures discussed in my Introduction, it attracted a smaller audience than any of the apparently 'minority' NCE films I discuss in Part II.

Masó aimed to make his money from subsidy, not the box office, in this film; in this endeavour, *La gran familia*, the first film backed by his own company (Hernández Ruiz 1997: 516), was a resounding success. Its celebration of the conservative ideology that underpinned Francoism, attractively packaged as light, or 'white', family comedy,[2] and supported by popular stars, pushed all the right buttons on the classification board, which awarded it the coveted subsidy. Indeed, even though the dictator's name is never mentioned in the film, its apparently perfect alignment of state policy with domestic life suggests it might be renamed Franco's Great Family:[3] the father is head of the household, the mother, the angel of the hearth, and the purpose of their marriage, procreation. In this sense, watching *La gran familia* is like watching a 104-minute version of Franco awarding a prize to the parents of a large family, a favourite subject of the NO-DO newsreels at the time. Art would have appeared to match life for audiences viewing NO-DO reports of such awards in theatres prior to the screening of the film,[4] then observing a year in the life of a family that had received such an award in the film itself.[5]

Like the NO-DOs, *La gran familia* might therefore be considered a tool of propaganda to support government policy. If today Western governments accept immigration (in theory at least) as a means to maintain workforces in response to declining birth rates, in Spain under Franco, a policy of pronatalism was adopted to re-stock a country whose population was depleted by the Civil War, and whose birth rates had been falling anyway (Grugel and Rees 1997: 135). Even though contraception, sterilisation and abortion were banned from 1941 (Brooksbank Jones 1997: 84), pronatalist policy under Franco failed. As Anny Brooksbank Jones points out (1997: 94 n. 3), despite the prohibition of its use,

> contraception was practised throughout the Franco years, as reflected in the decline in family size between 1930 (when 38% of married women had more than four children) and 1970 (when this figure had fallen to 17%) . . ... In 1963, 82% of doctors reportedly believed their patients were using some form of birth control and in only 34% of cases was this thought to be the withdrawal method.

Economic hardship explains why many parents chose to have fewer children in the post-war period, and, for those missing out on the economic boom, poverty was also the reason for smaller families in the developmental years. In addition, from the 1960s onwards, middle-class couples postponed and reduced child-bearing owing to increasing female attendance of universities and participation in working life.

Issues surrounding gender, therefore, throw into relief the tensions triggered by social change. As Brooksbank Jones notes, 'Throughout the 1960s, women remained at the epicentre of tensions between the competing demands of their official domestic role and the regime's growing need for an enlarged workforce' (1997: 77). This uneasy alliance of tradition and modernity is revealed by the government's contradictory actions in the early 1960s: while on the one hand its Ministry of Labour legally recognised certain women's rights in the workplace in the 1961 'Law of Political, Professional, and Labour Rights of Women', on the other, its Ministry of Information and Tourism awarded the pronatalist *La gran familia* the

'National Interest' prize, which led to the top level of subsidy of 50 per cent and benefits in promotion and distribution (Gubern 1981: 133).

To read *La gran familia* as straightforward propaganda, therefore, overlooks its more complex response to the contradictory context from which it arose: the failed promotion of pronatalism and simultaneous timid encouragement of female participation in the work force. Since the film focuses on a middle-class family, it does not address the economic reason for the decline in child-bearing – continued poverty meant fewer children – nor does it focus on the economic need for the women of working-class families to work. Rather, it responds to, and condemns, the new situation in the 1960s whereby middle-class couples postponed and restricted parenthood owing to changes in women's roles. *La gran familia* celebrates the twin cults of motherhood and domesticity that underpinned the nineteenth-century gender ideology of the 'ángel del hogar' (angel of the hearth). (Francoism's return to these anachronistic Victorian-style values was given legal expression in the re-adoption of the 1889 Civil Code in 1938.)[6] Unlike the authors of the historical epics of the 1940s and 1950s, Masó, the film's producer and scriptwriter, Rafael Salvia and Antonio Vich, its other scriptwriters, and Palacios, its director, do not choose period costume drama to advocate anachronistic values, but set the film in the present of 1962 Madrid, and even reinforce its contemporaneity by references to current events, like the marriage of the future monarch Prince Juan Carlos to Princess Sofia, which had taken place on 14 May 1962. Rather than avoid the confrontation of tradition and modernity through a period setting, then, *La gran familia* seeks instead to conceal the contradiction between its contemporary setting and anachronistic values by naturalising their reconciliation.

This chapter will therefore analyse first how the film conceals contradictions to construct a conservative vision of the family that was convincing enough to win over the 'National Interest' awards board. Genre, plot, musical score and performance style are harnessed to naturalise Franco's 1960s Great Family and show that the current economic boom happily coexists with traditional family structures. However, there are fault-lines running through the film that, even if they do not entirely undermine it, at least weaken this construction of conservatism. While mindful of the undesirability of approaches to popular film that skew textual evidence in their enthusiasm to read against the grain, in the second part of this chapter, I will none the less contend that *La gran familia* sustains a reading that reveals its tentative critique of Francoism in the 1960s. Peter Evans has already demonstrated that there is a 'discernible pattern of dissidence' in an analysis of Masó's *Familia* trilogy that emphasises its questioning of masculinity and parent–child relations (2000: 85). Focusing on the first of the three films, I develop these insights by paying particular attention to the role played by the veteran comic actor José Isbert and the discourse of claustrophobia that is emphasised in the film by cinematography and editing.

'¿Estás contento por algo?' (Are you happy for any particular reason?)

'Yo siempre estoy contento por mucho' (I always have lots to be happy about) the father of *La gran familia* replies to the mother's enquiry if he is happy about anything in particular, in one of the last scenes of the film. Even though at this point there is a particular reason – it's pay-day and, furthermore, the day for collecting the tax allowance the father is owed for his family of fifteen children – the general reason echoes like a refrain throughout Palacios's film: happiness is synonymous with the family, and the bigger the family the better. If we read *La gran familia* as an act of persuasion, its purpose is above all to naturalise this subjective opinion as objective fact. If happiness means having a large family, then unhappiness is caused by a lack of children – not economic hardship or political repression – and unhappiness within a large family is simply not 'natural'.

An arsenal of film resources is deployed to naturalise this message, which relates in particular to the input of Masó, Salvia and Vich on the script, Palacios as director (aided by Salvia as assistant director) and Adolfo Waitzman, who composed the film's original score. First, *La gran familia* proceeds according to the generic conventions of familiar settings and stock characters of the *comedia sainetesca*.[7] Its characters are not only recognisable, but are introduced in the opening sequence as types rather than individuals. The credits feature no proper names, but present the adults by family role – father, mother, grandpa, godfather – and the fifteen children by nicknames related to their activities – 'el petardista' (firework fan), 'la enamorada' (the girl who's in love) – or physical characteristics – 'la mellada' (the gap-toothed girl), 'los gemelos' (the twins). The setting of the film also conforms to expectations. Most of the action occurs in an interior studio re-creation of a lower-middle-class family flat, and the Madrid location is conveyed through references to emblematic sites in the script and in exterior shots. For instance, when the father describes his dream of the future, he sees the Gran Vía scattered with placards advertising his son as architect and himself as master builder, or again, when he admonishes another son for playing football in the flat, he asks, '¿Tú te has creído que esto es el estadio del Bernabéu?' (Did you think this was the Bernabéu stadium?).[8] The only exterior shots of recognisable city land-marks are associated with male adult family members; in keeping with her role as an angel of the hearth, the only public spaces in which the mother is seen are the covered market, where she buys food for the family, and the department store, where she chooses a first communion dress and sailor's outfit. The father is associated with contemporary, modernising Spain when he visits a building site on the Paseo de la Castellana,[9] and the grandpa is connected to traditional Spain when he goes Christmas shop-ping in the Plaza Mayor, which is emblematic of Madrid's Habsburg architecture. Characterisation according to family role and the setting in Madrid follow conventional expectations and thus serve to naturalise the status quo staged by the film: if the characters and the setting are 'normal', so is the happy life of a large family presented.

This status quo is shored up further by its disruption and restoration. The loss of Chencho, the family's youngest male child, on a Christmas shopping-trip with some of his siblings and grandpa in the Plaza Mayor, and his subsequent kidnapping by a childless couple, briefly expose the family as vulnerable in the urban environment. (As Evans [2000: 86] points out, this event also indicates the criminal desperation to which an other-wise pleasant couple are driven by their childlessness in a society that assigns all value to having children.) However, this vulnerability galvanises the family, leading its members to declare their enthusiasm for both its size and unity, and of course Chencho's return bolsters it further. After handing him over, the childless couple makes a desperate plea to the father for the boy to remain with them as they have no children, whereas the Alonsos have so many. This proposal allows the father to dismiss any notion that a child might benefit from being in a smaller family, and thus champion Franco's policy of pronatalism:

> Ya sé que son muchos hermanos, pero precisamente por eso han de estar juntos todos. . . . No se trata de que [Chencho] esté mejor o peor atendido, sino que esté donde debe estar: en su casa. (I know that there are lots of brothers and sisters, but that's precisely why they all have to be together. . . . It's not a question of whether [Chencho] would be looked after better or worse, but rather that he is where he should be: in his home.)

In this sequence we are further led to believe that the joy experienced by the family on the return of the child is so great that it makes them oblivi-ous to the presence of his kidnappers standing next to them outside the television studio: one might reasonably have expected the family to rebuke them for their criminal act.

The loss and return of Chencho also allow the film's authors to indicate, in passing, the efficiency of state bureaucracy. Through four soundbridges, four different sets of state officials are shown to combine their efforts in what constitutes no less than a paean to bureaucratic efficiency. Extra-diegetic music connects the first sequence of the initial phone call reporting the child's loss to the police switchboard, to the second image of the police commissioner receiving the report, and to the third image of the police on duty in patrol cars, and finally to the fourth image of the state radio presenters broadcasting the news of Chencho's loss to the nation. Moreover, and more importantly, the disruption and restoration of the status quo through the loss and return of the child allow scriptwriters and directors to signal the compatibility of family life and the modern city. Chencho gets lost owing to the threat posed to the family by the anonymous modern city, but he is found thanks to television, a synecdoche of that same modernity: the family appeal for Chencho's return in a television advert, and when the boy recognises his parents on screen, it pricks the consciences of his kidnappers. This happy coexistence of family and modernity is confirmed by the final sequence of the film. It is Christmas Eve, and the reunited fifteen children gather round the new television, which has been sent to them as a gift from the guilt-ridden kidnappers. They tune in to hear the 'Hallelujah Chorus' of Handel's *Messiah*, which is here restored to its 'proper' religious place after such irreverent treatment by Buñuel in the beggars' orgy sequence of *Viridiana* the previous year. Next, the mother announces the imminent arrival of child number sixteen, who will be called Jesús. On the soundtrack, we then hear the choir rejoice: 'And he shall reign forever and ever, King of Kings and Lord of Lords, forever and ever, Hallelujah'. Through the music played on the television (which may not have been grasped by all audiences as the words are in English, but would certainly have been clear to the composer Waitzman), the film makes an association that not only suggests that this Spanish mother is ideal, but that she is in fact a modern-day Mary who will give birth to a Messiah. Franco's Great Family, therefore, becomes none other than the Holy Family itself.

If the status quo is presented as 'normal' through predictable characterisation and setting, and shored up by its disruption and restoration, the scriptwriters and director further naturalise Franco's Great Family by structuring the plot of the film so that it follows the rhythms of one calendar year. This includes both the physical cycle of the seasons of spring, summer, autumn and winter, and the cultural cycles of the religious calendar – holy communion and Christmas – and the academic and working year – which alternate between periods of work, school examinations and holiday. The parallel between physical and cultural cycles renders both 'natural', and because the plot of the film is aligned with these cycles, so the message of the film is also presented as 'natural': the desirability of the more or less yearly birth of a child to a married couple. This process culminates with the mother's announcement of her fifteenth pregnancy. Though this event is based on the cultural choice of the couple not to practise abstinence or use contraception,[10] it is presented as natural, as is her husband's delighted reaction. Womanhood is, therefore, the vehicle that reconciles both the natural and the cultural. The fertile female body, which functions according to natural menstrual cycles, is used to naturalise the cultural choice to have a large family.

The composer Waitzman is another key contributor to the film's construction of conservatism. With the exception of Handel's work in the final sequence, the soundtrack of the film consists of Argentine-born Waitzman's original composition. It functions first to complement the narrative, and second, like the 'Hallelujah Chorus', to reflect and reinforce the film's promotion of the family. With respect to the first function, the use of the extra-diegetic music ranges from the inclusion of orchestral strings to signal romance (as when the parents are alone together), the inserts of percussion to highlight comedy (as when the crowd of children visit the godfather's patisserie and – to his consternation – relieve him of most of his freshly baked cakes), or the addition of music to emphasise the narrative (as when circus music complements the children and grandpa's circus game). With respect to the second function of reinforcing the promotion of the family, leitmotif is used effectively to underscore filial and fraternal bonds. This is vital in a film that attempts to convince its audience over just 104 minutes of running time that the fifteen children, who are physically dissimilar as they are played by actors who are not blood relations (with the exception of the identical twins), are in fact siblings.[11]

The film opens with a still frame of the family at what we later realise is a first communion ceremony, followed by a still frame in medium shot of the father and mother. These images are accompanied by the sound of a full choir and orchestra performing Waitzman's composition (Figure 1.1), which looks forward to the full rendition of the 'Hallelujah Chorus' of the final sequence. 'La gran familia' (The Great Family) sing the sopranos and altos, then the phrase is repeated in the same melody by the baritones and basses, which indicates the complementary roles played by men and women in the construction of such a 'Great Family'. Waitzman's opening and Handel's ending of the film are not only comparable because of the full choir and orchestra; their melodic profiles of rising and falling intervals, particularly the perfect fourth, are also similar (compare Figures 1.1 and 1.2).

Figure 1.1. Adapted excerpt of musical score from *La gran familia*, Pedro Masó P.C.

Figure 1.2. Excerpt of the 'Hallelujah Chorus' of Georg Friedrich Handel's *Messiah*.

Figure 1.3. Adapted excerpt of musical score from *La gran familia*, Pedro Masó P.C.

Following this Handel-inspired musical introduction to the great family, there follows a descending scale on strings that links the image of the family in the public space of the church to the introduction of the family in the private space of the home. A new musical phrase (Figure 1.3) played on bassoon accompanies the medium shot of the grandpa, and this phrase will become the Alonso family leitmotif used throughout this film and its sequel, for which Waitzman was also composer.[12]

As the credits roll, we meet each member of the family in medium shot as they sleep (save the parents in the marital bed, whose sleeping arrangements are decorously referred to by the image of their slippers and of their youngest child, the baby, in the cradle by their bed). The leitmotif is repeated on the soundtrack, with variations of pitch and tempo and on different instruments, so that the audience cannot fail to make the connection between the musical phrase and the blood bond that links these members.

This musical portrayal of the blood bond also confirms and celebrates the role of the father, as at the end of the first sequence we hear him whistle the leitmotif as he leaves the flat for work.[13] His role as progenitor is therefore announced and underscored by the fact that he is the only character who links non-diegetic music (Waitzman's score) to diegetic sound (his whistle). (His paternity is similarly confirmed through music when he sings the Christmas carol 'Marimorena', and his children gradually join in [Hernández Ruiz 1997: 517].) After extensive treatment in the opening sequence, the Alonso family musical leitmotif recurs throughout the narrative to remind the audience of blood relations, like a kind of acoustic representation of the family genes. In other words, the relationship between family members is not only the subject of the narrative of this film of family happiness. Waitzman's score suggests that blood bonds are so important that their representation extends beyond both narrative and imagetrack to the film's soundtrack.

The persuasiveness of the conservative message of *La gran familia*, which we may measure by its award of the institutional prize, if not by an upturn in the declining birth rate, is also due in large part to its excellent cast, an aspect that was stressed in contemporary reviews of the film.[14] While the director and co-director coax plausible performances from its team of child actors,[15] the picture is carried by the expensive stars, Alberto Closas and Amparo Soler Leal, who play the father and mother, complemented by José Isbert and José Luis López Vázquez, playing grandpa and godfather, as their comic sidekicks.[16] Closas plays a key role in *La gran familia*, just as the father is central to the family in the narrative of the film, and the patriarch is the mainstay of Francoist ideology. It is important that he is seen both at home and at work, as this underscores the parallel between his domestic and public roles: just as the father must provide authority as head of the household and money as bread-winner, so men must lead and work for Spain's current economic boom (were this a 1940s film, the empire might have been evoked in this context). Indications of a cross-over between these two roles further underscore the indivisibility of the two. For instance, we see the father work on his building plans at home; then we see him accidentally use a baby's dummy instead of an eraser at work, a comic incident that causes his colleague to recall the time when he delivered a plan wrapped up in nappies! The choice of the father's employment as a master builder also emphasises the indivisibility of the father's dual domestic and public roles, for he is both building the new modernising Spain and populating it. While the foreman at one of the building sites where he delivers his plans disapprovingly remarks that he has 'demasiados trabajos, demasiados hijos' (too many jobs and too many children), the exchange between another two builders represents more faithfully the optimism of the film: '¡Si a este hombre le dejan, hace él sólo la Torre de Madrid!' (If they let him, this man would build the Torre de Madrid himself),[17] comments one. '¡Y además la llena de chicos!' (And he would fill it up with children too!) quips the other.

The persuasiveness of this naturalisation of the male role as builder and populator of modern Spain hinges on Closas's convincing performance as the eternal optimist. He cheerfully performs both roles, and is unperturbed by the series of setbacks suffered by the family, like the lack of money to pay for the first communion, his 'oveja negra' (black sheep) son's failure in his exams and the loss of Chencho. If in the on-screen performance the mask of optimism does not slip – even when Closas delivers the most implausibly cheerful lines – the actor's off-screen persona surely punctures this utopian rhetoric. Evans points out that Closas's notorious womanising undermines his clean-cut portrayal of the father: 'he was an inveterate Don Juan, the Spanish cinema's equivalent of the endlessly divorcing Hollywood prototype, married seven times, his first marriage at twenty-one in 1942 lasting only three months, his second producing five children' (2000: 84). However, as Evans also shows, this off-screen star-image is possibly harnessed by the film for its on-screen promotion of conservatism, for 'paternity and marital fidelity are all the more convincing if embraced by a sexually desirable male with a history of sexual experience' (2000: 85).

Just as the role of the father is complemented by that of the mother in the narrative of the film, part of Closas's success derives from his convincing interaction with his co-star, Soler Leal, who plays the mother, and who was the only one of the four principal actors of the film to receive an award for her performance (Figure 1.4).[18] Drawing on centuries of representations of saintly motherhood, and especially Catholic Marian iconography and the domestic 'angel of the hearth' of nineteenth-century and Francoist female conduct manuals, Soler Leal embodies the perfect wife and mother fondly imagined in these texts. At only twenty-nine, the film also somewhat implausibly imagines the youthful beauty of this mother of fifteen – the actress playing the eldest child (María José Alonso) is in fact only seven years Soler Leal's junior. Like her husband, the mother is excessively optimistic in much of the picture. For instance, 'ya me las arreglaré' (I'll find a way) is her confident, fatalistic response to their inability to pay for the first communion, which is ultimately resolved not by her, but by the godfather's charity.

None the less, her performance becomes more nuanced and interesting following the loss of Chencho. On the one hand, the actress's ability to handle tragedy heightens her portrayal of the all-suffering mother, as when she clutches her husband Carlos in anguish on hearing of the child's loss, or when she delivers a heartfelt description of her son to the authorities in a static medium shot that underscores and glorifies her maternal despair (we have never seen her take much notice of Chencho up to this point, but

Figure 1.4. Amparo Soler Leal and Alberto Closas in *La gran familia*. Pedro Masó P.C.

somehow she is intimately acquainted with the idiosyncrasies of his linguistic and motor development). However, the tragic situation also provides
her with a single scene in which she may display anger, and Soler Leal seems
to relish her hearty outburst rather too much to be fitting for a domestic
angel. 'Tú, que estás fuera de este mundo' (You're in a world of your own),
she snaps at the grandpa, who was responsible for looking after the children, 'La culpa la tengo yo por dejarles ir solos contigo. Ellos no tienen
conocimiento, y tú no sabes tenerlo' (It's my fault for letting them go with
you on their own. They don't have the understanding, and you don't know
the meaning of the word). This sequence of rebellion is short-lived: the
father reprimands her, and her temper is soon controlled and remains so for
the rest of the picture. It is none the less tempting to read it as a premoni-
tion of the actress's future roles. Her portrayals of terrifying and aggressive
women in dissident cinema of the 1970s deconstruct the angelic motherhood of this picture (see, for instance, *Mi hija Hildegart* [*My Daughter
Hildegart*, Fernán Gómez 1977] and *Crimen de Cuenca* [*The Crime of
Cuenca*, Miró 1979]). This shift in her career has been attributed to Soler
Leal's marriage to the producer Alfredo Matas (head of Jet Films) in 1969
(Aguilar and Genover 1996: 615), but her refusal to repeat the role of
mother in the second and third films of the Masó *Familia* trilogy indicates
an earlier desire for a change of direction.

Closas's off-screen persona and earlier portrayal of the tortured hero in Bardem's dissident masterpiece *Muerte de un ciclista* (*Death of a Cyclist* 1955), and Soler Leal's future rejection of the role of beatific mother perceived in her angry outburst, are cracks in the mask of marital and parental bliss otherwise presented in the film. If those cracks are ultimately papered over by the processes of naturalisation, structure of plot, sound-track and performance style, other aspects of the film are more resistant to concealment.

'¡Superman no se rinde nunca!' (Superman will never give up!): José Isbert and Francisco Franco

If Closas and Soler Leal carry the family elements of this family comedy, Isbert and López Vázquez, two of Spain's greatest comic stars, provide the comedy. López Vázquez plays to comic type, drawing on his trade marks of exaggerated gesticulation and verbal excess to embody the grumpy but lovable godfather and provide the film with its moments of textbook situ-ation farce, as when he is ambushed by the children in the patisserie, courts the school teacher in pitiable French, is attacked by a parachuting crab from the children's rocket and almost ends up in a television nativity play – false beard and a live lamb hung around his shoulders and all. If these interludes serve as moments of light comic relief in the film, Evans also argues, in his consideration of the *Familia* trilogy as a whole, that the char-acterisation of López Vázquez's godfather plays the more important role of bolstering the family institution by representing an undesirable alter-native to it. First, his 'benign, ridiculous' masculinity (2000: 83) throws Closas's portrayal of the masculine ideal into relief, and second, his choice of an alternative life-style (he marries, but has no children) is sent up as ridiculous, thus reinforcing the family life championed by the film and 'innoculating' it against alternatives that threaten its existence (2000: 84). In keeping with the overall act of naturalisation performed by *La gran familia*, childlessness is not only figured as unnatural, but, in the case of the childless couple who resort to kidnap, it is criminal, and in the case of the godfather, absurd.

Isbert's grandpa apparently offers similar comic relief. The humour of his role appears to derive from simple comic reversal. He is the oldest family member, yet while age defines the parents and older children as adults, excessive age reverses the developmental scale and renders the grandpa a child (as it did in his hilarious portrayal of the mischievous big kid in the dark comedy scripted by Rafael Azcona and directed by Marco Ferreri, *El cochecito* [*The Little Car* 1960]). While the grandpa's pension suggests his former membership of a salaried, adult world, the amount he gets is insufficient to contribute to the 'grown-up' expenses of the household, and he spends it instead on cinema tickets, sweets and comics – which are also the favourite leisure items of the young children. The only other purchase he makes is of a comically emaciated turkey for the family Christmas dinner, which allows him simultaneously to exalt and deflate the stoic forbearance that characterised Spain's impoverished post-war years, through which he would have lived: the bird is 'flaco, pero honrado' (skinny, but honourable) he pompously declares.

Notwithstanding occasional interactions with the adult characters about not having much money, the injustice of retirement and whether he can cadge a cigarette, the script renders most of Isbert's verbal interventions indistinguishable from those of the younger children. In particular, the remarks he makes during the children's games, which include battles (in which he plays superman), space trips, rocket launches and circuses, are indistinguishable from the children's chatter. This makes him an enthusiastic child participant in, rather than an adult supervisor of, the games. His nutritional habits reinforce his characterisation as a naughty little child: when the family watch a film and the voice of the mother is heard warning that eating too many sweets leads to worms, she is talking to the grandpa, not one of the little kids. Indeed, when the younger ones fall ill after eating too many cakes at the first communion, the adults and older children remain well, but the grandpa falls sick too.

'Eres más crío que los críos' the mother reprimands him on arriving home during a particularly raucous battle-game, which idiomatically translates as 'you're just a big kid', but literally means 'you're more of a kid than the kids'. Indeed, the film draws parallels not just between the grandpa and the kids, but the grandpa and the youngest male child Chencho, the rather dim toddler with whom he shares a bedroom. Both eat biscuits at the breakfast table owing to their lack of teeth, and the speech of both is similarly difficult to decipher. The grandpa is occasionally almost unintelligible thanks to Isbert's famous rasping croak – at this stage in his career this was actually caused by the onset of laryngitis, an illness that forced him to give up acting in 1964, two years before his death (Aguilar and Genover 1996: 291). Chencho too is difficult to understand as he hasn't learnt to speak properly yet. This is no surprise, as the grandpa is the one responsible for teaching him: 'ga – lle – ta' (bis – cuit) he wheezes to him in a language lesson at the breakfast table, which, unsurprisingly, the boy is unable to repeat. 'Ni tú me entiendes a mí, ni yo a ti' (You can't understand me and I can't understand you), the grandpa concludes at another meal scene with the boy, reinforcing the similar linguistic unintelligibility of the two.

Evans highlights both the visual and acoustic aspects of Isbert's physicality in reading his performance as critical of the current political regime:

> His diminutive, gnome-like stature and rasping voice [are] the signs of Francoism's delivery of mutant forms of humanity . . . . Like López Vázquez he represents a complex alternative form of masculinity, tolerated because of its comic reversal of hegemonic forms, but also slightly troubling because its hyperbolic deviant expression registers the repressions and pressures to which all Spanish men had been subjected. (2000: 83)

Isbert's contribution to the film may be more troubling than Evans proposes because, unlike López Vázquez's godfather, his performance of a 'comic reversal of hegemonic forms' is imperfect. Like the godfather, he has married, but unlike the godfather, he has evidently been a parent and chosen family life. Therefore he is simultaneously both the quintessential patriarch, because he is the original progenitor, and a comic reversal of the patriarch, as his performance is occasionally indistinguishable from that of the younger children. This confusing conflation gives rise to great comic moments, as when the grandpa simultaneously champions the father – the inheritor of his role – yet challenges him. For example, he tells the children off for starting to eat before the father joins the head of the dinner table, yet, like one of the naughty little children who cannot wait, he himself nibbles his biscuits before the father's arrival. But the amalgam of both the normal and the comic in Isbert's role in *La gran familia* is more profound as it troubles that very 'normality' by blurring boundaries. If deviancy from the norm is, in Evans's words, 'slightly troubling', imperfect deviancy, whereby aspects of the deviant are combined with the norm, is more troubling, for it poses a challenge to normality by questioning its very existence.

Consider, for instance, the war game between grandpa-superman and the children. Isbert is hilariously decked out in the children's space helmet and toy gun, but a military medal can also be clearly seen, swinging on a chain around his neck (Figure 1.5; in this still the medal is concealed). We may assume that the medal was awarded to him when he was a young man fighting for the Nationalists, for while there is no explicit mention of the grandpa's military past in the film, it is likely that a man of his age would have fought in the Civil War.[19] This scene, in which Isbert is play-acting as an American cartoon action-figure, recalls the celebrated dream sequence of Berlanga's *¡Bienvenido Mister Marshall!* (1952). In Berlanga's film, Isbert plays a village mayor who dreams of being an American sheriff. In the depiction of this dream, we see Isbert appear in a spoof Hollywood western dressed in a cowboy outfit, complete with over-sized shiny

Figure 1.5. José Isbert and Amparo Soler Leal in *La gran familia*. Pedro Masó P.C.

sheriff's badge, of which the glinting medal dangling around Isbert's neck in *La gran familia* is a visual reminder. In *¡Bienvenido Mister Marshall!*, the authority of Isbert's mayor is sent up through this comic appearance in a re-created American film in the dream. In *La gran familia*, Isbert's character's frame of reference is similarly derived from American popular culture: Superman comics and space adventure films replace the western. But whereas the 'real-life' role as mayor is critiqued by the private dreams of cowboys and Indians in *¡Bienvenido Mister Marshall!*, this is reversed in the game sequence of *La gran familia*. Here, the fantasy world of the grandpa's war game is punctured by the reference to his 'real-life' military experience. The presence of the medal, therefore, gives the lie to the childish game by incongruously introducing the adult world of war, yet also simultaneously reduces the war – which brought the current government to power – to the level of a childish game. Rather than a comic reversal then, Isbert is an incongruous adult presence in the children's world, just as elsewhere in the film he is an incongruous childish presence in the adult world.

Isbert's role as grandpa evokes another incongruous figure in Spain at the time: Francisco Franco. The medal may remind audiences of the Caudillo, who was often seen by the public decorated in military paraphernalia, but a further parallel between the two lies in the fact that Isbert played the grandpa in *La gran familia* just when Franco was relishing the same role. With seven children born to his daughter Carmen between 1951 and 1964, the dictator was enjoying presiding over his own Great Family,[20] and Franco as benevolent grandpa was considered a suitable way to present him to the nation as he aged.[21] In 1962 Franco was seventy and Isbert seventy-six, and both were slightly rotund, diminutive old men. Palacios's Great Family is therefore Franco's Great Family because, through his on-screen surrogate Isbert, the dictator is present in the film as the grandpa. This parallel renders the script rich in double meanings. For instance, the grandpa's hilarious declaration in the middle of the battle-game that '¡Superman no se rinde nunca!' (Superman will never give up!) becomes a biting satire of both the dictator's inflated sense of masculinity and his refusal to relinquish power. The previously mentioned reference to Juan Carlos and Sofia's wedding is a further nod to this increasing preoccupation about Spain's future post-Franco, which was to become one of the major political issues of the 1960s, until the dictator finally named the prince as his successor in 1969.

Thus, rather than a comic reversal of normality, Isbert's portrayal of a 'tonto lelo' (silly twit) – as Chencho calls him in one of his few coherent phrases in the whole film – is a troubling deconstruction of normality itself, not least through reference to the figure of Franco, the nation's role model. Despite its location in this quintessential example of consensual cinema, Isbert's role in *La gran familia* might therefore be understood as a dress rehearsal for his celebrated role as a retired state executioner in another dissident Berlanga masterpiece, scripted by Azcona, of the following year, *El verdugo*. Steven Marsh notes in his reading of this film that 'Isbert plays a type Spaniard, he is always referred to as "normal", and undoes Spanishness in the playing of it' (2004: 127). Likewise, what is disruptive about Isbert's presence in *La gran familia* is not so much his 'hyperbolic deviancy', but his problematic normality. To paraphrase Marsh, in *La gran familia*, Isbert undoes the normal family by playing its grandpa.

'Estamos a punto de llegar a Saturno' (We're about to reach Saturn): Travel and Entrapment

If Isbert's role constitutes a connection between consensual and dissident cinemas in the period, further evidence of cross-fertilisation between the two is provided by the film's editor, Pedro del Rey. Scanning the list of his work in the 1960s gives the lie to any attempt to separate 'Old' and 'New' cinemas in the period, for *La gran familia* was cut by an editor who had worked with all the respected art directors of the day, including Buñuel (on *Viridiana*), Ferreri (on *El cochecito*) and Saura (on *Los golfos*), and would work on two of the NCE films studied in depth in this book, *La tía Tula* and *Nueve cartas a Berta*. While it would be naïve automatically to expect a critical edge from this editor just because he had worked in the opposi- tional cinema, his treatment of space in Palacios's film does create a sense of claustrophobia and entrapment that, like Isbert's performance, under- cuts its otherwise relentless utopianism. This sense of claustrophobia and entrapment created through editing also provides the impetus for an alter- native reading of aspects of the script, plot and *mise en scène* that refer to movement and travel.

With eighteen inhabitants (fifteen children, parents and grandpa), the Alonso family flat is overcrowded. At the start of the film, however, cine- matography counters the sensation of claustrophobia. We meet the family as they sleep, and even though there are in some cases four or five children to a room, each child is assigned their own space by the camera through their introduction in medium shot. (The exception is the twins, who share a medium shot as they share a bed.) However, after the credit sequence, the family flat is represented above all through long shots and relatively long takes.[22] Often the camera is static, with movement provided by the various family members scurrying in and out of the frame, or backwards and for- wards through depth of field, either playing games or attending to domes- tic chores. On the one hand, the movement of the actors within these scenes allows the cinematographer Juan Mariné to convey the cheerful hustle and bustle of family life, but on the other, his static camera creates an impression of claustrophobia that is emphasised by Del Rey's length of take. Núria Triana-Toribio calls the sequences featuring numerous family members in this film 'choral scenes', which, she argues, are fundamental to the film's promotion of '*desarrollismo* and National-Catholic strategies. The film's portrayal hinges on choral scenes with middle-class characters which emphasise that the production of (many) children, and the con- sumption of goods are the desirable goals for the Spanish Catholic family' (2003: 79). When the length of take transforms such choral communality into claustrophobia, it follows that the conservative message of the film regarding capitalist and family values is therefore weakened.

If the desirability of Franco's Great Family is questioned by figuring proximity as claustrophobia, then this is complemented by the represen- tation of Franco's Spain not in terms of the dynamism of change that underpinned *desarrollismo*, but in terms of stasis and entrapment. While the plot of the film includes one real journey to the Catalan coastal resort of Tarragona, it also evokes a number of fantasy journeys through the children and grandpa's games. Stimulated by space adventure films they have seen at the cinema, in one scene they re-create extra-terrestrial travel in a spaceship in the hall of the flat. But while in the films that they see at the cinema new planets are discovered and explored, their spaceship is – symbolically – grounded in the Madrid flat. 'Estamos a punto de llegar a Saturno' (We're about to reach Saturn) the grandpa informs the mother when she interrupts the game, a declaration that conveys both the fascination for travel and the impossibility of its realisation, and therefore encapsulates the film's portrayal of frustrated escape. Just as the mother interrupts the gang's space travel when they are about to land on Saturn, so their attempt to send a rocket to the moon is also frustrated by another family member. The rocket, along with its parachuting crab-astronaut, lands on top of the godfather during his courtship of the school teacher. It is therefore always the family that blocks escape. In fact, the only place outside Spain reached in the entire film is heaven, when the *petardista* sends a rocket up to God in the last image to thank him for the return of Chencho. In other words, the film proposes that in Franco's Spain, the only contact needed in the outside world is heaven – an ironic contrast with the military, business and political ties the regime sought with the West at the time.

In the context of this discourse of claustrophobia and entrapment, we might re-examine the script and *mise en scène*. The father's previously mentioned reference to the flat as the Bernabéu stadium might be reconsidered in this light as an ironic comment on its cramped nature. Likewise, when he complains at work about the city traffic, his remarks encode a condemnation of the city as a whole as cramped. '¿Usted ha visto cómo está la circulación?' (Have you seen what the traffic is like?) he grumbles good-humouredly to the site manager, 'En Madrid ya no se cabe. Tendríamos que hacerlo de nuevo, pero mucho más ancho. Y además hay que extenderse. Ciudades satélites. Alcalá, Guadalajara, Aranda . . .' (People don't fit in Madrid anymore. We ought to build it again, but much more spaced out. And what's more, we need to spread out. Commuter towns. Alcalá, Guadalajara, Aranda . . .).

The following exchange between the mother and father also refers to the claustrophobic flat and the desire to move further afield. When the mother tells the father that the baby will soon be walking, he responds, '¿Hacia dónde?' (Where to?). Although Closas delivers the line in a joking tone, it seems rather incongruous, given the parents' usual banter about the great futures that await all their children.[23] The idea that walking, movement or travel is pointless in Franco's Spain because there is nowhere to go is reinforced by the mother's retort: 'De momento como todos, pasillo arriba, pasillo abajo' ('For the moment like all of them/us, up the corridor and down the corridor). Though this line is cheerfully delivered by Soler Leal, it confirms the suggestion of entrapment. Furthermore, 'todos' could refer to 'all the children', or 'all of us', the latter suggesting that the whole of Franco's Great Family is trapped in the claustrophobic corridor of a flat, with nowhere to go. The prominent placing of paintings of images of transport in the family home might also be re-read in this context: the images of the sailing ship in the hall and of the railway station in the dining room suggest travel and escape that throw into relief the claustrophobia of the living space.

While textual analysis shows how film form naturalises Francoist ideology in *La gran familia*, it also reveals possibly unexpected overlaps between consensual and dissident cinema in this period. Just as there are similarities between Isbert's contribution to *La gran familia* and *El verdugo*, the references to claustrophobia and frustrated journeys in this commercial comedy also look forward to dissident Spanish cinema's treatment of the same subject. Tula is unable to escape from the ideological imprisonment of her suffocating life in *La tía Tula*, just as Lorenzo is symbolically trapped in Salamanca at the end of *Nueve cartas a Berta*, or Enrique is captured by both Spain's divided past and Saura's freeze-frame at the end of *La caza*. In Víctor Erice's *El espíritu de la colmena* (*The Spirit of the Beehive* 1973), the little girls, Ana and Isabel, might be psychologically disturbed rather than improbably cheerful like the children of *La gran familia*, but none the less, they are all fascinated by symbols of transport. In Palacios's film these may be comic props, like an astronaut's helmet, and in Erice's, lyrical images, like the train tracks disappearing on the horizon, but both pessimistically point to journeys that these children may never make.

Notes

1. For instance, in *Nuestro Cine*, José Luis Egea (1963) condemned the film as 'cine engañoso y cine mal hecho, cine-mentira. Cine-deshonestidad. Cine inmoral' (deceptive and poorly made cinema, a cinema of lies. Dishonest cinema. Immoral cinema).

2. Álvaro del Amo contrasts consensual 'white comedies' with dissident 'black comedies' (1975: 22); Núria Triana-Toribio suggests that in the mid-1960s romantic comedies were replaced by family comedies (2003: 76–7).

3. The adjective 'Gran[de]' means both 'big' and 'great'. Peter Evans (2000) and Triana-Toribio (2003) translate the title as 'Big'; I have chosen 'Great' to foreground the film's pretensions of grandeur, as well as the size of the family depicted. The subtitles of the DVD version of the film, recently released by Suevia Films, also use this translation.

4. For instance, no. 1003B of 1962 (included on the video selection of reels that accompanies Rafael Tranche and Vicente Sánchez Biosca's *NO-DO: el tiempo y la memoria*) might well have played before a screening of Palacios's film, which was released on 21 December 1962. These newsreels were obligatorily screened prior to films from 1943 to 1975.

5. When a journalist visits the family flat towards the end of the film, he and the parents recognise each other from his previous report of their large family prize.

6. Consequently, comparisons of late nineteenth-century and Francoist culture are revealing. See Stephanie Sieburth's comparison of novels of the 1850s–1870s and 1960s (1994) and my work on film adaptations of late nineteenth-century novels in the 1970s (2004: Chapter 4).

7. The *sainete* is a subgenre of Spanish popular comedy, which began in the theatre and was successfully adapted to film. It uses techniques of *costumbrismo* – the detailed, picturesque evocation of local setting and character. In both play and film versions, *sainete* characters include such types as *vejetes* (comic old men), *paletos* (country bumpkins), clumsy, well-meaning nuns and dim-witted maids, who populate a recognisable and often working-class Madrid. The genre's conventional plots present the status quo (or evoke it in the recent past), disrupt the status quo, then restore it to bring about satisfying closure, sacrificing narrative verisimilitude in order to follow this formula. Humour in these films is situation- and character-based.

8. Completed in 1947, this is the home ground of Real Madrid, the football team supported by Franco.

9. The 'barrio de Corea' is mentioned, a colloquial name given to the area to the north of La Castellana. I would like to thank Maruja Rincón Tapias for providing me with this information.

10. It is contentious to state that not using contraception, which was illegal, was a cultural choice, but statistics on the decline of family size and medical reports reveal that it was widely used (see the previous quotation of Brooksbank Jones 1997: 94 n. 30).

11. Apart from the twins, the only actors who are actually related are José Isbert and his daughter María, who plays the second family maid. This bit-part makes a wicked counter-reading of the film possible. The grandpa looks physically like neither Alberto Closas, the handsome father, nor Amparo Soler Leal, the beautiful mother (it is not clear whose biological father he is supposed to be), nor any of the grandchildren. However, as Isbert and his daughter have a family resemblance, her casting raises the thought in the audience's minds that the old man's only blood relative may be a daughter conceived outside marriage.

12. In order to reinforce the connection between the films, the Alonso family leitmotif is played at the opening of *La familia y uno más*, then at further key narrative moments such as when Antonio passes his architecture exams or when the family blow out the candles of the surprise birthday cake. Rather than the

diegetic use of Handel's 'Hallelujah Chorus', the leitmotif provides the extra-diegetic sound for the second film's affirmative ending. Carlos holds his first grandchild and proclaims 'ya hay uno más en la gran familia' (now there's one more in the great family), as the leitmotif confirms the continuation of the bloodline on the musictrack.

13. In Walter Lang's *Cheaper by the Dozen* (1950), which Evans shows is the source of Masó's trilogy (2000: 80), the father's whistle also plays an important role, as he uses it to summon his children to gather together. Both films promote large families and traditional parental roles (interestingly, at the end of Lang's picture, the mother takes on the father's business role) and condemn modern practices such as birth control. Both also share scenes such as the illness of the children, the re-creation of government practices – both of dictatorship and democracy – in family meetings, the trip to the seaside and the attraction of an elder daughter to a young beau on holiday, which is conveyed by his musical performance against the backdrop of the sea.

14. See the extracts from *El Alcázar* and *Marca* in *Cine-Asesor* (1962).

15. In the interview on the *El País* DVD, Masó recalls assistant director Salvia's skill at directing the younger children, which included tricks such as showing the boy who plays Chencho a hypodermic syringe to make him cry. He also reminisces that the atmosphere on set was like that of a 'big family', rather than a group of actors.

16. Closas, one of the most highly paid actors of Spanish cinema in the period, received half a million pesetas from the budget of 6,250,000 pesetas, which was also one of the highest in Spanish cinema at the time (Hernández Ruiz 1997: 517).

17. Standing at 142 metres of height over thirty-four floors in the city's central Plaza de España, this was the tallest building in Madrid until the completion of the Torre Picasso in 1989. Designed by the architects Julián and Joaquín Otamendi, and completed in 1957, it is emblematic of fascist architecture under Franco.

18. According to Carlos Aguilar and Jaume Genover, who list main prizes only, she won the Círculo de Escritores Cinematográficos prize in 1962 and the Placa San Juan prize in 1963 (1996: 615).

19. As well as American popular culture, the grandpa's other frame of reference is war. For instance, when he sees the sailor's outfit to be worn by the *petardista* for his first communion, he comments that all he needs now is a battleship. His participation on the Nationalist side in the Civil War is also indicated by his comment that the bottle of vodka contained in the Christmas hamper that the family is sent in error must have been sent by a 'rougé'.

20. The first boy was named Francisco Franco (the order of surnames for the child was reversed by special decree), indicating the old dictator's ultimately unrealised dreams of founding a dynasty (Preston 1993: 596, 636).

21. See, for instance, NO-DO reels 567B (1953), 974A (1961) and in particular 1004A (1963) (all included on the video that accompanies Tranche and

Sánchez Biosca 2002). The latter begins with the public presentation of the dictator reading his end of year speech as the imagetrack cuts between images of Franco and crowds of adoring supporters all over Spain. In the text of the speech (much of which was written by *aperturistas* Manuel Fraga Iribarne and Laureano López Rodó [Preston 1993: 706]), he refers to Spain as 'nuestra familia' (our family). The reel then switches to the private portrayal of the dictator with his wife and grandchildren, which complements this emphasis on the happy family. The reel is dated 7 January 1963, so was very likely to have been played in theatres before Palacios's film, which ran over the 1962–3 Christmas period.

22. The spaceship game is portrayed with a take of 34 seconds (14 minutes into the film) and the war-game take lasts 40 seconds (1 hour 13 minutes into the film).

23. Key public roles within the Spanish state, like a politician and a diplomat, are positions earmarked for the boys. While the older girls are characterised as future angels of the hearth, it is gratifying that the younger girls may look forward to being a translator ('la traductora') and an opera singer ('la soprano').

CHAPTER 2

Civilising the City in *La ciudad no es para mí* (*The City's Not For Me*, Lazaga 1965)

In *La ciudad no es para mí*, Pedro Masó's goal shifts from government subsidy (the aim of *La gran familia*) to the box office, where the producer had equal success. *La ciudad* became the most profitable film of the 1960s, and one that is still considered a blockbuster. This success was thanks in part to the commissioned director, Pedro Lazaga. One of the most prolific (and least studied) directors of Spanish film history, with ninety-five features to his name over his career as a whole (1948–78), Lazaga brought the considerable experience and expertise in commercial comedy gained over the 1950s and 1960s in films such as *Los tramposos* (*The Con Men* 1959) to Masó's commission. But the runaway success of the film is mainly attributable to the casting of the adored theatre actor of the decade, Paco Martínez Soria, who starred in and directed the play on which the film was based.

Modern Madrid, which is evoked in *La gran familia* in order to show its compatibility with the traditional family, apparently takes centre stage in *La ciudad*. The city dominates the opening credits, triggers the plot, underscores characterisation and gives the title to the film. Unlike *La gran familia*, which locates the status quo in the contemporary period, in *La ciudad* it must be retrospectively evoked through older relatives, who embody the nostalgic pull. If a rural past is implicit in Palacios's film – through the reference to the mother's knowledge of how to grow vegetables, for instance[1] – it is apparently the explicit focus of Lazaga's picture, which repeats the familiar formula of the country versus the city. *La ciudad* responds to the rural exodus that characterised the shift from the post-war, autarkic years to the 1960s, developmental years. In the earlier period, Spaniards were persuaded to remain in, or return to, the country to work to feed a nation aiming at economic self-sufficiency. In 1947, Franco announced freedom of movement for Spaniards within the country (Richardson 2002: 11–12), and if migration to the city was then tacitly encouraged to foster the industrial boom, urban immigration was actually included as state policy by the first

Development Plan of 1964–7 (Schubert 1990: 210). A straightforward change economically, urban immigration was more compex to justify ideo-logically, owing to the energy invested in the vilification of the city and cel-ebration of the country in post-war ruralist propaganda. The Falangist director José Antonio Nieves Condes's *Surcos* (1951), for example, champi-ons just such a return to the country at the end of a narrative that charts a family's moral decline in Madrid.[2] Conversely, Lazaga's *aperturista* film tries to reconcile the contradiction between the ideological rhetoric of country values and the economic need for liberalisation, and concomitant urbanisation.

In the first section of this chapter, I will analyse the ways *La ciudad* civilises the city through its nostalgic appeal to the country. Martínez Soria is the principal conduit of conservatism in the film, and his mission to clean up the family's moral life in the city is supported by a plot that insists upon the right, or proper, place. A general anxiety about people being in the wrong place in the period – the city, rather than the country – is thus projected onto particular examples of people and things being in the wrong place in the film. As in *La gran familia*, aspects of the musical score com-plement this enterprise (for instance, the sound of traditional castanets accompanies shots of the portrait of Antonia), but I will pay particular attention here to the way *mise en scène*, in particular the use of paintings and costume, is deployed to underscore the film's act of persuasion.

As in *La gran familia*, the contributions of certain members of the technical crew none the less create ripples in this smooth surface of con-formity. Cinematography, editing and music in the credit sequence, for instance, take advantage of current technical innovations in cinema to give the initial impression of a film that celebrates, rather than condemns, the vibrant, modern city. If this short portrayal of a Swinging Sixties Madrid is insufficient to sabotage the ruralism otherwise promoted, its location at the opening of the film none the less announces a possible alternative reading from the very beginning. Furthermore, in terms of plot, *La ciudad* repeats a tired comedy formula (which popular film inherited from the popular theatre) of the trials and tribulations of a likeable *paleto* (country bumpkin) in a hostile city. In the second half of this chapter, I propose first that the audience's attention, which is scarcely required to follow this pre-dictable plot, is drawn to the comic exaggeration of its execution. Second, I argue that the ostensible aim of the film to civilise the city is projected onto an attempt to civilise women through the characterisation of the female protagonist. Reconsidered in this light, the conservative message of the film emerges as awkwardly over-determined, and the role played by Luchy becomes surprisingly disruptive.

'La ciudad pa' quien le guste, que como el pueblo ni hablar' (The city's for those who like it, but there's nothing like the village)

Paco Martínez Soria's role as the conduit of conservatism in *La ciudad* confers on this comic character a paradoxically serious narrative function that was entirely absent from Isbert's contribution to *La gran familia*. While in Palacios's film the grandpa occupies a richly comic, but ideologically unsettling, liminal space between masculine normality and childish absurdity, Martínez Soria's character embodies the quintessential patriarchy that is central to the conservative message of Lazaga's picture. Tío (Uncle) Agustín, as he is affectionately called in his Aragonese home village Calacierva, is the axis about which the film turns. He is the narrative agent who evokes and restores the status quo, which, thanks to our adoption of his point of view, we are led to believe has been disrupted by city life. Tío Agustín's memories of his wife, son and daughter-in-law in the village conjure up an image of traditional family life in a rural environment. He tries to restore this status quo by fortifying the family, even though the film stops short of advocating their return to the village. Thus the narrative begins when Tío Agustín packs his suitcase, tucks a hand-painted portrait of his deceased wife Antonia under one arm, hangs a basket of squawking chickens over the other and pays his son and family a visit in Madrid. It develops as he discovers to his horror that they have fallen prey to the evils of urban existence. His son, Gusti, is a workaholic, and his daughter-in-law, Luchy, is teetering on the verge of adultery (the censorship norms of 1963 banned its actual portrayal on screen). The narrative is resolved through Tío Agustín's interventions, by which he restores a status quo that has never actually existed. Gusti newly sensitive to his wife's needs and Luchy forced to be an angel of the hearth, the film ends with Tío Agustín's triumphant return to Calacierva, where a street-sign is unveiled bearing his name and the villagers (all of whom seem to live off his charity) cheer when they hear he will not be returning to the city. He states the title of the film for the first time on explaining his decision not to return to Madrid to his family: 'La ciudad no es pa' mí' (City life ain't for me). There follows a second epilogue, not found in the original play, which is superfluous in terms of narrative, and extremely heavy-handed in execution. It is a second celebration in which the villagers sing and dance a *copla* (popular song or ballad) for their avuncular patron, the lyrics of which attempt to dissipate all conflict, 'Bien has hecho en regresar, Baturrico, la ciudad pa' quien le guste, que como el pueblo ni hablar' (You've done the right thing by coming back, Aragonese countryman, the city's for those who like it, but there's nothing like the village).

This portrayal of 'un pedazo de pan – un patriarca' (a real sweetie – a patriarch), as the voice-over of the film's prologue calls him, is dependent on a strong script and Martínez Soria's performance. Vicente Coello and the producer Masó wrote the former, adapting the enormously successful *sainete* play by Fernando Ángel Lozano.[3] Their script is largely faithful to the original, but adds sequences that take advantage of filmic resources like *mise en scène*. Thus the prologue in Madrid is added to reinforce the significance of this setting, as is the subplot on the portrait of Antonia, and the entire sequence at the Hotel Richmond, which underscores characterisation and plot through paintings. However, the dialogue retains the flavour of the original, and much of it is transposed verbatim from play to script. Thus, in both play and film, fast-talking Tío Agustín retains his patter, which is delivered through a thick Aragonese accent. It is laden with verbal tics, like the addition of the diminutive form '-ico' to the noun, confusion of direct and indirect objects and verbal puns. For instance, as the polite second-person verbal conjugation is identical to the third-person singular in Spanish, Tío Agustín misunderstands the traffic warden's references to the traffic lights changing colour as statements referring to his own humour ['ponerse verde' means both 'to turn green' and 'to be inexperienced or jealous'] (in the play, see Lozano 1965: 25). Similarly, when the maid asks him to find a tin of shellfish in the supermarket, he puns on the polysemy of 'navaja' (both 'razor shell' and 'knife') to suggest she looks for them in Albacete (the town famous for producing cutlery in Spain) (not present in the play). Moreover, Tío Agustín's language is replete with religious and rustic expressions. '¡Qué peregrinación!' (literally, 'What a pilgrimage!') he mutters to convey how long his journey has been, for example, or '¿van en carro?' (are you going by horse and cart?) he asks his granddaughter and friend, misunderstanding their jargonistic use of 'carro' for 'automóvil' (car), or again, 'Ha volado' (He's flown away) he says to Luchy to indicate that Ricardo has left (the reference to 'carro' can be found in the play [Lozano 1965: 41]). Tío Agustín's speech is also a repository of basic vocabulary, like 'moquero' for 'pañuelo' (equivalent to 'hankie' for 'handkerchief', though 'moquero' is etymologically linked to 'moco' – 'snot') or 'corona' (crown) for 'cofia' (coif) (the second example occurs in the play [Lozano 1965: 24]).

Although these linguistic idiosyncrasies read as painfully contrived on the page, on the screen Martínez Soria makes them just about plausible by his era-defining portrayal of a bumbling but well-meaning *paleto*. *La ciudad* won Martínez Soria the Placa San Juan Bosco prize in 1966 (Aguilar and Genover 1996: 375) and inaugurated what Nathan Richardson calls the 'subgenre' of *paleto* cinema in Spanish film, which included *El turismo es un gran invento* (*Tourism is a Great Invention*, Lazaga 1967), and *El abuelo tiene un plan* (*Grandpa Has a Plan*, Lazaga 1973), and lasted till the mid-1970s (Richardson 2000: 61). Martínez Soria's all-talking, all-gesticulating performance was honed to perfection through his portrayal of the same character in the play, which, as Lozano stated in the prologue of its publication (1965: 5), was conceived uniquely as a vehicle for this star, and which Martínez Soria directed himself. His Tío Agustín character passes off downright rudeness and busy-body meddling as benevolent paternal concern, though a contemporary audience would find his implicit recommendation of domestic violence particularly hard to stomach (he makes a gesture to indicate throttling Luchy and raises his hand as if to strike the maid).

If we approach *La ciudad* as *aperturista* propaganda, its purpose is to reconcile the key contradiction of 1960s Spain: tradition (here figured as the country) and modernity (here represented by the city). It cannot champion a reversal of the rural exodus like *Surcos*, as by the 1960s such a reactionary move would jeopardise the Francoist economic boom. Thus despite its seemingly relentless presentation of city life as inferior, the logical conclusion to this state of affairs – the return of Tío Agustín's family to Calacierva – is never even suggested. Although the moralising narrator of the film's prologue falls silent when the narrative begins, his preceding condemnation of Madrid through a series of impersonal statistics, and glorification of Calacierva through tender observations about its inhabitants, ring in our ears throughout the film. Subplots and apparently incidental background details set up oppositions that are intended further to persuade us of the desirability of country life. For instance, when Tío Agustín arrives in the capital, a crook attempts to sell him an envelope of blank papers that he pretends are 1,000-peseta notes. Tío Agustín refuses, of course, and encourages him to deposit them in a bank.[4] This first occurrence in the city therefore presents it as a place of crime, as opposed to the village, which, like its representative Tío Agustín, is a cradle of integrity. (Tío Agustín's cheating at cards to fleece the taxcollector in the village is a different matter, of course, as he does so in the name of the villagers; even the priest turns a blind eye.) The incident with the con man also contrasts the city's fraudulence with the country's authenticity, for the crook pretends to be a crippled simpleton, whereas Belén of Calacierva is genuinely disabled.

To compensate for the impossibility of returning the family to the countryside, its proper place, the film develops a number of subplots that return people, and things, to their proper places. The implication is that if everything else is in the proper place, then life in the city, the wrong place, is tolerable. *La ciudad* proposes that Gusti, Tío Agustín's son, is in the wrong place, as he spends time at work as a surgeon in the hospital, not at home. Furthermore, the film suggests that Gusti's money is in the wrong place because it remains symbolically inside his wallet, rather than being used by Tío Agustín for the charitable benefit of the village. Gusti's excessive absence from the home is remedied by a lecture on family responsibilites from his father, and, sure enough, at the end of the film he takes an afternoon off work to take his wife to the cinema (that such an absence may cause the cancellation of operations is a consequence of his actions that the film does not concern itself to explore). Likewise, Gusti accedes to Tío Agustín's plea for cash donations, opening his wallet and allowing his father to take thousands of pesetas to spend on gifts for the Calacierva villagers.

More dangerous for the family honour, the mother is in the wrong place as she leaves the home. We learn, through the maid, that she is forever out and about, either playing cards, seeing friends (a Roberto is mentioned) or doing charitable work. In the film, we see her leave the home twice, once to go to her husband's hospital, where she accidentally-on-purpose bumps into Ricardo, and again to go to the hotel bar on a date with this would-be lover. These outings lead her to the verge of adultery – she is almost, therefore, in the wrong bed. Again, Tío Agustín's intervention averts the crisis: he sends would-be lover Ricardo packing and tells a few home truths to his wayward daughter-in-law, which compel her to become an angel of the hearth. By the end of the film, Luchy seems to acknowledge that leaving the home got her into trouble in the first place, and she is even reluctant to leave the flat to go out to the cinema with her husband ('¿Por qué no nos quedamos en casa?' [Why don't we stay at home?]).

Finally, two comic subplots reinforce this thesis of the proper place. First, we learn that the maid has been in the wrong place, or bed, by getting pregnant before marriage. Tío Agustín puts her in the right place by insisting her boyfriend marries her, under threat of fifteen years in Ocaña, Madrid's famous jail. Finally, a subplot on the proper place runs through the film concerning which picture should hang in the sitting room of the Madrid flat: an original Picasso that displays the family's wealth and modernity, or the old-fashioned portrait of Tío Agustín's wife, the dead matriarch, Antonia.

Dressing Up and Dressing Down

The attention paid to *mise en scène* in *La ciudad* is indicated by the fact that the technical crew included an art department of three (Luciano Arroyo, Tomás Fernández, Jesús Mateos) to support the set decorator Antonio

Simont (who was also responsible for décor in *La gran familia*). The place occupied by Antonia's portrait reflects the development of the plot of the film, which is reinforced by the narrative use of other portraits and paintings: the original Picasso owned by the family that hangs in their sitting room (it is the *Still Life with Guitar* [1922]); the photographic portrait of Luchy, also placed in the sitting room; and finally the picture of the old man with two prostitutes and the portrait of a *maja*, both found in the hotel bar.[5]

Antonia's portrait (see Figure 2.1) vies for central position on the wall of the Madrid flat with Picasso's *Still Life with Guitar*, a confrontation that underpins the struggle between tradition and modernity in the film. The opposition between the two pictures is dramatic, in both pictorial and symbolic terms, and cannot be missed by the audience, especially as it is reinforced by the script. The portrait of the matriarch evokes the essence of traditional values: executed according to realist convention, the plump and comely Antonia, decorously dressed in a high-necked loose blouse, and with her long black hair tied up in a traditional bun, smiles out from within the rustic wooden frame. Tío Agustín exclusively controls the meaning of the portrait. When we first see it, he informs us that Antonia 'era una santa' (was a saint). Further, he interacts with it as if it were a flesh-and-blood

Figure 2.1. Paco Martínez Soria and Gracita Morales in *La ciudad no es para mí*.
Video Mercury Films.

woman, explaining 'es mi mujer' (this is my wife) when a fellow passenger helps him carry it/her off the train (one wonders if there would have been any difference between his engagement with this piece of paper, wood and glass and with his wife when alive). He is even the medium that allows us to hear Antonia's voice from beyond the grave when he recalls Gusti's departure for Madrid and imitates her fretting over what he would eat there. The controlling presence of the portrait of the dead matriarch repeats the role of a similar picture in Nieves Condes's *Balarrasa* (1950). *La ciudad* borrows the earlier film's use of arrangement within the frame to underscore the portrait's meaning. In *Balarrasa*, the portrait of the mother dominates the background at key narrative moments such as Javier's return to the family home after he has taken the decision to become a priest (Gómez 2002: 581). Likewise, in *La ciudad*, the image of Antonia casts her silent approval over scenes such as the reunion of father and son: the two embrace in the foreground, while the wife and mother in the portrait smiles down on them in the background.

In contrast, Picasso's painting stands for the modernity that *aperturista* Spain craved in the 1960s. By using a still life of an uncontroversial subject matter, the film ignores the awkward facts that Picasso was a Spanish artist who lived in exile in France (he moved there permanently from 1901) and that his work condemned Spanish fascism. The international admiration garnered by this co-founder of Cubism encodes the kind of success the *aperturistas* fondly imagined for the NCE, but in Lazaga's film, which was not intended for foreign audiences, this example of high art simply becomes a straw man to be knocked down. It symbolises first, the acquisition of wealth for its own sake, and second, the distortion of family values. Gusti and Tío Agustín's conversation about the painting and the portrait summarises the opposition. Tío Agustín describes it as 'Uno muy raro que no se sabía lo que era' (A weird one where you couldn't see what it was of). Rather than defend the artistic merits of Cubism, Gusti simply responds, 'Pero padre, que vale un millón' (But Dad, it's worth a million pesetas). This enables Tío Agustín to counter with a line that celebrates morals over money, 'Y esto, ¿no vale más para ti? Es tu madre' (And isn't this worth more to you? It's your mother). Tío Agustín's dismissal of the aesthetic merit of the Picasso painting is echoed by the film's second mouthpiece of traditional rustic values, the maid Filo, who refuses to keep it in her room as it makes her feel sick ('me da mareos' [it makes me feel dizzy]). Although Luchy is never aligned with the picture through juxtaposition within the frame, she is nevertheless Picasso's champion in the film, because she is the one who insists the still life hangs in the sitting room rather than Antonia's portrait. This desire for the housewife to decide on the decoration of her own home seems reasonable, but it is given a symbolic dimension because of Luchy's near-adultery. When she speaks to Ricardo on the telephone during the tea party, the Picasso still life is visible in the background of the shot, and on the day of her adulterous date with him, the sequence begins with a medium shot of the painting. Thus her distortion of family values by contemplating adultery is pictorially represented by her association with the 'distortion' of still life forms in the Cubist masterpiece.[6]

The condemnation of the challenge to patriarchy is also represented pictorially in the scene at the hotel bar. Ricardo has arranged to meet Luchy at Hotel Richmond in order to begin their adulterous affair. *Mise en scène* underscores the moral distortion implicit in this plan, as the would-be lover is juxtaposed in the bar with the picture of the old man with two prostitutes. Just as the picture describes the perverse sexual relationship between a decrepit old man with walking sticks and a scantily clad, buxom young prostitute (Goya explores a similar opposition in *La Boda* [*The Wedding* 1791–2], though the treatment of the figures here recalls his *Aún aprendo* [*Still I Learn* 1824–8] and *Las Caprichos* [*The Caprices* 1799]), so we are led to understand that Ricardo and Luchy's adulterous union would be similarly perverse. Furthermore, when Luchy arrives at the bar, her position before the *maja* painting condemns her would-be adultery as both artificial imitation and as prostitution. Through the pictorial alignment, Luchy and the *maja* are condemned as impersonators, which picks up the idea of the fraudulence of the city alluded to elsewhere in the film. In the eighteenth century, the fashion for upper-class Madrid women to wear the clothes of lower-class *majas* for playful erotic effect was immortalised in Goya's portraits *La Duquesa de Alba* (*The Duchess of Alba* 1797), *La Reina María Luisa con mantilla* (*Queen María Luisa Wearing a Mantilla* 1799) and *La Marquesa de Santa Cruz* (*The Marquess of Santa Cruz* 1797–9), of which the painting in Lazaga's film is clearly an imitation. In fact, rather than a member of the upper class imitating the fashion of the lower class, Luchy is a new member of the middle class. The daughter of a poor rural family in Calacierva and a former village dressmaker, she is anxious to consolidate her newly acquired status by displaying the kind of cultural 'distinction' analysed by the French sociologist Pierre Bourdieu.[7] In a Spanish cultural context, she would therefore be described as a *cursi*.[8] Eager to imitate all things foreign to compensate for the pace of her social ascendance, she has changed her name from the Castilian 'Luciana' to the foreignified, Italianate 'Luchy', drinks tea and spirits instead of coffee and wine,[9] and prefers Picasso to the traditional family portrait. During the tea-party sequence, one of the marquesses, who, as a member of the aristocracy, is a custodian of 'genuine' taste, immediately sees through the

pretensions of Ricardo's love-letter, which Luchy takes seriously. She dismisses its opening address, 'adorada Luchy' (My adored Luchy) as '¡Qué
cursilada!' (How cheesy!)

The connection between Luchy the middle-class *cursi* and the *maja*
depicted in the painting is therefore that both are fraudulent imitators.
The painting serves a further purpose, however, in condemning Luchy's
adulterous temptation. The *maja* painting is a sexed-up version of Goya's
more subtle representations of erotic female spectacle on display. The
painter exaggerates the bust and bottom, and places the woman on a
balcony – the quintessential site of display. She coquettishly lifts her skirt
to reveal a shapely calf and dainty foot imprisoned in a pointed shoe.
Through her juxtaposition with the portrait it is suggested that Luchy is
decked out in a 1960s version of the *maja*'s temptress outfit. Her tight-
fitting glittery cocktail dress and fur coat[10] replace the *maja*'s lace petti-
coats and *mantilla*, her hat stands in for the elaborate bow displayed on the
head of her eighteenth-century predecessor, and she carries an evening bag
instead of a fan. The similarity of both the attire and the pose of Luchy
and the *maja* is underscored by the positioning of the actress before the
picture for a full 8 seconds of the 17-second take that records Luchy's
arrival at the hotel bar. Furthermore, just as the *maja*'s gaze beckons an
implied male admirer to the right out of the picture frame, so Luchy looks
for Ricardo to the right out of the cinematic frame. In both cases, the excessive, and artificial, erotic display is condemned as prostitution, as both
women peer out of picture and cinema frames for male lovers or cus-
tomers.

The work in costume design (Humberto Cornejo and Matías Montero
Nanette) and makeup (Paloma Fernández and María Elena García) in the
Hotel Richmond sequence is typical of the whole film, which underscores
its characterisation of Luchy as would-be adulteress through her clothes
and cosmetics. What Luchy wears is as interesting as what she says and
how she says it, for although Doris Coll camps up her portrayal, dragging
on her cigarettes like a textbook *femme fatale*, Coello and Masó's script
stifles her performance through lines that are little more than banal
clichés.[11] Our first sight of her is on the balcony of the flat (a nice touch
that looks forward to the balcony on which the *maja* is displayed), where
she wears a modern outfit of leggings, vest and sweat band as she completes
her keep-fit exercise routine. Next we see her in an elegant white dress
and matching pendant earings, fully made up with thick eyeliner and
false eyelashes, as she receives her marquess friends for afternoon tea (see
Figure 2.2). During this sequence her father-in-law reveals her humble
origins as a village dressmaker, which indicates to us that she would be

especially sensitive to the fact that what she wears conveys her newly acquired class status. Her outfit for the adulterous encounter with Ricardo at the hotel bar summarises her elegance, wealth and confidence in her own sexuality, but, as we have seen, this display is parodied by its juxtaposition with the *maja*.

Tío Agustín, of course, rescues her from the edge of adultery, and insists she becomes the angelic wife and mother of patriarchy. Logically, her compliance with his orders is represented sartorially. The action shifts from the hotel bar back to the flat, where we see smug Tío Agustín contentedly sprawling spread-legged on the sitting room armchair. Luchy has changed her outfit, but on a symbolic level, Tío Agustín has punished her by stripping off her fur coat, fancy hat and sexy cocktail dress, and reclothing her in a dowdy, hand-knitted cardigan, with the tiny triangle of flesh that might have been visible at its V-neck decorously shrouded by an ugly neckerchief and old-fashioned brooch. Knitwear encodes the village in *La ciudad*, through the saccharine characterisation of the disabled girl Belén, who always appears wearing a knitted scarf, and who gives Tío Agustín a knitted cardigan that he wears in the last scene of the film. Literally and figuratively dressed down by Tío Agustín, Luchy's new look makes her instantly appear older and plumper, robbing her of the sexual confidence she exudes elsewhere in the film. In other words, the visual manifestation of her transformation into the angel of the hearth has made her a version of Antonia. The film therefore condemns sartorial luxury as sexual lust, punning on the shared root of 'lujo' (luxury) and 'lujuria' (lust) in Spanish. It is not incidental that Tío Agustín remarks '¡Qué lujo!' (How luxurious!) when he first sees the Madrid flat, at a point when Luchy is wearing the elegant outfit to receive the marquesses. In the last scene in the Madrid flat, the old meddler has saved the family from the dangers of luxury and lust by reclothing Luchy in ugly, asexual, village clothes.

This change is further underscored by the photographic portrait of Luchy, which becomes the mirror-image of the painted portrait of Antonia it faces on the opposite side of the sitting room in the Madrid flat. Earlier in the film we have seen Ricardo caress the framed photograph as he fondly imagines his future seduction, but in the penultimate sequence, when Gusti returns home from work early and Luchy greets him in the dowdy cardigan, the portrait is restored to its traditional role. When Gusti opens the door of the flat, the shot is arranged so that we see him enter in the background, while Luchy's portrait dominates the foreground. Like Antonia, Luchy is back in her proper place in the home, contained and controlled by a portrait, and symbolically tied to her husband through the connection of foreground and background in the cinematic frame.

Swinging Sixties Madrid

Just as the counter-reading of *La gran familia* proposed in the previous chapter emerged from the conflicting contributions of members of the technical crew such as composer and editor, I also suggest an alternative reading of *La ciudad* through an examination of the different interventions of members of its crew. Script, Martínez Soria's performance and *mise en scène* all emphasise the film's condemnation of adultery, which is aligned with urban life, and promotion of the family, which is aligned with rural life. However, the prologue of the film, which was added to Lozano's original play, proposes an alternative vision of a dynamic city full of possibility, as opposed to a static village immune to change. This is achieved through the input of Juan Mariné (cinematography) and Alfonso Santacana (editing), and the inclusion of an instrumental by 'Los Shakers' on the soundtrack.

The film opens with Mariné's long shot of the recognisable Madrid cityscape, which is recorded through a slow pan and long take from the large park on the city's western edge, the Casa de Campo. While the cityscape is visible on the skyline, the trees and vegetation of the park dominate the foreground. The slow pan and long take are therefore associated with rural space through the position of the camera in the park. The title of the film (presented by an intertitle) declares antipathy to city life, but this conflicts with the interesting architectural collage of Madrid's monuments and buildings glimpsed in the long shot. The rock music played on the soundtrack underpins this view of a dynamic modern city. 'Los Shakers' were bang up to date in 1965: a Uruguayan band formed in 1963, they sang in English and specialised in music that imitated 'The Beatles'. The rapid tempo struck by the electric guitar and drums contrasts with the slow pan from left to right, emphasised by a long take of 36 seconds. We associate the fast-paced rock music with the cityscape seen in the background, and the slow pan and long take with the rural park in the foreground. This first sequence of the film seems to respond to the attraction of the cityscape, as it ends with a zoom into the city, which takes our attention and interest with it. There follows a cut, then a matching zoom out from a lampost to reveal the Plaza de España. This opening arouses our interest in the city, and satisfies it by the movement from rural to urban space by means of the matching zooms.

Like the 'Los Shakers' soundtrack, the use of the zoom is very contemporary, as this was one of the technical innovations that date from the end of the 1950s in Spain (Sánchez Biosca 1989: 89). The cinematographer Mariné takes advantage of further technical developments in the whirlwind filmic tour of the capital that follows, which records both its monuments and most emblematic buildings (such as the Plaza de la Cibeles and the Metrópolis building) and the activities of its inhabitants (we see pedestrians crossing the busy streets, passengers riding on buses or in cars and filmgoers entering a cinema). The rock music of the soundtrack and rapid editing are also crucial to this breathless presentation of an exciting city. Santacana only allows shots to rest on monuments or buildings long enough for us to recognise them. The strong beat of the 'Los Shakers' track generates excitement and also makes Madrid appear a Spanish version of contemporary Swinging London. When night falls, this city portrait becomes more formally experimental. From minute 1, 55 the music increases in tempo and Santacana steps up the frequency of the montage.

Taking advantage of the creative possibilities allowed by new technology that critics have thus far explored only in the art house NCE films in this period, *La ciudad* therefore registers their impact on the commercial cinema too. The introduction in 1960s Spain of new light weight equipment like the German Arriflex camera (Llinàs 1989b: 214–15) allows Mariné to locate his camera in interesting places, like the front of a car, which affords us its perspective speeding through the city both above and below ground. Furthermore, new extra-sensitive film stock reduced the need for artificial lighting, expanding the possibilities of filming at night (Torán 1989: 103–4), both here and in more formally experimental films like *Nueve cartas a Berta*. Finally, in this nocturnal Madrid scene, the imagetrack is speeded up to fast forward, a shift that promotes exhilaration rather than disorientation, because there is no change of subject, and we revisit places at speed that we have already seen at normal pace. Taken together, this presentation of the whole city exudes the youth and energy associated with the contemporary club scene, a feeling that is confirmed when Sara, friends and Tío Agustín visit a nightclub later in the film and we see 'Los Shakers' perform live the tune we have heard in the prologue.

The vibrancy and velocity of this 1960s city are then crushed by the voice-over that begins at minute 2, 18. The disembodied male voice tries retrospectively to align formal experimentation with a condemnation of the city. He reads a list of damning statistics about Madrid, which echoes the changes of perspective offered by the editing, and condemns the fast pace of life in the capital, which recalls the fast-forward images and rock music. This pompously authoritative voice-over is a version of the narrative commentary that accompanied the NO-DO newsreels, and this obvious association with the mouthpiece of the state may have led some members of the audience to treat it sceptically. Furthermore, Spanish audiences were used to hearing disclaimer voice-overs added by censors at the start of films, informing them, for instance, that what they were about to see was fictional and in no way representative of Spain (for instance, *Calle Mayor* [Bardem 1956]), or downplaying any possibly subversive content in the film that followed (for example, *No desearás al vecino del quinto* [*Thou Shalt Not Covet Thy Fifth Floor Neighbour*, Fernández 1970]). In addition, Núria Triana-Toribio speculates that 'These prologues may be there only because they are fashionable or familiar to the audience', but that none the less, 'they can also be read as an implicit acknowedgement of the presence of censorship' (2003: 101). It is clear, then, that audiences' responses to these prologue voice-overs were knowing, which raises the possibility that some may have been sceptical of them, others may have ignored them and still others may have bloody-mindedly adopted the opposite view, simply because they were being told not to.

A resistant reading of the voice-over's intervention in *La ciudad* is therefore plausible. Its insistence that the city is 'unnaturally' large is straightforward to deconstruct as it relies on a simple listing technique to create the impression of overwhelming size. Statistics referring to inhabitants, marriages, births, deaths and crime are reeled off, and nouns describing excess are repeated: 'montañas de . . .', 'toneladas de . . .', 'kilómetros de . . .' (mountains of . . ., tonnes of . . ., kilometres of . . .). The narrator's sigh of relief is audible when, at minute 4, 36, we move to the village, and he reflects, 'Ay, menos mal que todavía existen sitios más tranquilos' (Ah, just as well that quieter places still exist). As if to reward the countryside-obsessed narrator, two long takes offer the pictorial recreation of stereotypical bucolic images. First, the camera zooms out from the image of two donkeys tied to a post in front of a whitewashed wall, and second, it zooms in to an abandoned, horse-drawn cart leaning against another whitewashed wall. In parallel, the narrator offers a nauseatingly paternal and contrived description of the village and its inhabitants, which replays, in a conservative and authoritative key, the famous voice-over prologue to *¡Bienvenido Mister Marsall!* (Berlanga 1952), read by Fernando Rey and scripted by Bardem and Berlanga. However, in its eagerness to portray the ideal village, the film contradicts itself. For while pictorial *mise en scène* and the narrator idealise tranquility, we also see a group of screaming young children running down the street, and further commotion sets in at the news of the birth of a baby boy. The idea is presumably to show that the village can reconcile opposites and be both a repository of timeless tradition and motor of new life. However, cinematography and editing during the village sequence recoil from the technical innovations of the city prologue, and rather recall the slow pan and long take of the initial shot from the Casa de Campo. So, despite the narrator's celebration of the village, the energetic children and the news of the birth, the creeping pace of camera movement and editing support a counter-reading of this rural eulogy as static and stultifying, in contrast with the dynamic urban environment we have previously seen.

Conservative Comedy Against Itself

If the prologue is read against the grain as a celebration of the city, it casts a different light over the ensuing narrative. In Álvaro del Amo's tongue-in-cheek analysis of the predictability of Spanish film comedy, he notes that the *paleto* plot, inherited by the cinema from pre-war theatrical traditions of the *sainete* and the *zarzuela*, turns around 'las desventuras de pueblerinos (que recibirán la denominación de "paletos") en su contacto azaroso con la ciudad' (the mishaps of country people [who will be called 'country bumpkins'] in their hazardous contact with the city) (1975: 18), and that the *paleto* will inevitably be characterised by 'la boina, la maleta de madera y una caja atada con cordel en donde se guardan sólidas, contundentes muestras de la bollería local y jugosos embutidos' (his beret, wooden suitcase and box tied with string, in which examples of heavy and filling local breads and pastries and succulent sausages are kept). Based as it is on a *sainete* play, *La ciudad* follows this plot and characterisation to the letter,[12] attracting audience sympathy for Tío Agustín as he comically grapples with manifestations of urban modernity like traffic lights, telephones and supermarkets. Sure enough, Tío Agustín does not fail to underscore the opposition of country and city through food and drink. Whereas the Madrid family eat tinned food and cold dinners (according to the maid), have tea and fancy cakes (as we see at the teaparty) and drink spirits from a collection of glass decanters, Tío Agustín brings live chickens to make a tasty soup, along with the inevitable *chorizo*, cheese and bread, and drinks village wine from the *porrón* that he wields with Martínez Soria's trademark flourish.

Whereas conventional setting and characters in *La gran familia* served to naturalise its conservative message, the predictable plot and characterisation of *La ciudad* point to self-parody. There is a difference, after all, between conventionality and predictability, and Lazaga's film takes predictability to such an extreme that its conservative message collapses under the weight of exaggeration. For instance, Martínez Soria's role in the film tries, and fails, to reconcile two opposites. He is simultaneously charged with the serious role of instigator of propriety, and the comic role of *paleto*. As well as the excessive verbosity and gesticulation typical of a *sainete* character, Diego Galán suggests that his performance style also draws on the

world of circus clowns (1983). The intention is for the humour of his performance to give a friendly face to his reactionary conservatism, but
instead it discourages us from taking that conservatism seriously. Tío
Agustín ends up joining the ranks of the other symbols of authority parodied in the film, like the mayor, the traffic warden, the taxcollector and even
the dictator himself – as Richardson points out, the porter of the Madrid
flat is set up, through his military-style outfit, as a Franco-surrogate whose
pretensions are mocked (2000: 68).

Take, for instance, the uproarious sequence of the marquesses' visit for
afternoon tea. Tío Agustín is the defender of family honour here, as he has
sussed out Luchy's situation by overhearing her read the letter from
Ricardo and eavesdropping on a telephone call. But this serious function
is undercut by the comic excess of his participation in the tea party. He
begins by stamping his feet to announce his presence, then continues by
sitting next to the marquesses on the sofa and lecherously drooling over
them with the embarrassing excess that would become typical of the Sexy
Spanish Comedy of the 1970s (Figure 2.2). The sequence ends with a
moment of textbook slapstick farce in which he drops a spoonful of sugar
down one marquess's top, scatters the remaining contents of the sugar
bowl over himself and then accidentally sits on top of the other marquess

Figure 2.2. Doris Coll, María Luisa Ponte, Paco Martínez Soria and Margot Cottens in
La ciudad no es para mí. Video Mercury Films.

(the scene is lifted straight from the play [Lozano 1965: 33–4]). This conflict between his earnest narrative role of saving Luchy from the adulterous affair her friends encourage her to begin, and its comic execution during the tea party, is exacerbated by the excessive theatricality of Martínez Soria's performance. He is above all a theatre actor (Aguilar and Genover 1996: 375; Gracia Pascual 2002: 44), a fact alluded to in the script of *La ciudad* when a marquess describes him as a 'tipo de sainete' (a typical *sainete* character). The mismatch between stage and film performance styles has interesting effects in other Spanish films. For instance, Aurora Bautista's stage background meant her roles in CIFESA's historical epics were characterised by melodramatic excess, which had the effect of conferring her heroines with a vigour that undercut the otherwise patriarchal content of the films. Similarly, Martínez Soria's comic theatricality in *La ciudad* translates into exaggerated excess on screen. He debunks the traditions he is meant to embody, causing conservative comedy to implode.

Consider, further, the role played by Tío Agustín's beret. It emerges that both the supposedly frivolous daughter-in-law and apparently wholesome Tío Agustín are equally attentive to their headgear. On the one hand, the beret declares Tío Agustín's rural background, as when the traffic warden looks him up and down and comments 'Estos turistas de pollos' ('These country bumpkin tourists', literally, 'These tourists with chickens'), or when the maid assumes he is a peasant selling local produce when he first arrives at the flat. But, on the other, it becomes overdetermined as a symbol of patriarchal honour, either as a sort of cloth, which cleans up the family honour, or a kind of weapon, which repels the family's would-be attackers. In the village sequences, Tío Agustín does not touch his headgear, which conveys the security of his values in this space, but when he arrives at the entrance of the Madrid family flat, he whips the beret off his head and uses it to polish the brass plaque bearing his son's name. This action looks forward to the unveiling of the street sign bearing his name in Calacierva at the end of the film, and also neatly conveys Tío Agustín's role as symbolic cleanser of the family honour. Again, when he finds the portrait of Antonia in the junk cupboard (see Figure 2.1), the beret is removed and used to polish the glass so the ideal wife and mother can be seen more clearly in order to project the patriarchal values for which she stands. More amusingly, the beret-*qua*-sword is brandished to repel the enemies of the family honour. Like a warrior of yesteryear, resheathing his trusty weapon after slaying a foe, Tío Agustín removes his beret and slaps it on his hand a few times after he gets rid of the the marquesses who are encouraging Luchy to have an affair, or dispatches the would-be adulterer Ricardo in the hotel bar. This repeated and excessive use of the hat transforms it into a comic patriarchal prop, which has the ultimate effect of weakening the traditions it is meant to uphold.

If the comic characterisation of Tío Agustín undercuts the conservatism in whose name he acts, those very actions also seem to do more harm than good. For instance, he meddles in his son's marriage in the name of patriarchal honour, but in so doing questions the authority of the husband, for Gusti remains blissfully ignorant of his near-cuckolding and is thus infantilised. On the very day of his wife's adulterous date, for instance, he whistles a tune that evokes the romantic bliss that the spectator knows is in jeapardy, Beethoven's *Für Elise*.[13] In the film's subplot, Tío Agustín enforces a marriage between the maid and the Don Juan egg-seller who seduced her, but her new husband is lazy, jealous and dominated by a tyrranical mother, so action in the name of the institution of marriage timidly questions that institution. It would appear that Tío Agustín's only success is in rescuing Luchy from adultery, a fact that invites us to reconsider what this film is really about.

The opposition between country and city is spurious. It is a smokescreen that covers the real opposition of *La ciudad*: that between the faithful wife and the adulteress. This is not a film about civilising the city, but one about civilising women. On closer examination, country and city, which the voice-over narrator tries so hard to oppose in the prologue, are not so different after all. For instance, before focusing on an establishing long shot of Calacierva (which matches the Madrid cityscape of the opening of the film) Mariné holds the camera on the electricity wires that connect the village to the outside world (this detail is also noted by Richardson 2000: 66). The fact that the village is not immune to modern technological advance is also shown by the arrival of Belén's knitting machine. Furthermore, the prologue of the film, which is meant to oppose country and city, reveals that multiple employment is present in both: in the city, the narrator addresses a character with five jobs; in the country, Venancio has at least four – bellringer, sacristan, town-crier and general odd-jobs man – which means he doesn't even have time to visit his newborn son as he has to ring the church bells, then read the official letter announcing the arrival of the taxcollector. Moreover, the country does not have exclusive ownership of community and family values. Tío Agustín comes to the city to 'save' the family, but prior to his arrival we witness pleasant exchanges between Sara and her parents, one in the flat with her mother, and one on the telephone with her father. The crook may attempt to fleece Tío Agustín when he walks out of the railway station in Madrid, but otherwise he encounters a host of benevolent strangers: a kindly gentleman, who helps him unload his luggage from the train, an obliging traffic warden, who helps him cross the road and gives him directions, and a responsible tour operator, who makes up for his mistake of bundling him on the wrong coach by giving him a lift to the flat. The film also points out that Madrid is a city of rural immigrants. Gusti and Luchy may wish to ignore their past thanks to their economic and social ascendance in the capital (on three occasions Gusti claims not to remember his old village friends when Tío Agustín tells him about them), but the less successful maid Filo is fond of evoking her *pueblo*. Finally, even Tío Agustín's embodiment of a *paleto* is incoherent. He may get confused by the traffic lights on his arrival in Madrid, but he otherwise shows a ready facility for modern technology, such as the switchboard, which he deftly manipulates in order to uncover Luchy and Ricardo's arrangements for their date.

In his account of *La ciudad* as an example of *paleto* cinema, Richardson likewise rejects the country versus the city conceit. 'Tío Agustín's triumph', he argues, 'is not so much the triumph of the premodern *paleto* but rather the victory of the modern capitalist' (2000: 64). Richardson challenges the assumption that *La ciudad* perpetuated the ruralist propaganda of the regime and argues that its conservatism is instead located in the film's implicit promotion of consumer values. The scene in which the Calacierva *cacique* (local patriarch) Tío Agustín extracts Gusti's city money in order to do rural charity is crucial, as it dissolves the difference between country and city by showing that both form part of the consumer culture enthusiastically embraced in 1960s Spain. As Richardson notes, 'while the *campesinos* [peasants] proclaim disinterested love for their former neighbour, they shower him with requests and feel betrayed when the desired goods fail to appear' (2000: 69). Furthermore, Richardson argues that the village itself is commodified as an object of consumption by the end of the film, which offers a coherent interpretation of why Coello and Masó add an otherwise superfluous second epilogue to the script. The ending reifies the countryside, according to Richardson, as an object of consumption for both rural tourists, like the family visiting for the day for the street-naming, and for fans of *paleto* cinema, who pay their ticket entrance to enjoy the clichéd representation of the countryside on screen.

While sharing Richardson's revisionist approach, I would add that the interpretation of Tío Agustín's role as a champion of consumerism, or *aperturista* hero, is undercut by the exaggeration of Martínez Soria's comic performance. Furthermore, Richardson's suggestion that the film 'interpellated Spanish citizens as modernisation-friendly consumers who could appreciate the market value of the rural', leaves no room for the kind of resistant reading of popular culture proposed here. Finally, Richardson does not take into account the centrality of the representations

of womanhood in the film, such as the portrait of Antonia and the characterisation of Luchy. This centrality leads me to the different conclusion
that *La ciudad* is above all concerned with the control of female sexuality.

As a formulaic conservative comedy the film, naturally, repeats the tired
opposition of woman as an angel of the hearth (Antonia) against woman as
adulteress (Luchy prior to Tío Agustín's arrival), and attempts to reconcile
these representatives of tradition and modernity by conflating the two
(Luchy following Tío Agustín's departure). If this reading makes Mariné
and Santacana's potentially subversive celebration of the city and condemnation of the country at the beginning of the film less important, it also
renders the ending of the film more open to resistant reinterpretation. In
the epilogue, Tío Agustín returns to Calacierva accompanied by his young
family, and the welcome home party laid on by the villagers is acted out with
absurd exaggeration. After the unveiling of the 'Agustín Valverde' street-
sign, the returned prodigal son makes a saccharine speech to the adoring
crowd, interrupted by heartfelt exclamations of '¡Viva Tío Agustín!' (Long
live Uncle Agustín!). Perhaps Lazaga wanted to dampen this excessive
enthusiasm, as rainfall mercifully interrupts the celebration. But the aspect
of the sequence that is of particular interest, given the attention paid to
costume throughout the film, is the portrayal of Luchy. Although the script
has her play the domestic angel and beg Tío Agustín to stay and live with
the family in Madrid, we notice that she has exchanged the dowdy cardigan, which symbolised her domesticity in the previous sequence, for a
matching checked coat and hat, pearl accessories, sling-back high-heel
shoes, full make-up and stylish hair-do, which symbolised her adultery. The
film might end with medium- and close-up shots of the tearful 'pedazo de
pan' patriarch weeping with happiness at the success of his conservative
enterprise, but Luchy's reappearance in her sartorial finery adds a surprising disruptive note. Fashion and clothing may be conventionally regarded
as frivolous, or even considered symbols of women's collusion with their
own oppression by early feminists. But in *La ciudad*, costume may also be
read against the grain as a celebration of the female agency that the rest of
this film tries to curtail.

The fact that *La ciudad* is based on a popular *sainete* play explains both its
success and its failure. Adapting an already profitable play is an obvious
choice for a producer out to make money, and re-casting its popular lead
further ensures its success. But even if scriptwriters aim for maximum
fidelity, the act of transferring the plot from stage to screen leads,
inevitably, to changes. In *La ciudad*, a prologue that sets the picture in
Madrid is added, but this enables cinematographer and editor to evoke an

exciting, dynamic city, complemented on the soundtrack by the music of a trendy young rock band, which challenges the conservative ruralism of the plot. Furthermore, the attention paid to costume in the film means that the would-be adulteress, who is symbolically contained and punished in the home in the penultimate scene, may incongruously reappear in the epilogue, exuding sexual confidence through her clothes and makeup. Finally, the re-casting of the original theatre actor in the film paradoxically works against the conservatism he embodied in the play, for on screen, Martínez Soria's comic theatrical performance is so excessive that it parodies the very traditions of country life and patriarchy that his character tries to promote.

Notes

1. In the sequel, *La familia y uno más*, rural nostalgia is confirmed by the revelation that the mother always wanted the family to move to a house in the country.
2. On ruralism in Spanish cinema, see Richardson (2002) and Faulkner (2006).
3. First staged in Palencia on 13 June 1962, then in Barcelona on 8 August 1962, and in Madrid on 6 Febuary 1963 (Lozano 1965: 6), the play was performed thousands of times throughout Spain (*Cine-Asesor* 1966). For a definition of the *sainete*, see Chapter 1, n. 7.
4. This excruciating episode repeats the trick performed by Tony Leblanc in *Los tramposos* (1959), also directed by Lazaga, in which the gullible victim is fooled.
5. *Majas* were working-class Madrid women, who were also often prostitutes. Goya painted a number of portraits of these women in the eighteenth century, and *majas* remained a popular picturesque theme in the nineteenth. In the film, both the *maja* painting and the picture of the old man are poor quality imitations of Goya's treatment of these popular themes.
6. In Juan Antonio Bardem's *Muerte de un ciclista* (1955), adultery is also associated with modern art through the blackmail sequence between Rafa and María José at the art gallery.
7. Bourdieu's analysis of class and taste is based on a survey of French social mores carried out in a period contemporary with this film, 1963 (1999: 503).
8. Noël Valis, in her book-length study of *cursilería*, notes that 'This word is hard to define since all the English synonyms typically given in dictionaries to explain it – "in bad taste, vulgar," "showy, flashy," or "pseudo-refined, affected" – merely point to its symptoms, not its underlying condition, cause, or context' (2002: 3). These, she argues, are Spain's uneven modernity, where the old and the new coexist in uneasy proximity. Although she does not mention 1960s Spain, the rapid transformations of this decade are typical of this uneven modernity.

9. In Saura's 1967 *Peppermint frappé*, he aligns the Spanish bourgeoisie with the consumption of the fancy tipple from which the film takes its name, a concoction that combines the visual inauthenticity of its impossibly green colour (this was Saura's second colour film), with the linguistic inauthenticity of its conflation of the English noun 'peppermint' and the French adjective *frappé* (iced).

10. When Cabiria of Fellini's *The Nights of Cabiria* (1957) exchanges prostitution for respectability she abandons her fur stole.

11. This is because in the play from which the script is drawn, Luchy is treated as an object of mockery. The stage directions specify that she dresses elegantly, but also insist that she is forty-two years old and and wears glasses (Lozano 1965: 22). Through Tío Agustín, the play misogynistically dismisses Luchy's near-adultery as an embarrassing attempt by an older woman to regain her youth (Lozano 1965: 69). The repetition of this attack on female ageing in the film seems rather absurd, for Coll is relatively young and attractive.

12. I use the term *sainete* in the sense of deploying a number of characteristics of the theatre genre. In his study of the *sainete* in Spanish cinema, Juan Antonio Río Carratalá uses the term more strictly, which means that, for him, while films starring Paco Martínez Soria may contain many aspects of the *sainete*, they are not film *sainetes* as the 'omnipresence' of this actor obliterates a picturesque treatment of setting and customs (*costumbrismo*) and a choral tone (1997: 148–9).

13. This weakening of the patriarch is original to the film, for in Lozano's play Gusti himself writes the love letters to Luchy in order to test her fidelity (1965: 72–3).

PART II

THE *NUEVO CINE ESPAÑOL* (*NEW SPANISH CINEMA*)

CHAPTER 3

Reality and Pretence in *Los farsantes* (*Frauds*, Camus 1963)

Director or Producer? Models of Authorship in the *Viejo Cine Español* and the *Nuevo Cine Español*

In the first two chapters of this book I offered close readings of representative films, paying attention to production as well as socio-historical contexts, to argue that the commercial cinema should not be condemned as uniformly conservative. The same approach is adopted in the rest of this book, necessarily modified to account for the comparative wealth of critical material on the NCE. If the films examined in Part I reveal that the VCE contained elements of dissent that have previously been overlooked, so the example of *Los farsantes* shows that the NCE was closer to the commercial industry than has been suggested hitherto. In this opening section I will chronicle the confrontation between the two distinct models of film authorship of the producer-led commercial cinema and the director-led art cinema in the genesis of *Los farsantes*.

According to the director-led, auteurist model of cinema authorship, the NCE may be considered a cinema that explores contradiction as its directors critiqued the tensions within *aperturista* Spain in their films. Following this model, I argue that Mario Camus's attempt to define, and condemn, reality and pretence in *Los farsantes* exposes these contradictions. The film follows a group of travelling actors and sets up an opposition between the apparently artificial sphere of popular spectacle, represented by theatrical performances and religious ceremony, and the actual struggle for survival of the actors and their provincial audiences, for whom the 1960s seem indistinguishable from the post-war 'años de hambre' (years of hunger). Camus's film, therefore, looks back to the telling contrasts highlighted by Berlanga and Bardem in the 1950s between the supposedly glamorous worlds of film, theatre and advertising and the grim realities of working-class urban and rural life in *Esa pareja feliz* (1951) and *¡Bienvenido Mister Marshall!* (1952).[1]

According, again, to the director-led model of authorship, this early film of the NCE also seems to exemplify the movement's promotion of realism through both theme and form. Although the four examples discussed in this book reveal considerable diversity within the NCE over the question of form, critics have taken its adaptation of Italian Neorealism to the Spanish context to be its aesthetic blueprint (see Introduction). In the early 1960s it seemed doubtful that Camus would be the Film School student to direct a picture that pioneered the formal characteristics of the movement. Saura, for instance, has spoken of his conviction that Camus would be a writer (Sánchez Noriega 1998: 29), and the director himself has admitted on a number of occasions that he planned to be a scriptwriter (Cobos and Sebastián de Erice 1963: 746; Monleón and Egea 1965: 11; Sánchez Noriega 2003: 252). None the less, his collaborative work in the late 1950s and early 1960s with a number of the students who would become the key figures of the NCE explains why his first film pointed a way for the rest of the movement. Camus co-wrote the scripts for Saura's first two features, the pivotal 1959 *Los golfos* (with Saura and Daniel Sueiro) and *Llanto por un bandido* (*Lament for a Bandit* 1963) (with Saura), as well as the scripts for three films that were never made, *La boda* (*The Wedding*) (based on Unamuno's *Abel Sánchez*, with Saura), *El regreso* (*The Return*) (with Saura and Sueiro) and *Jimena* (with Joaquín Jordá, Francisco Regueiro and Miguel Picazo). He was also involved in the production of Basilio Martín Patino's two shorts, *El noveno* (*The Tithe* 1959)[2] and *Torerillos, 61* (*Amateur Bullfighters, 61* 1961) (Sánchez Noriega 1998: 32). Particularly noteworthy here is the collaboration with contemporary writers such as Sueiro, the author of the original short story on which *Los farsantes* is based, and co-scriptwriter for the film: as Kathleen Vernon has pointed out, Camus was the bridge between developments in the novel in the 1950s and cinema in the 1960s: 'building upon his initial collaborations with Ignacio Aldecoa and Daniel Sueiro, [he] codified a vein of Spanish critical realism that persists today' (2002: 262).

A reading of *Los farsantes* as auteur cinema therefore reveals the aesthetic influence of Italian Neorealism and Spanish literature on the NCE. However, the film owes its practical existence to the VCE in the form of the unlikely figure of Ignacio Iquino. Director of some eighty-seven popular films over half a century of filmmaking from 1934 to 1984 (including six works in just one year, 1943), and producer of thirty-six pictures from 1949, when he set up his IFI production company,[3] Iquino's support for the art house cinema of a young Film School graduate is explained by the government's intervention in film production in the 1960s. The subsidy system meant that the state itself acted as a production company, leading, as Casimiro Torreiro has pointed out, to two opposing production phenomena (2000: 155). First, thanks to reduced financial risks, new producers began in the business, and some of them shared the NCE directors' intellectual commitment to critique Franco's Spain.[4] Second, established producers of popular cinema backed the work of the young NCE directors for financial reward. Even if the resulting films are very different, Iquino therefore backed *Los farsantes* for the same reason that Masó did *La gran familia*: pre-production subsidies that would cover the costs of the film (Masó successfully gained 'National Interest' classification for Palacios's film; Iquino only a 2A for Camus's). Eduardo Rodríguez Merchán describes this confrontation between NCE directors and VCE producers as a paradox that 'se repetirá en diversas ocasiones: son los productores veteranos, los artífices del *"cine de muñequitas pintadas"*, tan denostado por los nuevos autores, los que permitirán a éstos desarrollar sus ideas y fabricar un cine que hable de la realidad cotidiana desde una veta profundamente realista' (will be repeated on various occasions: it is the veteran producers, the makers of the *'cinema of painted dolls'* that the new authors insulted so often, who will enable these same authors to develop their ideas and construct a cinema that talks about everyday reality from a profoundly realist vein) (2003: 399, quoting Miguel Picazo).

Camus experienced this paradox with Iquino, a producer whose behaviour in business Óscar de Julián describes as 'go-getting and sharp' (2002: 57). Learning that the government was offering special subsidies for films made by former students of the state Film School, Iquino phoned the graduates of 1962 and offered to produce a film of their choice (Monleón and Egea 1965: 10; in an earlier interview the director recalled that at first Iquino only asked for scripts [Cobos and Sebastián de Erice 1963: 745]). Camus accepted the invitation to direct a film, presumably encouraged by the freedom he had experienced in choosing a script, which Iquino had told him needed only slight modification (Monleón and Egea 1965: 10), and locations (Cobos and Sebastián de Erice 1963: 746). He chose an adaptation of a short story by Sueiro, which he co-wrote with the author, and shot the film in Castile, where he himself, along with Patino and Luis Ciges (who would play Justo in the film) had participated in a student travelling theatre group in Holy Week, 1957.[5]

Notwithstanding this freedom, Camus's experience with Iquino, who produced his first two films, was to be a steep learning curve for the fresh-faced graduate and stages the clash between director-led and producer-led models of film authorship. Although later in his career Camus would work on commercial film commissions (such as his Raphael and Sara Montiel star-vehicle films of the late 1960s), his film background in his late twenties was that provided by the Film School. As discussed in the Introduction, the School trained directors to be auteurs. Its students considered themselves intellectuals, prized their independence and learning, and dismissed their national popular cinema as anathema. Iquino altered Camus and Sueiro's script, dictated the length of the shoot (approximately two months) and the entire cast and technical crew, basically offering Camus the personnel who had just finished work on the now forgotten *José María, el tempranillo* (Forn 1963). This included the cinematograper Salvador Torres Garriga (who only worked on these two films for Iquino), editor Ramón Quadreny (who worked on ten of the producer's films from 1950, but who went on to collaborate in the Barcelona School after *Los farsantes*), composer Enrique Escobar (who worked for Iquino on every film from 1961) and set decorator Andrés Vallvé (who worked on eleven from 1955 to 1971). Noteworthy among the cast are Film School-trained Ciges (who later become an important actor of the Barcelona School) and the excellent Margarita Lozano (who had played Ramona in Buñuel's *Viridiana* [1961]).

Despite their employment by what José Luis Sánchez Noriega terms the 'Iquino factory' (1998: 58), it is therefore possible that Camus found likeminded collaborators among this group, especially given some of their previous and future roles. Emmanuel Larraz has also pointed out that the low-budget techniques of Neorealism fitted perfectly with the notoriously stingy Iquino's desire to keep production costs to a minimum (2003: 5). Overall, we have conflicting accounts of Camus's experience, though interviewers have tended to ask him about working with Iquino, not specific members of the crew. In 1965 he recounts, a little defensively, that he made both *Los farsantes* and *Young Sánchez* 'con una libertad absoluta . . . Iquino estaba realmente de acuerdo conmigo y, además, conmigo se portó muy bien' (with absolute freedom . . . Iquino really was in agreement with me and, what's more, he behaved very well towards me) (Monleón and Egea 1965: 14). However, in more recent interviews he has compared his own experience to that of his fellow students with progressive producers in a rather self-pitying tone: 'yo siempre pensé que cualquiera de los otros trabajaban con amigos' (I always thought that any one of the others was working with friends) (Sánchez Noriega 2003: 253). He recalls, for example, that prior to the *Young Sánchez* shoot Iquino warned him that if he used more than 8500 metres of film, he would have to pay for it himself (Julián 2002: 57)! The director's statements are therefore to be treated sceptically. For instance, while on the one hand he has stated that his cast was pre-selected (Julián 2002: 57), he has also claimed that he chose Lozano, the female lead, himself (Sánchez Noriega 2003: 252). Furthermore, while he recalls that, after Iquino asked to see the material shot after a few days, he gave him complete freedom (Frugone 1984: 53–4; Sánchez Noriega 2003: 254), Sánchez Noriega reports that the producer later forced Camus to include a flamenco sequence to take advantage of the actor José Montez, who plays Currito, and insisted that 40 minutes of the final material was cut (1998: 61).

What is certain is that the production context of *Los farsantes* was one of paradox: the first feature of a director promoted by the state as a would-be art house auteur, made by the creative and technical teams of a producer notorious for churning out material of questionable quality – 'el esta-janovista del cine' [film's Stajanov], as Sánchez Noriega describes him (2003: 253). After the completion of the film, *Los farsantes* fell victim to the contradictions of the state's policy towards cinema in the period. According to the director, the censors cut it by almost 15 minutes (Monleón and Egea 1965: 14), removing, first, the scenes that dealt with homosexuality and second, the soundtrack of the Holy Week procession drums from the final section of the film. Next, the producer – who had covered his costs through the subsidy – neglected its distribution (see Monleón and Egea 1965: 14) and *Los farsantes* was scarcely exhibited.[6] The film was never screened in Madrid, and shown only in re-release theatres in other cities, although it was apparently successful abroad (Sánchez Noriega 1998: 68). We consequently have little record of reception – even reviewers were unable to see the film.[7]

The plot of *Los farsantes* follows Don Pancho's group of nine travelling players, who perform two plays and a variety act as they travel through four different Castilian villages in the weeks preceding Holy Week, and ends with the actors' near-starvation in the days before Easter Sunday, which they spend lying low in a flat in Valladolid because theatre is prohibited in this period.[8] In the last sequence of the film, the city's bells herald the resurrection and the actors continue on their way. The basic conceit, which draws on Alberto Lattuada and Federico Fellini's *Variety Lights* (1950) (Torreiro 1995b: 313; Sánchez Noriega 2003: 252), is to contrast the nature of human existence illustrated on-stage, with that experienced by the performers off-stage.[9] From this opposition of reality and pretence, there develops a study of the dangers of distraction. We see spectators submit to the supposedly easy emotions stirred by sentimental theatre and popular religious spectacle, but we are encouraged to condemn this diversion of their attention away from the more urgent concerns of their own poverty and lack of freedom. Likewise, the actors are engrossed by petty jealousy and deceit, and thus fail to attend to what we are encouraged to understand as the more pressing issues of bettering their own humble circumstances and ending their dependency on Pancho. Integral to this story is Camus's allegorical condemnation of Spain's continued dependency on a dictatorship that, in 1963, entered its twenty-fourth year. The film suggests that, like the characters of *Los farsantes*, Spaniards under Franco are also distracted by everyday concerns, diverted by popular culture and consoled by popular religious ceremony, and consequently fail to address the reality of their repression and dependency.

If we consider it an auteurist, or director-led, film on the basis of the fact that Camus chose the script and locations, *Los farsantes* is therefore an attempt to lift the scales from his audience's eyes, and to this end champions both the aims and methods of Italian Neorealism. Its contradictory production context reveals, however, that the auteurist NCE was practically dependent on the popular VCE that it intellectually condemned, a fact that is often hidden in accounts of the movement. *Los farsantes* is particularly interesting in this regard because it addresses this production context within the film narrative itself. We might first consider the link between production context and creative expression as Camus's attempt to bite the hand that feeds him: *Los farsantes* aims to condemn the distorting and distracting effects of popular theatre and spectacle, which encodes a critique of the popular cinema for which Iquino was well known. However, and possibly despite Camus's intentions, *Los farsantes* itself uses its intended object of critique, popular culture's appeal to emotional identification, to highlight the characters' plight. Its attack of Franco's Spain is executed partly through a Neorealist denunciation of reality, and partly through the audience's emotional identification with Tina. This is thanks to the strength of Lozano's performance, the pre-selected star imposed on Camus in a manner typical of producer-led cinema. Thus, perhaps despite itself, this early example of the NCE in fact benefits from the backing of the VCE in artistic as well as practical terms.

Condemning Popular Spectacle

The critical consensus that the aesthetic and political concerns of the NCE derive largely from Italian Neorealism has led to work on the nature and extent of its influence on particular films (e.g. Arocena 2003), and how it interacts with other developments in world cinema of the 1960s. This latter focus leads Carlos Heredero to consider the NCE in a European context, and conclude that the movement is situated 'En la estela de la modernidad: entre el Neorrealismo y la *Nouvelle Vague*' (In the wake of modernity: between Neorealism and the *Nouvelle Vague*) (Heredero 2003). An alternative approach has recently been defended by Santos Zunzunegui, who sets the NCE within the national context of indigenous cultural tendencies (2002a; 2002b). He argues that, notwithstanding exceptions like Julio Diamante's *Los que no fuimos a la guerra* (*Those of Us Who Didn't Go to*

War 1961) (which the director renamed *Cuando estalló la paz* [*When Peace Broke Out*] when the censors objected to the original title), the NCE privileged Neorealism at the expense of Spanish comic traditions, in particular the *esperpento*. Zunzunegui shows that, despite the wicked satiric success of this idiom of grotesque, dark comedy in the films scripted by Rafael Azcona like *El pisito* (*The Little Flat*, Ferreri 1958), *El cochecito* (Ferreri 1960) and *Plácido* (Berlanga 1961), the NCE rejected this fertile creative vein to conform to a narrow, Marxist understanding of the purpose of art. The movement adopted the ' "realismo" . . . en su formulación de corte luckasiano' ('realism' . . . in its Lukácsian formulation) (2002a: 482)[10] championed by Juan Antonio Bardem (whose presence Zunzunegui describes, punning on the title of an Antxón Eceiza film, as a 'cadáver cinematográfico . . . "de cuerpo presente" ' [cinematic corpse . . . 'present in body'] [2002a: 477 n. 18]), to the exclusion of alternative dissident tendencies. For the critics of *Nuestro Cine*, the problem with the *esperpento* was that it was seen as 'de "fácil digestión" para una burguesía que no se daba, decían, por aludida ante "lo insólito del monstruo o del esperpento" ' ('easily digestible' for a bourgeoisie that, they would say, didn't get the hint when confronted with 'the unusual spectacle of the monstruous or the *esperpento*') (Zunzunegui 2002b: 106, quoting José Luis Egea). 'De esta manera,' Zunzunegui concludes,

> se decretaba desde los púlpitos de la denominada crítica progresista [*Nuestro Cine*] la marginación de una serie de raíces culturales que van desde el Arcipreste de Hita hasta Valle-Inclán pasando por la picaresca o Goya, bajo el argumento de su difusa mordiente política. (Thus, from the pulpits of the so-called progressive criticism [*Nuestro Cine*], it was decreed that a series of cultural influences, from the Archpriest of Hita up to Valle-Inclán via the picaresque or Goya, should be sidelined, according to the argument that their political critique was vague.) (Zunzunegui 2002b: 106)

Los farsantes, a film not mentioned by Zunzunegui, seems typical of the NCE's embrace of realism. Eduardo Rodríguez Merchán confirms that Camus

> había decidido decantarse por un *postneorrealismo moral* que se desmarcaba de la tradición deformante y paródica, cuyo paradigma se situaba en las recientes obras maestras del dúo Azcona-Berlanga, para sumergirse en un criticismo más realista, más objetivo o – si se prefiere – más 'verdadero'. (had decided to opt for a *moral postneorealism* that distanced itself from the deforming and parodic tradition, whose paradigm could be found in the recent work of the Azcona-Berlanga duo, in order to immerse himself in a more realist, objective or – if you prefer – 'true' criticism.) (Rodríguez Merchán 2003: 398, quoting Santiago San Miguel; original emphasis)

Camus's aim in *Los farsantes* initially appears clear: to toe the *Nuestro Cine* party line and depict Spanish 'reality' – to be understood in the Marxist sense of a portrait of the class struggle – while condemning the distorted versions of the 'reality' offered by popular spectacle.

However, it is significant that Camus chooses to focus on a group whose poverty evokes the misery of the post-war years. In an interview published in *Film Ideal* following the film's release, the director notes that travelling players had become increasingly rare in 1960s Spain, only surviving in some parts of Castile and Extremadura (Cobos and Sebastián de Erice 1963: 746). On the one hand, the choice of this group allows Camus to contrast the poverty of the actors with the relative affluence of the bourgeoisie and thus condemn the uneven modernisation of 1960s Spain. But on the other, it raises the question of how far this fast-disappearing group could be representative of 'reality' in the 1960s. Pancho's vagabond theatre company could scarcely be further away from the revitalisation of the Spanish stage that was actually taking place in the 1960s (Zatlin 2002: 229). Camus acknowledges this lack of realism later in the interview:

> *Los farsantes* quizá no sea muy realista, el término realista está muy fastidiado ya . . . la historia es una historia de ficción mía . . . no tiene ningún fundamento realista en el sentido que tú lo dices . . . tiene un realismo en otro sentido. Es un realismo mío personal. (*Los farsantes* is perhaps not very realist, the term realist is very vexed now . . . the story is my own work of fiction . . . it doesn't have any realist basis in the sense that you mean . . . it's realist in another sense. It's my personal realism.) (Cobos and Sebastián de Erice 1963: 746)

Unfortunately, the interview is poorly edited and the question ('in the sense that you mean') that gave rise to this response is omitted, but we might conjecture that it queried the director's commitment to *Nuestro Cine*'s Marxist definition of realism.

Finally, however, in an interview cited by Juan Carlos Frugone in 1984, which is unfortunately undated, Camus declared that Italian Neorealism was an influence on his first two features. He mentions Cesare Zavattini – the scriptwriter of key works like *Bicycle Thief* (De Sica 1948) and frequent visitor to Spain – who became a major source of influence for Spanish writers and directors from the 1950s onwards (Heredero 1993: 289–90):

> Yo pertenezco a una generación que creía en una revolución. Sigo creyendo en eso. Zavattini decía: 'Lo que uno intenta es conmover al hombre con todo lo que sucede a su alrededor en el mundo. Y en particular lo que sucede hoy o en un inmediato ayer.' Esto dio resultado en *Los farsantes* y en *Young Sánchez* . . . (I belong to a generation that believed in a revolution. I still believe in that. Zavattini would say: 'What one tries to do is to get people to be moved by everything happening around them in the

world. And in particular by what is happening today or in the immediate past.' This
bore fruit in *Los farsantes* and *Young Sánchez* . . .) (Frugone 1984: 53)

It is perhaps more sensible to leave aside interviews, with their hidden
agendas of questions of political allegiance, and compare *Los farsantes* with
its two immediate sources of influence. First, unlike Lattuada and Fellini's
Variety Lights, Camus avoids revelling in the glamour of the showbiz
world, thereby insisting that his audience focus on the film's politics and
condemn theatrical spectacle as a source of distraction. Second, the
changes Camus makes to the narrative perspective of Sueiro's original
short story also seem to indicate his desire to make a film that encourages
intellectual detachment, rather than emotional involvement. The perspective of Sueiro's first-person narrator Rogelio is removed as Camus appears
to offer a choral film in which the actors form a collective protagonist, and
no single character becomes the object of our identification. This attempt
to check identification is consistent with Brechtian aesthetics as it is
intended to channel our attention away from individual concerns towards
the political message portrayed instead. Camus's choice to focus on a social
group that is scarcely representative of 1960s Spain as a whole reveals that
his aim was not to offer the Lukácsian realism demanded by *Nuestro Cine*.
By focusing on the world of travelling players, his aim was, rather, to
oppose reality and pretence.

The object of Camus's attack in *Los farsantes* is the perniciously distracting and distorting effects of 'farsa' (farce), which divert attention away
from 'reality'. While denunciation may be less ambitious than the creative
appropriation of Spanish farcical traditions Zunzunegui so admires in
directors like Berlanga, Camus does not, therefore, ignore these traditions.
Further, the 'farsa' of Camus's title does not narrowly refer to 'farce' as in
light-hearted carnivalesque buffoonery, which is only touched on in the
striptease performance. Camus puns on the polysemy of 'farsa' in Spanish,
meaning both poor quality theatre and pretence or deceit. This play on
words is original to the short story on which the film is based (see, for
instance, Sueiro's reference to 'la farsa se detiene' [the farce stops] [1988:
79]) although Camus brings it to the fore by replacing both Sueiro's original title, 'La carpa' (The Big Top), and the title of the first version of the
script, 'Fin de fiesta' (End of the Festivities), with *Los farsantes*.[11]

Los farsantes, therefore, condemns the distorting and distracting effects
of pretence and privileges the drive for an authentic representation of
reality that was the mainstay of Italian Neorealism. It consequently
opposes popular performances with a portrayal of reality using Neorealist
practices such as on-location shooting (although there are some studio sets

too), documentary sequences (the images and sounds of the Holy Week processions were shot and recorded in Valladolid as a documentary prior to the rest of the film)[12] and an emphasis on *mise en scène*. On the latter point, Camus affirmed that a concern for *mise en scène* characterised his early work (the two shorts, *El borracho* [*The Drunkard*] and *La suerte* [*Luck*], and two features *Los farsantes* and *Young Sánchez*) (Monleón and Egea 1965: 10–11). In *Los farsantes* the long shots that sweep across the barren Castilian landscape constitute a visual refrain in the film. These exterior shots contrast with the artificial worlds evoked in the company's performances, and explain the poverty of the actors and villagers who inhabit such lands. The use of these techniques, which Florencio Martínez Aguinagalde describes as an 'aesthetic of defeat' (1989: 148), allows Camus to denounce a reality that characters and audiences ignore owing to their distraction by pretence.

The anti-clerical opening sequence of *Los farsantes* establishes this thesis of the opposition of reality and pretence. Each actor is introduced in medium shot as they wait in a theatre for the village priest to arrive and perform the last rites for their recently deceased companion, Manolo. The run-down setting of the village theatre contrasts with the elaborate costumes and backdrops left on stage. The intended clash is highlighted in the script, where the theatre is described as having a 'pared descarnada, con el cemento caído y los ladrillos al aire' (dilapidated wall, with the cement render falling off and the bricks showing), yet 'Aún está armado en la tarima un decorado que representa la fachada de un lujoso palacio y los árboles de un jardín' (Scenery representing the façade of a luxurious palace and the trees of a garden is still set up on stage) (Camus and Sueiro 1963: 3, 4). After taking in these differences, we witness Pancho rebuke the group of actors for their indifference regarding their companion's death. He instructs them to feign mourning for Manolo's passing for the benefit of the villagers: 'Demostrad que lo sentís' (Show that you're sorry). Thus just as the theatrical props are artificial, so too is their grief.

When the priest and altar boys arrive to perform the rituals of mourning, the actors therefore respectfully gather round the body and bow their heads. However, Camus rather playfully has Justo cast aside one of the costumes as he takes up his position in the group of mourners – thus exchanging one type of performance for another. Telling also is the cinematographic arrangement of the shot of the last rites. It is a long take from the perspective of a camera placed on the stage, which suggests an equivalence between theatrical and religious performance and highlights the pretence implicit in both. The next sequences make this clear. In the script Camus and Sueiro specify that at the interment, Pancho, 'con un

ademán digno de un gran actor, tira un puñado de tierra contra la caja'
(with a gesture worthy of a great actor, throws a handful of earth against
the coffin) (1963: 14). Next, Pancho entreats the village mayor to sympathise with his company's mourning of their deceased companion – and
thereby write off the debts they have incurred – while back in the theatre
we observe that the actors' true preoccupations go no further than putting
food on their plates and a roof over their heads. It is important to under-
line here that this introduction to the film is not a condemnation of the
callous self-interest of the actors. Camus attends to the details of their miserable existence, emphasising their shabby dress and dilapidated surroundings through *mise en scène*, and their attitude of dejection through
performance style, and thus provides ample explanation for their attitude.
Los farsantes rather censures the pointlessness of religious observance in
a situation where the mourners have more urgent material concerns.

Reality and pretence are likewise opposed in Camus's treatment of the
two plays we see the theatre group perform. First, a version of *Genoveva
de Brabante*[13] is staged in two villages. In the first village, Tina and Rogelio
act out Genoveva and Segisfredo's betrothal, in the second, they perform
the couple's reunion after Segisfredo had been tricked about his wife's dis-
honour and death. Although parts of the performances may have been cut
on Iquino's instructions, what remains of the treatment of the play and its
juxtaposition with events off-stage reveal that Camus's apparent purpose
was to satirise the artificiality of melodramatic, historical theatre, whose
cinematic equivalent was the bombastic, historical cinema produced by
companies like IFI España, or CIFESA. While the performances themselves showcase fancy period costume and elaborate rhetoric, these illu-
sions of grandeur are deflated through the editing of the two extracts. The
first sequence follows the group's escape from the first village, when they
sit on the back of the van in the open air, and we see the first of many argu-
ments between Rogelio and Avilés over Tina. The introduction of the play
by means of a fade highlights the jarring contrast between the preceding
sequence of physical hardship and petty jealousy off-stage, and the ornate
costumes and high-register language of Tina and Rogelio on-stage as
Segisfredo addresses his betrothed using the standard bucolic imagery of
love poetry:

> Mi Genoveva querida,
> jardín de olorosas flores,
> ídolo de mis amores,
> vida de mi propia vida;
> y a la hora apetecida,
> llego a hacerte dichosa,

> desde hoy serás mi esposa.
> (My beloved Genoveva,
> garden of fragrant flowers,
> idol of my love,
> life of my own life;
> and at the longed-for moment,
> I come to make you happy,
> from today you will be my wife.)

The attentive viewer might, however, note that Genoveva's misgivings about her marriage on-stage reflect Tina's difficulties in the love triangle off-stage:

> desterrar no puedo,
> de dentro del alma mía,
> extraña melancolía,
> y presentimientos tales,
> cual si nuestros esponsales,
> nuncios fueran de agonía.
> (I cannot banish,
> from my heart,
> a strange melancholy,
> and a sense of foreboding,
> as though our betrothal,
> were a harbinger of great suffering.)

The sequence ends with a fade to a close-up of Pancho and Pura's hands counting peseta pieces, the camera then zooming back to reveal the whole group gathered round the takings. This juxtaposition of the two shots again highlights the gulf between the noble sentiments expressed on stage and their irrelevance in the context of desperate poverty. In what may have been a fruitful collaboration with editor Ramón Quadreny here, Camus, therefore, contrasts the Neorealist depiction of hardship with the fake portrait of humanity offered by the play, which reinforces the thesis of *Los farsantes*: that performance is a source of falsification and distraction, and characters and audiences alike should focus on the everyday trials of life depicted.

In the second performance of a different section of the play, Camus refers explicitly to audience reception. As in the first performance, Quadreny's editing again contrasts two situations. When Segisfredo re-encounters his long-lost wife, their reunion is announced by his declaration:

> Te creo Genoveva desdichada.
> Ven a mis brazos
> y deja que ellos sean
> un trono para tu honor.

> (I believe you unhappy Genoveva.
> Come into my arms
> and let them be
> a throne for your honour.)

These words evoke the tearful responses of two female members of the audience, which are illustrated with cross-cuts. The technique of parallel montage is rather obvious and the acting of the members of the audience is poor, but its self-referentiality is noteworthy. The sequence appears to instruct us how to react to the film we are watching. It seems to suggest that an emotional response is undesirable and, because two women are depicted, 'feminised'. In contrast, it apparently promotes detachment: we should respond in a non-emotional, intellectual or 'masculinised' way to Camus's denunciation of poverty and hypocrisy.

In the second play, the title of which is given on the group's promotional posters and the side of their van as *Vanidad y Miseria* (*Vanity and Poverty*), Camus once again contrasts on- and off-stage worlds. Up to this point in the film, Camus shows that for the company of actors, religious observance is a matter of indifference. Pancho insists on keeping up appearances, such as publicly mourning Manolo's passing, and concealing the extramarital relationships of Tina and Rogelio and Milagritos and Lucio (in the original version of the film these would have included Currito and Vicente's gay partnership too). But this only serves to highlight the meaninglessness of clerically sanctioned behaviour for the group. Indeed, the first time we see Pancho scold the older couple for their lack of discretion about their sexual relationship, Camus places a picture of the Virgin behind him, in the first of many instances of ironic contrast in the film. Given this context of patent atheism, the players' performance of the Passion play, in which Camus even has the randy Lucio in the role of the Messiah, is an obvious critique of pretence. The treatment of this play is an instance of Camus's encoded critique of Spanish popular cinema, as it slyly overturns the premise of the pro-Franco film made by Iquino himself, *El Judas* (*The Judas* 1952), in which the actor who takes on the role of Jesus in the Holy Week play is morally improved by the character he embodies.

The village priest is another target of this anti-clerical assault. First, Camus changes Sueiro's original so that in the film the priest insists on checking the play prior to its performance, whereas in the short story it is a teacher (Sánchez Noriega 1998: 67). But the priest is not just a source of censorship in the film. As the actors get changed in the sacristy, Camus also has him uncharitably instruct his sacristan to lock away the silver, for fear it will be stolen. There follows a sequence that again indicates Camus's gift for setting up ironic contrasts between sound- and imagetracks. As the actors rehearse their lines and read out loud the pious sentiments of the play, the priest's sacristan puts the valuables under lock and key, much to Rogelio's annoyance. After the sequence in the sacristy, it is difficult to interpret the performance of the play in the church atrium as anything but empty theatricality. The *mise en scène* of the church's façade, on which the Falangist symbol is prominently displayed, also points to the anachronism of the sentiments expressed, for in an earlier sequence the priest has admitted that the building is in need of repair, just as its flock of faithful is ever dwindling.

Camus's condemnation of the distracting nature of popular theatre and religious ceremony also extends to the official rhetoric of *aperturista* Spain, which is referenced in the film with a Radio Nacional de España report on foreign relations between the United States and Europe. After the performance of *Vanidad y Miseria*, Tina and Rogelio accept an invitation – or rather, given their hunger, force an invitation – to have lunch with Rogelio's old army friend and his family, while their companions play cards and drink in the local bar. Frugone has interpreted the couple's behaviour in the bourgeois home as further proof of the actors' fraudulence, for they imitate their bourgeois hosts as soon as they are left in the house alone by having sex, like man and wife, in the marital bed (1984: 55). The still reproduced as Figure 3.1 shows how *mise en scène* is constructed to convey the similarities and differences between the actors and their bourgeois hosts (in the version of the film currently available in the Madrid Film Archives this image has been cut, presumably because it precedes the sex-scene). Tina is juxtaposed with an image of the Virgin on the left side of the screen, while the framed image of Rogelio in the mirror matches the framed photograph of Antonio in military uniform on the right. This not only reveals that the penniless actors are willing to perform bourgeois roles. More incisively, it also suggests that those religious and military bourgeois roles are themselves nothing more than performances, since they can be acted out with such ease by others.

However, the real object of critique in this sequence is not Tina and Rogelio's understandable desire to enjoy the home comforts of their wealthier friends, but rather the opposition highlighted by Camus between the actors' activities and the radio report by means of diegetic sound. The sequence opens in the bar, where the actors play cards and tease Avilés about his jealousy of Rogelio, and the news begins on the radio. There follows a soundbridge to Tina and Rogelio as they cavort in Antonio's house and the report on the European Union and the latest German–American alliance continues. An ironic contrast is therefore drawn between the wordy

Figure 3.1. Margarita Lozano in *Los farsantes*.
Video Mercury Films.

description of international relations we hear and the picaresque tale of Avilés's jealousy, Tina and Rogelio's lust and the ensuing violence as the sequence ends in a drunken brawl between the two rivals we see. *Los farsantes* shows that the *aperturista* government's concern with Spain's role in the international arena is misconceived. Franco's Spain in the 1960s attempted to act as a modern European power on the international stage (in the early 1960s it tried, but failed, to join the EEC), but Camus's revelation of the squalid reality of Spanish life exposes this as empty rhetoric that distracts attention away from the poverty and dependency of its citizens.

This condemnation of pretence culminates with Camus's treatment of the variety act performed by the actors for the group of upper-bourgeois day-trippers we see arrive in the village during the religious play. These bourgeois characters are not included in Sueiro's short story, so we may take this original sequence as one of particular interest to Camus. Their inclusion enables the director to critique the two key social groups from which Franco drew his support. Some of the group are members of Spain's landed gentry, as they own a mansion in the countryside, and the others belong to the new entrepreneurial bourgeois class that benefited from Spain's economic liberalisation, as they drive luxury cars suggesting their arrival from the city. The inclusion of these bourgeois pleasure-seekers also enables Camus to expose the huge disparities of wealth consequent of 1960s Spain's uneven modernisation. Camus's film makes clear that the economic polarisation of the classes was as much a target of critique in the 1960s as the dictatorship itself. The three long shots and takes of the arrival of the bourgeois in the village offer a striking image of these disparities of wealth: the well-heeled, car-owning friends sit alongside the pious old women clothed in black to watch the play. Pancho's penniless actors also look incongruous in the luxurious surroundings of the bourgeois holiday home, where they arrive to perform the variety act. Camus's inexperience perhaps shows in the exaggerated portrayal of the bourgeois characters' staggering snobbery, although it recalls similar attacks found in the contemporary Spanish novel.[14] 'Yo no me explico cómo puede vivir esa gente' (I don't understand how these people can live) scoffs one of them after the actors arrive, 'para mí son como marcianos' (to me they're like Martians) agrees another, 'auténtico gente de otro planeta' (really people from another planet) adds a third.

The treatment of performance during the variety act sequence is more successful, however, because Camus returns to the thesis of reality and pretence he has developed to this point. Of the various acts the groups performs, which include Pancho's rendition of Calderón's *La vida es sueño* (*Life's a Dream*), the bourgeois are only interested in the striptease. American jazz is played on the flashy new record player, and the English lyrics of the female vocalist, especially the repetition of the word 'Manhattan', evoke a modern, Western and urban world to which Franco's *aperturista* Spain aspired. But Camus's treatment of the striptease exposes the artificiality of the bourgeois characters' aspirations of modernity and sophistication. The sequence is excruciating to watch: it is an erotic spectacle reflected in the concave mirror of Valle-Inclán's *Luces de Bohemia* (*Bohemian Lights* 1920).[15] Tina's version of sophisticated erotica is a grotesque deformation, thanks to Lozano's brilliant performance as the poor, ageing, exhausted and famished actress. She cannot keep time with the American music – suggesting Spain's uneasy transatlantic alliances – and discards her clothes with all the artfulness of a child. When the record is put on fast-forward she even hops and trips as she steps out of her skirt, and ends up half-falling, half-slumping in the corner in a state of undress and distress. Like the play-within-a-play of Shakespeare's *Hamlet*, this performance reaches a wider truth: the fake artificiality of Tina's puppet-like act exposes the actual artificiality of the bourgeois characters.[16] The modern ambitions of *aperturista* Spain are therefore exposed in *Los farsantes* as a sham.

A comparison of the *esperpento* treatment of Tina's performance with other directors' use of this idiom of exaggeration is revealing of Camus's approach in *Los farsantes*. In the dark comedies of Berlanga or Ferreri, grotesque exaggeration evokes laughter, not shame: consider, for instance, the comic effects of Nino Manfredi as reluctant executioner in *El verdugo* (1963). In contrast, Tina's pitiable performance evokes compassion not amusement; a point underlined by Avilés's interruption at the end of the sequence when he denounces the audience's voyeurism, yelling '¡Fuera! ¡Si quieren ver a una mujer desnuda, echen mano a una de éstas!' (Get out! If you want to see a naked woman, try one of these!), gesturing towards the bourgeois women. The effect of this outcry within the film is further to condemn the bourgeoisie. But, through Avilés, Camus also challenges us, for at this point we too are voyeurs, having shared the bourgeois characters' point of view as they watch the performance. Thus Avilés's denunciation also entreats us to sympathise with Tina as a suffering subject, not laugh at her as a pathetic erotic object.[17] This sequence shows that, even in the context of Neorealism, the insights of the *esperpento* were not ignored, as Zunzunegui affirms, but rather inverted. If, 'In its declared intention to show the comedy in tragic situations, the *esperpento* required the elimination of empathy and identification', as John Lyon observed in his work on Valle-Inclán (1983: 105), in *Los farsantes*, Camus shows the tragic in comic situations, which conversely requires an emphasis on empathy and identification.

Identification and Critique

This is an important turning point in *Los farsantes*, as from here on Tina ceases to be one of a group of characters, and emerges as a tragic individual with whom we are encouraged to identify. From the striptease sequence onwards, the film begins to adopt her perspective in both narrative and cinematographic terms. As the plot unfolds, her feelings are emphasised, from her embarrassment during the performance, to her dejection following Rogelio's betrayal, who we have seen steal the money she suffers so acutely to earn. During the final Holy Week section of the film, it is Tina who initiates a sexual encounter with Avilés,[18] and she then emerges as the only character willing to rebel against the actors' dependency. This shared narrative perspective is reinforced by the subjective cinematography with which mainstream narrative cinema fosters audience identification. For instance, on the morning following the striptease, after a 180° pan reveals that the actors have spent the night sleeping in the open, Tina is framed in medium shot for a long take of 1 minute, during which the camera registers her wordless despair as, off-screen, the others discuss Rogelio's betrayal. Similarly, the impact of Rogelio's return is also felt through a point-of-view shot from Tina's perspective as she sees him in the corner of the café in Valladolid. It may be argued that this focus on Tina's personal distress distracts our attention from the denunciation of the collective experience of poverty. However, Camus has been so careful to present the reasons for the actors' behaviour in a wider context earlier in the film, that *Los farsantes* condemns a general situation through Tina's particular despair.

The importance of this identification with Tina in the film, therefore, seems to contradict Camus's apparent condemnation of emotional engagement explored in his treatment of the tearful audiences of *Genoveva de Brabante*. We may account for this discrepancy as the result of producer-pressure, whereby Camus was forced to expand Tina's role to take advantage of Lozano, the most famous actor in the cast – confirmed by the fact that her name appears first in the credits – though it would be an exaggeration to label her a bankable star.[19] However, we have no record of Camus's discomfort with the cast. On the contrary, he declared in a contemporary interview that if there were a remake, he would use the same actors (Cobos and Sebastián de Erice 1963: 746), and, as we have seen, even claimed to have cast Lozano himself. It seems likely that Camus's development of her character, and encouragement of his audiences to identify with her, were intentional. The shift in emphasis away from a film with a collective protagonist to one with individual characterisation corresponds to Camus's description of his work with the actors: 'A medida que ellos iban interpretando yo iba creando los papeles como les iban mucho más a ellos. Así, el papel iba de acuerdo con las posibilidades de cada uno' (As they acted, I adjusted the roles so they would fit them better. That way the role matched the abilities of each one) (Cobos and Sebastián de Erice 1963: 746). Thus Camus fitted the film round Lozano's abilities and consequently expanded her role. Camus's next film confirms this shift away from a collective to an individual protagonist. Just as Tina becomes a focus for *Los farsantes*'s denunciation of the continued poverty experienced in Spain despite economic liberalisation, in *Young Sánchez*, Camus's censure of the lack of prospects of working-class urban youth likewise hinges on our identification with the protagonist, Julián Mateos's ambitious young boxer.

Tina's characterisation in *Los farsantes*, therefore, reveals that, perhaps despite himself, this NCE director was willing to adopt some of the strategies of popular culture that he also seemed simultaneously to condemn. So, while he appears to critique the tearful spectators of *Genoveva de Brabante* as emotionally indulgent, he evokes the very same sentiments of pity and empathy in his own audience through his treatment of Tina. The difference, Camus might contend, is that the former is triggered by the pointless distraction of sentimental melodrama and the latter by the urgent denunciation of the class struggle. However, taken as a whole, *Los farsantes* demonstrates the possible contestatory effects of both popular culture – in its appeal to emotional engagement – and art house cinema – with its entreaty to address intellectually the situations presented. This not only confirms that popular culture under Franco, so often dismissed and derided, could play a potentially subversive role. It also shows that auteurs of art cinema, who in theory dismissed Spanish popular culture, in practice adopted its strategies of identification.

Rather than the sanitised Marxist version of Italian Neorealism cherished by contributors to *Nuestro Cine*, *Los farsantes* therefore exhibits the contradiction that scholars have noted lies at the movement's heart. For instance, *Bicycle Thief* (De Sica 1948), one of the few films owned by the Film School and one that Camus saw so many times he claimed he knew it by heart (Sánchez Noriega 1998: 2), censures the distracting effects of Hollywood melodrama on the one hand – Antonio's bicycle is stolen as he admires a poster of Rita Hayworth – yet on the other the film itself explores the theme of family relations and uses the techniques of identification that were central to the American genre. Giuseppe de Santis's *Bitter Rice* (1948) also seeks to oppose the distractions of Hollywood film with the reality of female labour in the rice fields, though, just like his protagonist Silvana, the director betrays a fascination for American popular culture, thus undermining his political position. *Los farsantes* also censures popular spectacle, but through Tina, Camus harnesses its appeal to emotional engagement for his own critical ends. The treatment of the female audience of *Genoveva de Brabante* is therefore ambiguous: the emotions stirred by popular theatre may be diverting, but may also be channelled to denounce injustice.

Ceremony and Suffering

Popular religious ceremony is also presented in *Los farsantes* as a source of distraction, but its treatment is less equivocal than Camus's response to popular theatre. Two of Camus's characters declare their enthusiasm for the Church and its ceremonies, which points to its role as a source of solace in hard times. However, Camus and Sueiro's script ensures that both statements are undercut and cannot be taken seriously. Currito, who is the only believer of the group of actors, admonishes Rogelio for challenging the suspicious sacristan in the previously discussed sequence in the sacristy. But we cannot take seriously Currito's declaration 'tengo devoción y respeto' (I am devoted and respectful). Coming as it does after the group's uncharitable treatment by the priest, it seems ridiculous rather than pious.

Likewise, on their arrival in the flat in Valladolid, the maid eagerly describes the city's Holy Week celebrations to the group. Again, we cannot take her seriously when she states 'Dicen que la Semana Santa de Sevilla es muy buena, pero como ésta, ni hablar' (They say Holy Week in Seville is very good, but it's not a patch on this one), as she reveals that her pride is based on hearsay, not knowledge.

Camus's critique of the Catholic Church – the institution that gave moral legitimacy to the Franco regime – is, therefore, an anti-clerical thread woven throughout the film. *Los farsantes* begins by underlining the pretence enacted at Manolo's funeral, proceeds to satirise the message of the Passion play, and ends with a daring treatment of Holy Week, the most important event in the Christian calendar. Like the actors who are so engrossed in everyday concerns they fail to address the reality of their own situation, Camus shows that the faithful are also so distracted by public ceremony that they fail to address the actual suffering in their midst.[20] The point is encapsulated by the first sequence following the group's arrival in Valladolid. During a meal in a guesthouse, the distrustful owner tells Pancho that the group must leave. Given their obvious indigence, this seems reasonable, but Camus slyly makes his point through the presence of a poster on the wall behind the owner advertising 'Semana Santa, Abril 1963' (Holy Week, April 1963), on which Christ's Crucifixion alongside the two thieves may be clearly seen. Earlier in the film, as the group arrives in the village where they put on the second peformance of *Genoveva de Brabante*, Camus prefigures this association of the actors with Christ and the thieves through a long shot of their van passing behind three crosses that evoke the Crucifixion, and that consequently associate them with both the transgressors and the Messiah himself in his suffering. The poster reminds us that Christ, who preaches compassion to the poor, was himself 'numbered with the transgressors' when he was crucified beside common thieves (Mark 15: 28), and it is therefore an ironic comment on the owner's rejection of Pancho's appeal for charity. The proprietress may not charge the actors for their meal, but her refusal of lodging means she only partly fulfils the biblical injunction on the treatment of strangers (Matthew 25: 34–46).

Camus's critical treatment of the Valladolid Holy Week processions is an expansion of this idea of ironic contrast. Fundamentally, the pity and piety that is publicly displayed in the Easter processions are juxtaposed with the actual and acute suffering of the group of actors that is hidden from sight in two rooms of a private flat.[21] The contrast drawn between the representation of suffering in the processions and the actual suffering of the actors is original to Sueiro's short story. 'Esos días dramáticos, nebulosos, agónicos' (These dark days of drama and death), his narrator writes of Holy Week, 'para nadie lo son tanto como para nosotros, los de la carpa' (are particularly so for us, the theatre people) (Sueiro 1988: 80). Both the reader of the story and the viewer of the film are therefore invited to consider contrasts between the biblical story and the plot of *Los farsantes*. For instance, the fasting of the faithful in imitation of Christ's suffering in the wilderness is shown to parallel the actual starvation of the actors. Likewise, the pain experienced by the faithful in imitation of Christ's Passion on the cross by beating drums in the processions (which Sueiro mentions [1988: 117]) matches the actors' actual pain through lack of food. Our identification with the actors in their actual suffering reinforces the contrast with the imitation of suffering of the faithful.

This contrast is developed through editing, cinematography and soundtrack. The Holy Week section of *Los farsantes* is particularly interesting in terms of film form as, like the siesta sequence of *La caza* discussed in Chapter 6, it is not wholly driven by narrative; for while the actors' suffering is part of the story, the linear progression of the plot is not Camus's primary concern. Parts of this 22-minute sequence (the film is 82 minutes in total) transcend narrative to represent hunger, madness and the slow passing of time as the actors wait until the ban on theatre is lifted and they can work and eat again. Since the actors' suffering is physical, it is logical that Camus should focus on the body. An important association is made at the start of the sequence between the images of the suffering body of Christ on the Holy Week floats in medium and long shots, and the response of Currito as he looks on in medium shot. As Currito is a believer, we assume at first that Camus's parallel montage indicates his piety. However, Currito is also the character who goes on to suffer most from lack of food, so his association with Christ established through editing does not indicate religious belief, but the shared physical suffering of the body. Even if Camus was forced to include it against his will, the flamenco sequence (Figure 3.2) underscores this shared suffering. In a performance that is a far cry from the picturesque Andalusian spectacle of the *españoladas* (folkloric musical films), the close-ups of Currito's straining body and anguished face during the flamenco dance in the flat recall the agonised body and face of the images of Christ we have seen on the floats. On Easter Sunday, as the bells of the resurrection ring out, Vicente and Lucio carry Currito's almost lifeless body from the flat to the van, which also recalls the removal of Jesus from the cross. Camus also uses close-up to represent the suffering of other characters, such as the slow tracking shot in extreme close-up of Justo and Avilés's bodies, which emphasises their hands and feet, the two body parts by which Christ was nailed to the cross. This representation of starvation through the detailed attention to the experience

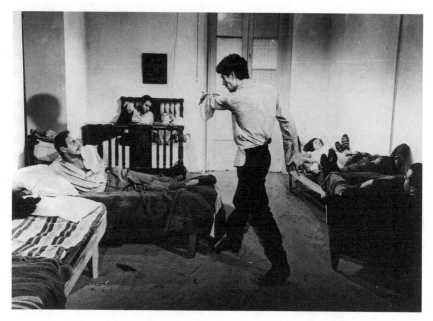

Figure 3.2 José Montez in *Los farsantes*. Video Mercury Films.

of the body has been called Camus's portrayal of 'the cinematographic physicality of the senses' (Rodríguez Merchán 2003: 400), and is achieved by extending Neorealism to a level of physical detail that approaches *cinéma-vérité*, a technique taken to an extreme by Saura in *La caza*. What is impressive here is that Camus pulled this off with the technical teams of Iquino's production machine, whereas Saura was working with arguably Spain's top art cinematographer of all time, Luis Cuadrado.

Camus's original intention may have been to represent the passing of time in *Los farsantes* by a similar emphasis on physical detail: the sound of the processional drums in the street outside would have magnified the slow passing of minutes and seconds for the actors trapped inside the flat.[22] However, the censors picked up on the association made between the drums and the actors' hunger and descent into madness by means of the sound-bridge, and forced Camus to add a new soundtrack to the last two reels of the film. In the currently available version of *Los farsantes*, the important diegetic sound of the Holy Week drums has been replaced by bland melody of the background music that is played during the credits and to suture sequences together. To deduce how this sequence might originally have sounded we at least have a version of it in Sueiro's original short story, which reveals the role the drums play in underlining the actors' gradual starvation, 'Los tambores habían retumbado en los cristales de las tres ventanas, con los mismos sonidos lentos, estremecidos, siniestros que deben acompañar a los condenados que van a morir en la horca' (The drums had made the panes of the three windows vibrate with the same slow, shaking, sinister beat that must accompany condemned men to the gallows) (Sueiro 1988: 105), and in emphasising the passing of time as the actors wait:

> Aquel tiempo sin horas y sin fechas, sin días ni noches, sin nada que hacer ni que pensar, nos tenía como idos de este mundo. El miércoles por la noche nos metimos en la pensión de la calle Teresa Gil y ya no volvimos a salir. Desde nuestra habitación oíamos continuamente, durante todo el día y buena parte de la noche, el paso lento, arrastrado, obsesionante de las procesiones, siempre acompañadas por el retumbar de los tambores, y, de vez en cuando, la estridencia de las cornetas. (That time without hours or dates, without days or nights, with nothing to do or think about, made us feel absent from this world. On Wednesday night we went into the guesthouse on Teresa Gil street and we didn't come out again. All day and for much of the night, we could continually hear from our room the slow, dragging, obsessive passing of the processions, which were always accompanied by the booming of the drums, and, occasionally, the shrill cry of the bugles.) (Sueiro 1988: 109–10)

In the final Holy Week section of the film, Camus, therefore, pays particular attention to the painful experience of the starving body and the slow passing of time to establish a provocatively anti-clerical parallel between the representation of the suffering of Christ in the biblical story, and the actual suffering of a group of poverty-stricken actors in provincial Spain. *Los farsantes*, therefore, condemns religious ceremony as distraction: the Valladolid faithful display penance in the public processions, but ignore the suffering of the actors in their midst.

Allegories of Dependency

Camus's denunciation of the distorting and distracting effects of pretence, in its various forms of popular theatre, Catholic ceremony, official rhetoric and erotic spectacle, may also be extended to an allegorical reading of the film as a whole. Audiences are called on to address what the director considers to be the worthy object of our attention, his version of Spanish reality, rather than be diverted by pretence. In this context the film may be read as autobiographical, as the relationship between the actors and Pancho allegorises Camus's own dependency on Iquino. However, the choice of the name Pancho for the manager of the theatrical group is not accidental, as it is a familiar form of Francisco, the dictator's Christian name.[23] Pancho's relationship with the group of actors is, therefore, much more than the encoded whingeing of an auteur director about his commercial producer. It in fact refers to Franco's relationship with Spain.

The critique is hardly subtle. Pancho directs a company of desperate, dejected actors, whose poverty and hunger rob them of ambition.[24] Their submission to him infantilises them and robs them of all dignity: they accept his regulation of their private lives in the name of keeping up appearances and put up with the miserable living conditions he provides without complaint. It is noteworthy that Camus does not simply condemn Pancho's actors, or Franco's subjects, for their dependency, but rather explains the reasons for that dependency by showing how their attention is diverted. The actors' immediate concerns engross them. One obvious instance of this is the sequence in which they fail to notice that Rogelio is robbing them because they are absorbed by Tina's striptease. In the film as a whole, the jealousy, rivalry and betrayal between the actors is shown to distract them from their desperate situation, which Camus highlights to the audience by emphasising their poverty.

Only during the long days of hunger during Holy Week do we witness any form of dissent from the actors. Their conversation in the flat, which ostensibly describes their own situation, might be readily understood as referring to the country as a whole. '¿Qué podemos hacer?' (What can we do?) asks a despondent Currito, to Vicente's empty retort '¿Qué vamos a hacer?' (What are we going to do?). Lucio's 'Hay que resignarse' (We'll just have to resign ourselves to it) characterises the group's defeatist attitude, and only Tina emerges as a character who tries to be the agent of her own destiny. As she lies in bed, the camera frames her face in extreme close-up as she reflects that 'Nadie dirá nada, aunque el hambre les vuelva locos. Esperarán tumbados, nadie será capaz de dar un sólo paso ni por comer. Y cuando [Pancho] llame, todos tan contentos. El único que se libró de esta vida fue Lorenzo, y por eso tuvo que morirse' (Nobody will say anything, even though hunger may drive them mad. They will wait, lying down, nobody will be able to walk one step, not even for something to eat. And when [Pancho] calls, they'll all be perfectly happy. The only one who escaped this life was Lorenzo, and to do it he had to die). The next day she announces '¡Vosotros aguantáis esto!' (You might be able to put up with this!), which could refer to the group's present predicament or the wider political situation, and her defiant 'Yo desde luego, ¡no!' (I certainly can't!) announces her attempt to feed herself through prostitution. When she strides out of the flat to a café to find a client, we follow her, accomplices in her rebellion. Her disappointment is therefore ours when her bid for autonomy is thwarted by the reappearance of Rogelio and she has to return to the flat only to be beaten by Avilés for her supposed infidelity.

Had Tina's rebellion succeeded, *Los farsantes* might have been a different film, ending with an optimistic allegory of rebellion against the dictatorship, rather than a pessimistic portrayal of its continuation. Instead, the final sequence is among the most despairing of Spanish cinema under Franco. Pancho returns, and the starving actors follow him, staggering and blinking, into the sunlit street of Easter Sunday as the bells of resurrection ring out. Tina, the potential rebel, does not even have the energy to protest when she sees Rogelio has rejoined the group. Justo then voices the most pessimistic line of the whole film. We have witnessed his gradual realisation that Pancho is a fraud, but rather than act on this knowledge, he simply accepts it. 'Mentira' (That's a lie) he says in response to the manager's extravagant promises, muttering to himself as he climbs on the back of Pancho's van, 'Por lo menos no vamos a engañarnos' (At least let's not fool ourselves). The church bells that mark the resurrection in this sequence may therefore be understood as one more instance of ironic contrast in the film. Rather than rebirth, they signify the symbolic death of the actors, entombed by their condition of dependency.[25] The end of the film, therefore, closes the circle: *Los farsantes* begins with the sound of the bells that mark the actual death of one of the actors, and ends with the sound of the bells that mark the symbolic death of the rest.

I began this chapter by considering *Los farsantes* as a site of confrontation between the differing models of authorship of the VCE and the NCE. Close analysis of production contexts reveals that while the NCE was financially dependent on state subsidies, many of these films were also practically dependent on the VCE as they were made by producers of popular cinema. *Los farsantes* shows that the relationship between the NCE and the VCE was artistic as well as practical. On the one hand, Camus, the Film School-trained, would-be auteur, responds creatively to this dependency by encoding a critique of popular cinema through his treatment of popular theatre in the film. On the other hand, the auteur collaborates fruitfully with Iquino's crew and cast. Having condemned the distracting artificiality of theatrical spectacle, *Los farsantes* then takes advantage of the range of Lozano's performance style for its own political critique. Likewise, the technical crew drawn from the VCE produce for Camus a film that exemplifies the Neorealist techniques championed by the NCE.

Notes

1. Bardem's portrayal of the world of theatre, *Cómicos* (*Actors* 1954), is a psychological study that is closer to Camus's *Young Sánchez* (1963) than *Los farsantes*, despite its subject matter.

2. Strictly, 'el noveno' refers to the payment of a ninth of tenants' goods to the landlord, not the tenth implied by 'tithe'.

3. According to Carlos Heredero, Iquino created his previous production company, Emisora Films, in 1934, but after legal wrangles with his brother-in-law, established IFI (1993: 86). Iquino's filmography reveals his objectives were entirely commercial: it ranges from the pious *El Judas* (1952), which secured the 'National Interest' award for its service to Catholicism, to *¿Podrías con cinco chicas a la vez?* (*Could You Do it with Five Girls at the Same Time?* 1979), which cashed in on the market for pornography during the *destape*.

4. The attraction of this new area to young entrepreneurs is referenced in the conversation between the group of friends on the beach in Jaime Camino's *Los felices sesenta* (*The Happy Sixties* 1962). For details of companies producing NCE films, see Torreiro (2000: 155–6).

5. Both script and locations, therefore, drew on Camus's own experience (Sánchez Noriega 1998: 61). The student theatre group performed Lucas Fernández's *Auto de Pasión* in a number of villages near Segovia (Sánchez Noriega mentions Sepúlveda, Turégano and Pedraza [1998: 22–3]). Camus sets parts of *Los farsantes* in those same villages, and also includes the performance of an *auto sacramental* (eucharistic play).

6. Camus claims the cost of the film was declared to be four and a half million pesetas (of which he was paid 120,000), and that it received a subsidy of two million following its classification as 2A (Sánchez Noriega 2003: 253–4). As it was common practice to exaggerate production costs, we can assume that the subsidy probably paid for the film. In a 1974 interview, Camus noted: 'A veces parece que el exhibidor no tiene interés ninguno en que la película vaya bien . . . aunque parezca aberración resulta que hay películas españolas que dan dinero aún sin estrenarse' (Sometimes it seems that the exhibitor has no interest in the film doing well . . . though it may seem an aberration, there are Spanish films that are profitable before they are released) (Castro 1974: 111–12), a point also made by Peter Besas in 1997. He notes that the Spanish film 'industry' (a term that Besas suggests might better be replaced with 'artisanry') continues to produce films whose 'financial return is often not made at the box office but in the financing stage' (1997: 243, 255).

7. For instance, Juan Cobos and González Sebastián de Erice reported that Iquino refused to let them see the original version as the censors had requested changes, and because the cut version was not ready, they ended up seeing neither (1963: 745).

8. Camus thanks the mayors of Sepúlveda and Pedraza in the credits. Juan Carlos Frugone states that the film was actually shot from 19 May to 20 July 1963 (1984: 151); in a contemporary interview Camus claimed the shoot began on 15 May (Cobos and Sebastián de Erice 1963: 745).

9. Another influence may have been the documentary-style section of *The Greatest Show on Earth* (De Mille 1952), which focuses on the work that lies

behind the erection of the big top that is ignored by audiences enthralled by the spectacles performed within it.

10. The communist literary critic Gyorgy Lukács held that the novel (Balzac's being exemplary) should be a realist illustration of the class struggle.

11. 'La carpa' was first published in a collection of the same title in 1958 (Schwartz 1976: 132). The title of the script that won third prize in the Sindicato del Espectáculo competition in 1957 was 'Fin de fiesta' (Sánchez Noriega 1998: 23) (Patino's 'Amanecida' [Dawn] won first prize). The script deposited in the Biblioteca Nacional in 1963 is entitled 'Los farsantes'. The translation of the title as *Frauds*, which I have adopted following Chema de la Peña's documentary *De Salamanca a ninguna parte* (2002), loses the reference to farce as theatre, but conveys the idea of pretence, both on the part of the actors and the hypocritical society that they encounter.

12. The intention was seamlessly to suture these sequences into the narrative, although the difference in their tone and grain is visible. At the time Camus claimed he shot this material (Monleón and Egea 1965: 746), but has more recently stated it is the work of a fellow Film School student, Miguel Chan (Sánchez Noriega 2003: 254).

13. A legend illustrating the rewards of virtue, *Genoveva de Brabante* has been the subject of numerous European novels, plays and films. Versions of this exemplary tale of female behaviour were common in 1940s Spain (Vázquez Montalbán 2003: 37), and there were a number of theatrical treatments on the post-war stage. Camus himself cannot recall which versions of *Genoveva de Brabante* and *Vanidad y miseria* he used in *Los farsantes*, but in correspondence with the author has revealed that the *Genoveva* text was lent to him by a group of travelling players who were still performing in 1962.

14. For instance, Juan Goytisolo's attack of the Catalan bourgeoisie in *La resaca* (1959) and Juan Marsé's critique of students from the same class in *Últimas tardes con Teresa* (1966).

15. Camus was the scriptwriter for Miguel Angel Díez's film adaptation of this play (1985).

16. Thanks to Nicholas McDowell for pointing out this reference to me.

17. Triana-Toribio has demonstrated that in Camus's *Los santos inocentes* (*The Holy Innocents* 1984), the character Régula stops both Quirce and the audience from laughing at the pathetic simpleton Azarías (2003: 130). This curtailing of the comic is similar to the situation that occurs here between the triangle of Avilés, the bourgeois audience and Tina.

18. This replacement of Rogelio by Avilés in Tina's affections is ironically prefigured by Pancho's instruction to Avilés to 'aprender los papeles de Rogelio' (learn Rogelio's parts).

19. Prior to *Los farsantes*, she appeared in seventeen other films from 1953, though mainly in secondary roles.

20. A literary precedent for this can be found in Chapter 8 of Goytisolo's *Fiestas* (1957). My thanks to Caragh Wells for pointing out this overlap to me.

21. The flat appears to belong to a rich, unnamed man, who keeps the former actress there as his mistress. Frugone suggests it is a brothel – 'gran ironía del film: pasar la Semana Santa en una especie de prostíbulo' (the great irony of the film: spending Holy Week in a kind of brothel) (1984: 56) – but there is not enough evidence to support this reading.

22. The Holy Week drums of Calanda are used by Buñuel to indicate the delusion of his protagonist in *Nazarín* (1958); similarly, they convey Julián's mental instability in Saura's *Peppermint frappé* (1967).

23. In Sueiro's original short story the association is made clearer by the inclusion of the detail that Pancho, like Franco, is Galician (1988: 87).

24. Larraz reads this film as a 'homage' to the 'dignity' of the actors, because he interprets the inclusion of the plays as a celebration of the 'magic' of theatre (2003: 8, 13), a view that leads him to a positive reading of the end of the film where the group continue in the hope of inspiring audiences with their art (2003: 14). But this interpretation overlooks both the ambiguous treatment of popular spectacle and the role of Pancho.

25. Sánchez Noriega suggests the bells represent sadness and disappointment at both the beginning and end of the film (1998: 63); I suggest a more extreme association with death.

CHAPTER 4

Repression and Excess in *La tía Tula* (*Aunt Tula*, Picazo 1964)

Miguel Picazo's *La tía Tula* is an example of the NCE films that Mario Camus described as made 'with friends' (Sánchez Noriega 2003: 253). It was jointly produced by Surco Films, a company set up by the novelist Nino Quevedo especially for the film (Iznaola Gómez 2004a: 32), and Eco Films, which was run by José López Moreno, Juan Miguel Lamet and Ramiro Bermúdez de Castro, who had previously backed Manuel Summers's *Del rosa . . . al amarillo* (1963) and *La niña del luto* (*The Girl in Mourning* 1964). Picazo's technical crew included the cinematographer and editor who were most closely associated with the movement, Juan Julio Baena and Pedro del Rey, and he secured his desired star for the picture, Aurora Bautista. Critical material on the film further confirms its status as an auteurist production. A combination of *La tía Tula*'s triumph at the 1964 San Sebastián film festival (where it won best Spanish-language film and best director),[1] its success at the domestic box office (see Introduction) and its coincidence with the centenary celebration of the birth of the author of the original novella, Miguel de Unamuno, ensured extensive coverage of this promising new director at the time of the film's release. Numerous interviews offered Picazo a platform to reiterate his authorial intentions ('Miguel Picazo' 1964; Martialay and Buceta 1964; Núñez 1964; Castro 1974). The unfulfilled potential that characterises the director's career from 1964 has also meant that more recent interviews still focus on *La tía Tula*, his first and finest film (Gavilán Sánchez and Lamarca Rosales 2002; Hernández 2003; Iznaola Gómez 2004a).[2]

Given the ample supporting material provided by interviews with the director, and the dominance of auteurism in Spanish film scholarship in any case, critics have adopted an auteurist approach to *La tía Tula*. This has led to the problem of how to deal with Picazo's complaints about the censorship of the film. Even though Picazo was entirely aware that the NCE directors' work was not immune from censorship from his own previous experience with scripts, he complained bitterly of the official treatment of *La tía Tula*. His attack on censorship in the press caused him to fall out of favour with the regime (Hernández 2003: 328), and in every interview he gave, he took the opportunity to condemn the cuts suffered by his film.[3] If, according to the auteurist approach, the director is the source of creative intention in the film, how does the critic respond to his lament that censorship meant 40–50 per cent of its impact was lost ('Miguel Picazo' 1964: 45)? In these circumstances, readings of the films may become elegies for the parts cut by the censors. John Hopewell's interpretation of *La tía Tula*, for instance, is a regretful analysis of the losses suffered by a film 'of such composed understatement every scene counted' (1986: 66), while Jorge Castillejo has used the emotive language of 'mutilation' to describe its censorship (1998: 138).

This chapter avoids the criticism of lament by adopting a revised auteurist approach that is sensitive to production contexts. First, for all Picazo's auteurist posturing, he, like all the NCE directors, was a product of the government's intervention in film in the 1960s. Trained at the Film School, it was only García Escudero's appointment as Director-General in 1962 that enabled Picazo to make his first film – a debt the director acknowledged at the time (Núñez 1964). *La tía Tula* was awarded subsidies when it was classified as 1A, which were increased to 50 per cent when that classification was revised to 'Special Interest' in the light of the film's success at San Sebastián. This ironic production context of a would-be independent auteur financed by the Francoist state suggests a new way of thinking about the treatment of contradiction in the film, for the exploration of rebellion and restraint in the narrative of *La tía Tula* matches the director's analogous experience in the film's creation.

This chapter also offers a revised auteurist approach by paying attention to the contributions of members of the technical crew and cast. Again, Picazo's statements must not blind us to the fact that, even in this quintessential example of the auteurist NCE, film is a collaborative art. Indeed, even the backing of two NCE production companies did not necessarily guarantee Picazo's total freedom: the Eco producers disliked the film and wanted to make the final cut, and only thanks to Quevedo's intervention did Picazo remain in control (Castro 1974: 332; Gubern 1997: 562; Gavilán Sánchez and Lamarca Rosales 2002: 98). Cinematography and editing, which were crucial to the impression of claustrophobia created in the film, are the work of Baena, the 'pioneer of modern cinematography' in Spain (Sánchez Biosca 1989: 90), and the seasoned NCE editor Del Rey. Both were veterans of the dissident Spanish cinema of the preceding five years, including Saura's *Los golfos* (1959) and Ferreri's *El cochecito* (1960), but both also had experience of the popular Spanish cinema (as we have seen with respect to Del Rey in Chapter 1). Picazo's casting of CIFESA's heroine, Aurora Bautista, has led critics to conclude that in *La tía Tula*, the auteur aimed to oppose the VCE, but I will suggest here that the relationship between NCE and VCE in the film might be more fruitfully reconsidered as one of overlap.

While we must attribute the exploration of the Virgin/Mother dichotomy to Unamuno, the author of the novella, Picazo's updating of the film means that his *La tía Tula* responds to the way the Francoist regime, especially in its neo-Catholic phase, enshrined the divorce between motherhood and sexuality, or sanitised motherhood, through the figure of the Virgin Mary. However, it is important to note the ways in which the gender ideology of the regime evolved. While Helen Graham has observed that in the 1940s the 'many incarnations of the Virgin provided the perfect role model' for women (1995a: 184), economic development in the late 1950s and 1960s saw the incorporation of middle-class women into the labour force (working-class women had always been part of it) with concomitant revisions to the regime's legislation on gender – the reform to the Civil Code of 1958, the 'Law of Political, Professional and Labour Rights of Women' of 1961 and the inclusion of women's work in the 1963 Development Plan (Amorós 1986: 42). Rosario Coca Hernando has chronicled the impact of this transformation in the 1960s in her study of the regime's Sección Femenina (Women's Section) magazine *Teresa*, the mouthpiece of official discourses of femininity. Parallel to the tentative legal reforms in favour of women's rights, she demonstrates that there appeared 'the image of the "modern" or "new" woman' (1998: 5). As was typical of the *apertura*, this figure was another contradictory reconciliation of old and new values, a woman who was, in the words of the Sección Femenina, 'antigua y siempre nueva' (old-fashioned and always up to date), or, as Coca Hernando summarises, representative of 'an ambivalent femininity which combined both the traditional and the modern' (1998: 7, 13).

Given this context of tentative change in women's roles, through the characterisation of Tula, Picazo denounces both the contradiction of the cult of sanitised motherhood and the anachronism of a continued adherence to such outmoded gender norms in provincial Spain in the 1960s. Tula's aunthood, or attempt to be a Virgin Mary, or sexless mother, is a *reductio ad absurdum* of the demand that women be 'pure' yet mothers.[4] Picazo shows that Tula's behaviour results in both repression (through her denial of her body) and excess (through Ramiro's enslavement to his body, which leads to an attempted and an actual rape). Saura recently summarised the first film of his ex-student and fellow member of the NCE with a concision that perhaps time has afforded: 'hay sobre todo la explosión del sexo y de la pasión amorosa que surge de la represión' (there is above all the explosion of sex and romantic passion that arises from repression) (2004: 205).

La tía Tula is a thesis on the interdependence of restraint and rebellion, which describes both the subject of the film and Picazo's experience in making it. It scrutinises the contradictions of Francoist ideology with respect to gender and sexuality, and recursively examines its own contradictory genesis as part of a government-sponsored movement, especially Picazo's equivocal experience of artistic freedom yet ideological restraint. In this chapter I therefore combine a focus on these equivocal historical and industrial contexts with close readings of film form. Repression and excess are explored in particular through the use of setting, off-screen space and the negotiation of the body. After considering the *mise en scène* of Tula's flat as a haunted house, I will examine three key areas of contradiction in the film: the portrayal of femininity; masculinity; and childhood. I will also account for the impressive mobilisation of filmic resources throughout, paying attention to script (plot and characterisation), casting (characterisation), *mise en scène* (particularly claustrophobic settings), cinematography (especially lighting and the use of off-screen space), editing (in particular the long take, as one of the remarkable features of this film is that the average take is an unusually lengthy 2 minutes) and, finally, sound (notably the significance of the switch between diegetic and non-diegetic sources).

Some of the frustration that Picazo pours into *La tía Tula*, which is palpable in every image, is explained by his experience up to 1964. The decade began well. His graduation short, *Habitación de alquiler* (*Rented Room* 1960) secured him first, a teaching post at the Film School that began the same year,[5] and second, an offer from Ferreri to produce his first film (Hernández 2003: 323). *Jimena*, with a script by himself, Camus, Joaquín Jordá and Francisco Regueiro, was to be a corrective version of the Cid myth to challenge the Samuel Bronston-produced film directed by Anthony Mann. The censors sent the script to the Real Academia de la Historia, who rejected it, while supporting the American version (Picazo has bitterly pointed out that this was because the revered Ramón Ménendez Pidal's son was the handsomely paid historical advisor to the Mann picture [Castro 1974: 331; Hernández 2003: 324; Iznaola Gómez 2004a: 31]). After the initial rush of success, then, there followed three years of disappointment for the aspiring filmmaker, in which the *Viridiana* scandal erupted, UNINCI (one of the projected producers of *Jimena*) folded and Ferreri's residence permit was refused renewal, which meant the return of Picazo's mentor to Italy. Prior to his departure, Ferreri had suggested Picazo read Unamuno's novella and adapt it for film, but it was García Escudero's legislation that finally got the project into production.

A comparison with Unamuno's original reveals the personal nature of

Picazo's treatment. In collaboration with fellow scriptwriters Luis Sánchez Enciso, José Miguel Hernán and Manuel López Yubero, he prunes the plot, eliminating Ramiro's first marriage to Rosa[6] and second marriage to Juanita. This allows him to focus on Tula's relationship with her brother-in-law, Ramiro, and niece and nephew, Tulita and Ramirín, and telescope the questions of repression and excess. Tula's understanding of 'aunthood' means that while she enthusiastically embraces the role of mother to the children, she rejects all physical contact with Ramiro. It is also significant that the scriptwriters empower Tula by having Ramiro and the children move into her house (in the novella Tula moves in with them [Unamuno 1996: 111]). After Tula rejects his marriage proposal, Ramiro becomes increasingly frustrated and attempts to rape her (this does not occur in the novella), but Tula succeeds in fighting him off. On another occasion, aroused by Tula's apparent advances, he does violate her cousin Juanita. The girl falls pregnant, Ramiro marries her and takes the children with him, leaving Tula alone.

Picazo and scriptwriters make the temporal and geographical settings of Unamuno's abstract original concrete. Picazo stated in numerous interviews on the film's release and subsequently that Tula reminded him of two women he actually knew ('Miguel Picazo' 1964: 44; Núñez 1964; Castro 1974: 332; Iznaola 2002: 32).[7] Thus the film is a tale of a woman in provincial Spain, shot in Guadalajara and Brihuega, set in a period contemporary to its production. Picazo further explains his intentions in the same interview in *Ínsula*:

> Unamuno crea un ser de excepción, desorbitado. En la película se ha intentado lo contrario; es decir, acercar el personaje al público actual, para que lo reconozca y se sienta próximo a él, tome conciencia del problema en su dimensión real y, al mismo tiempo, le haga pensar en las consecuencias que se derivan del comportamiento de Tula y de Ramiro. (Unamuno creates an exceptional, exorbitant being. In the film the aim has been to do the opposite; that's to say, to make the character accessible to today's audience so that they recognise and feel close to it, become aware of the problem as it really is and, at the same time, are made to think about the consequences of Tula and Ramiro's behaviour.) (Núñez 1964)

Unamuno's original abstract study thus becomes a film of specific denunciation ('the problem as it really is'). Our response to Tula is complex for we are at once encouraged to identify with her ('recognise and feel close'), yet condemn the consequences of her behaviour; although she is a victim of her environment, in turn, she makes others her victims too. Though in this interview Picazo dare not denounce that environment by name, it is clearly the gender ideology of Franco's Spain. The comment made by the interviewer about the ending of the film reveals the effectiveness of this critique of contemporary society, and the use of the word 'algo' (something) again indicates that the target cannot be named: 'Dan ganas de arremeter contra *algo*, para que tales cosas no ocurran' (It makes you wanted to attack *something*, so that such things don't happen) (Núñez 1964, emphasis added).

As an adaptation, *La tía Tula* foregrounds its place in Spanish literary history, but it is equally embedded in Spanish cinema history. Much has been written on the relationship of the NCE with foreign movements, especially Italian Neorealism and the French New Wave. In a recent interview Picazo rather mechanically mentions the influence of Neorealism (Hernández 2003: 326), but elsewhere he highlights the importance of his teachers at the Film School in his training, rather than foreign films or movements, stating in 1964, 'En el aspecto cinematográfico, la Escuela lo ha sido todo para mí. Yo no puedo hablar más que bien. Todo lo que sé de cine lo aprendí en la Escuela' (As far as cinematic matters are concerned, the School has been everything for me. I can only speak well of it. Everything I know about cinema I learned in the School) (Núñez 1964). His teachers included the filmmakers Berlanga, José Gutiérrez Maesso, Carlos Serrano de Osma and Saura, and in an interview with Javier Hernández, Picazo mentions in particular the classes of Camón Aznar (History of Art) and Enrique Alarcón (set decoration – Alarcón was responsible for the interiors of *Calle Mayor*) (2003: 320). In another interview, he stresses the influence of Serrano de Osma on his work (Gavilán Sánchez and Lamarca Rosales 2002: 94–5), who had directed six features between 1946 and 1951 and one in 1960, and whose filmography includes the Unamuno adaptation, *Abel Sánchez* (1946). It would be naïve to state that Picazo's frame of filmic reference in *La tía Tula* is, therefore, 'Spanish', as any notion of a pure national cinema is a fallacy that overlooks the transnational hybridity of film. However, it is the case that Picazo is less concerned with his place among European New Cinemas than other NCE directors (he never mentions trips to foreign film festivals, for instance). *La tía Tula* is clearly indebted to dissident Spanish cinema of the 1950s and early 1960s (when asked in 1964 which three Spanish films had most influenced him he named *¡Bienvenido Mister Marshall!* [Berlanga 1952], *Calle Mayor* [Bardem 1956] and *Viridiana* [Buñuel 1961] ['Miguel Picazo' 1964: 48]), which in turn drew on multiple international influences. Picazo's domestic drama bears the trace of the *film noir* deployed by Serrano de Osma in his Unamuno adaptation (Labanyi 1995b), the Hollywood melodrama used by Bardem in *Calle Mayor* and the gothic employed by Buñuel in *Viridiana*. The influence of Italian Neorealism is evident too, through both its aim to address and denounce Tula's class – the landowning upper bourgeoisie of provincial Spain from which Franco drew his support – and techniques like the use of direct sound.[8]

For all the oft-repeated rejection, the NCE did not operate in isolation from the VCE. Picazo states that he cast Aurora Bautista not because of her film work, but because he had seen her in a play (Hernández 2003: 325). Given the NCE's views of the VCE, Picazo's dismissal of Bautista's earlier roles is to be expected, but it is impossible that he did not know them well. Bautista's 1940s–1950s CIFESA pictures, like *Locura de amor* (*Love's Madness* 1948) and *Agustina de Aragón* (1950) (both directed by Juan de Orduña), were the blockbusters of the era. Jo Labanyi has noted that the famous image of Bautista firing a canon in the 1950 film 'passed into the popular imaginary through its reproduction in children's storybooks and on postage stamps, calendars and brand labels' (2000: 176). Furthermore, a fellow student has revealed that Orduña's films were studied at the Film School. Antonio Drove recalls that Berlanga, who also taught Picazo, would show *Locura de amor*, Bautista's smash hit, over and again in class, saying 'Este Orduña, hay que ver, se lo cree tanto que te contagia su emoción' (This Orduña, it's incredible, he believes it all so much that his emotion infects you) (Alberich 2002: 26). The casting of Bautista is therefore a highly visible connection with the VCE, and I will argue that there are further overlaps through the less visible contributions of *La tía Tula*'s technical crew.

Tula's Haunted House

Since *La tía Tula* attributes Tula's behaviour to the stifling traditionalism of the provinces, the construction of setting and *mise en scène* in Picazo's portrait of 1960s Guadalajara is especially significant. Picazo moved to this Castilian city as a child in 1940, and associates it with the hardships of the post-war years: 'era el ejemplo más claro de una sociedad triste y reprimida y que me supuso un nuevo planteamiento vital' (it was the clearest example of a sad and repressed society and made me approach life in a new way) (Castro 1974: 328). While *La tía Tula* may show that the hunger of these years has passed, the traditionalist mentality of the era, particularly in the realm of gender, remains. The shots of the city are not particularised, so the portrait of provincial Spain is general (unlike Bardem's *Calle Mayor*, which locates the action in Cuenca through establishing shots). The exterior shots evoke gloomy tedium (filming took place in Guadalajara in a grey autumn from 16 September to 3 November 1963 [Hernández 2003: 325]), which is occasionally punctuated by church bells or the hum of a moped.

Through lighting, Baena was careful to ensure a continuum between these exteriors and the studio interior shots of Tula's flat (Torán 1989: 113). This domestic space magnifies the oppressive atmosphere Picazo associates with the provinces. No mopeds offer a hint of modernity here, and it seems doubtful that the television set Tula mentions buying after receiving her tenants' rent in an early sequence could ever find a place in it – over the course of the film the set does not appear. Tula's flat is a kind of time capsule, redolent with tradition and death. The furniture belongs to her dead uncle Primitivo (as explained in the script [Hernán et al. 1964: 33]), who had been a priest, and there are two significant portraits that function as projections of her value systems. The first is of the conservative Pope Pius XII, who was already dead when the film was shot, replaced in office in 1958 by the more conciliatory John XXIII, who set up Vatican II, which recommended a series of reforms that shook the conservative Francoist establishment.[9] The second is of Tula's dead female cousin Gabrielita, who, according to the script, died from consumption at seventeen (Hernán et al. 1964: 43). This portrait is particularly admired by the little girl Tulita, who recounts the family story for our benefit: 'le avisó el Niño Jesús a la prima Gabrielita cuando se iba a morir' (Baby Jesus warned cousin Gabrielita when she was going to die), and who will later use the picture as a model in her dressing-up game.

Luis Argüello's set decoration (he also worked on Buñuel's *Tristana* [1970]) goes beyond melodrama's usual emphasis on *mise en scène* to create a house haunted by the ghosts of the past: a dead pope, a dead priest uncle and a prematurely deceased cousin. This gothic dimension is accentuated through cinematography and editing. Luis Enrique Torán notes of Baena's work in the film that 'los negros, fundamentales en esta obra, lucen en toda su profundidad' (the blacks, which are fundamental to this work, shine out in all their depth) and that the 'acusada profundidad de campo se adecúa perfectamente al juego escénico y a la inteligente planificación de Picazo' (rich depth of field is entirely suited to the way Picazo plays the scenes off against each other and his intelligent shot arrangements) (1989: 113). It is important to note that contrastive lighting and depth of field, techniques that Buñuel also used in his recreation of Jaime's gothic house in *Viridiana*, are not new technical innovations. They are in fact typical of *film noir* of 1940s Spanish cinema, such as the work of Picazo's teacher Serrano de Osma, which were shot according to the Guerner School.[10] Despite its NCE cinematographer, *La tía Tula* is therefore indebted to earlier practices in Spanish film photography, rather than the technical developments in vogue in contemporary European New Cinemas. The effects of contrastive lighting and depth of field are also dependent on long takes, a style of editing that further embeds the film in indigenous cinematic traditions. Pedro del Rey had previously used this technique with subversive effect in both the dissident cinema (in *Viridiana*, for instance, the long take underscores Jaime's gothic house) and popular film (in Chapter 1 I discuss his occasionally disruptive contribution to *La gran familia*, in which he uses the long take to imply claustrophobia).

In an interview of 1964 Picazo makes clear the dual function of Tula's haunted house. In terms of the narrative of the film it explains Tula's treatment of Ramiro, and in terms of the historical context it condemns the situation in Spain in general:

> la casa de Tula es una casa-trampa, es una casa horrorosa, es una casa monstruo, es una casa atroz, y . . . esta mujer le hostiga [a Ramiro] y le trata como un enemigo . . . No es una cosa de ciencia-ficción, es una cosa que se está dando en las relaciones humanas dentro de España. (Tula's house is a house-trap, it's a horrendous house, a monster-house, it is a terrible house and this woman harasses [Ramiro] and treats him like an enemy . . . This isn't science fiction, this is something that is happening within human relationships in Spain.) (Martialay and Buceta 1964: 486)

By linking her behaviour to the house and mentioning science fiction films, Picazo's comments conjure up the image of Tula as a spider weaving a deadly web to trap her victims. Tula's house is a web of deadening traditions. Only in the hidden shadows may life be found, as the children discover when they rummage around in the trunk in the back room[11] and find sexy women's clothes and Ramiro's love letters to Rosa. Tula's victims will include Tulita, who falls ill under her care, and Ramiro, who as well as illness, is driven to criminality – though her first victim is herself.

Femininity

Picazo indicates repression and excess in *La tía Tula* through the treatment of the body, oscillating between the extremes of Tula, who denies her body, and Ramiro, who becomes ruled by his. The credit sequence, which follows Rosa's funeral wake, foregrounds Tula's transcendence of her body. She sits on her own in a room and background activity can be glimpsed through a crack in the door. The viewer recognises that this is not a freeze-frame, and is led to believe that Tula is motionless for over 2 minutes, thus exercising incredible restraint over her own body (Picazo has subsequently revealed that this effect was achieved by suturing five frames together again and again [Castillejo 1998: 136]). Thus ideas of restraint and repression are linked to both the treatment of the body and to editing, as we assume this is a long take with no cuts. The soundtrack is also crucial in this sequence as it expresses the emotion of grief at the loss of a sister that cannot be found in Bautista's impassive face or motionless body.[12] It is important also that this sound is non-diegetic, which looks forward to a central theme in the film: that emotion and desire are located off-screen, be that off-screen space, like the trunk in the back room of Tula's flat, or an off-screen source of music.

In this credit sequence Tula transcends her body in terms of expressing emotion, but is in another sense trapped in her body by the static camera and trick long take, two cinematic techniques that become associated with imprisonment throughout the film. The treatment of Tula's body through close-up in later sequences is similar. She is defined, or trapped, by her body in the new domestic role she adopts after taking Ramiro and the children into her house. To indicate this, the first three sequences in her flat begin with close-ups of Tula's hands attending to domestic labour: first we see her hands clearing the dinner table, then ironing, then sewing. The way these close-ups replace establishing shots also contributes to the sense of claustrophobia in these scenes. Tula is also shown to transcend her body in a sexual sense. When Ramiro kisses her hands, for instance, we then see her wash them in disgust. There is a visual echo between the close-ups of her hands completing household chores, which tie her body to domesticity, and the close-up of Tula washing those hands, and denying her body in a physical sense.

As Picazo correctly predicted, though refused fully to explain, Bautista is the perfect actress for this role. Her star image is one of pure histrionic excess, and the repression of her performance style in La tía Tula enriches her portrayal of the repressed aunt in a particularly effective way. The lusty heroines Bautista embodied in Locura de amor and Agustina de Aragón, cry out as if imprisoned in Tula's every word and gesture, and serve as a constant reminder that excess is the flip-side of repression. This is not to say that Bautista's performance in La tía Tula is unconvincing, but rather that the choice of this actress is a particularly felicitous case of casting against type. The relationship between the VCE and the NCE highlighted in La tía Tula through the presence of Bautista is therefore not one of opposition, as Gubern argues (he calls her Tula role the 'counter-figure' of her previous work [1997: 562]), or as Castillejo proposes (he sees this role as 'totally opposed' to her earlier work [1998: 7]), but creative reappropriation. Even if unplanned, another biographical detail further adds to Bautista's embodiment of the contradictory aunt. In autumn 1963, Bautista was herself a newly-wed. She married in Mexico on 3 September (Castillejo 1998: 131), and, as she subsequently recounts, 'Ese personaje es el mejor que he hecho en mi vida, aunque lo hice *con tensión bastante fuerte,* porque tenía que interpretar a una solterona cuando en realidad estaba en luna de miel' (This is the best character I've played in my life, though I did it *feeling pretty tense* because I had to portray an old maid when I was really on my honeymoon) (quoted in Castillejo 1998: 46; emphasis added).

Bautista's performance as a repressed aunt oozes with the excess that the actress keeps in check. Only at the end of the film, when Ramiro announces his future marriage to Juanita just when Tula has finally resolved to accept him as a husband, does she unleash her anger and Bautista her dramatic delivery. Likewise, this tense narrative is occasionally punctured by moments of release that confirm the inseparability of repression and excess implicit elsewhere in the film. For instance, two sequences of female hysteria, one anguished and the other joyful, contrast with Tula's self-denial. First, when Ramiro and Ramirín visit Rosa's grave, we see a dishevelled woman run into the churchyard and hear her cry hysterically and enigmatically '¿por qué lo ha hecho?' (why did he/she/you do it?), before she is ushered out of our sight and earshot by well-wishers. Second, Tula attends a hen party along with her female friends from the 'Acción Católica',[13] in which the women get tipsy on punch, and giggle and dance like schoolgirls (Picazo recounts that he took particular care in casting the right actresses for this sequence, and that it was a genuine booze-up, recorded warts and all through long takes and direct sound [Martialay and Buceta 1964: 487]). Their intoxication is not only a moment of release that highlights the repression of the rest of the film, Picazo also uses it to condemn the women as foolish schoolgirls, whose lack of knowledge of sex is highlighted in their songs and jokes about the wedding night, stating, 'creo que lo más corrosivo de esa escena pudiesen ser esas mujeres, esas vírgines de 27 y 30 años, hablando del amor como si fueran niñas de 11 o de 12, portándose frente al amor de una manera totalmente infantil, sin ser adultas' (I think the most corrosive aspect of this scene may have been these women, these virgins of 27 and 30 years old, speaking about love as if they were 11- or 12-year-old girls, behaving in a completely childish way about love, not being adults) (Martialay and Buceta 1964: 487).

If these two moments of release, one negative and one positive, throw into relief the repression that governs the rest of *La tía Tula*, elsewhere release is located off-screen. With this in mind, we may approach one of the scenes cut by the censors, where Tula is shot in black lacy underwear, adjusting the suspender on her provocatively arched right leg (Figure 4.1).[14] For the viewer of the film as it stands, such a vision of Tula's voluptuous enjoyment of her body is never seen but may be imagined, especially as the style of underwear is in keeping with the type of clothing Tula hides away in the trunk in the back room. Though not Picazo's intention, the censoring of the

Figure 4.1. Aurora Bautista in *La tía Tula*.
Video Mercury Films.

image reinforces the idea of an out-of-sight, off-screen space, bursting, like
the trunk of sexy clothes in the back room, with repressed desire. This
reading may seem to invest audiences with an over-active, schoolboy imagination, but such over-determination was a consequence of censorship. For

instance, it was a widely held belief among Spanish audiences that Rita Hayworth's dance sequence in *Gilda* (Vidor 1946), where she removes her gloves, was a full striptease that was cut by the censors (Vázquez Montalbán 2003: 100). As a female cinema-goer recalls, 'As censorship was so terrible . . . imagination went beyond reality . . . do you remember when Gilda takes her glove off? Everyone assumed that the censors had cut that scene because she went on stripping' (Gómez-Sierra 2004: 94). In other words, repression through censorship led to an excess of imagination.

A sequence that takes place towards the end of the film when the family is on holiday in a country village (Brihuega) further demonstrates this thesis of out-of-sight, off-screen space as the site and source of sexual desire. The episode of the holiday replays the same tensions as the rest of the film, but indicates that they may be resolved. The family has left Tula's web-like haunted house, and formal differences in the portrayal of the village in comparison to the city invite us to expect a resolution. For instance, unlike the static camera of the credit sequence, the holiday episode begins with a dynamic rotation of the camera of almost 360°, which records the village main square, then the arrival of the family from Guadalajara on the bus. Furthermore, on their arrival in the country house, we see Tula and Ramiro share food for the first time in the film; significantly this food is fruit, in order to evoke Eve and the apple of temptation. In the night-time sequence at the country house we see Tula awake, consider her reflection in the bedroom mirror, then go to the kitchen to drink a glass of water, where she encounters Ramiro. This sequence both recalls and contrasts with the portrayal of their relations in the haunted house in the city. The long takes are similar, indicating entrapment and claustrophobia, as is the use of the mirror, which by this point in the film we have come to understand as a symbol of entrapment within the frame. The music, which we at first assume is non-diegetic, points to desire and emotion, as it has throughout the film. The difference in this sequence is our discovery that the music is diegetic as Tula later tells Ramiro that it has woken her up. Literally and figuratively awoken then, Tula seeks her object of desire, Ramiro. Just as the music shifts from a non-diegetic to diegetic source, so Ramiro emerges from off-screen into on-screen space, gliding into our field of vision when Tula has her back turned in the kitchen. The sexual tension of this sequence is more palpable here than elsewhere in the film. Tula drinks a glass of water, and whereas earlier in the film her maternal relationship with Ramiro is articulated through her feeding and watering him, here drinking and eating are associated with sexual desire, as Picazo implied with the sharing of fruit at the start of the sequence.

While these shifts from off-screen to on-screen space on the imagetrack, and from extra-diegetic to diegetic music on the soundtrack, hint at the resolution of repressed sexual desire, the film ends with repression. In the final sequence Ramiro leaves on a train, and is thus lost to Tula forever in off-screen space, while she remains at the station trapped in the frame, along with the abandoned, stationary rail carriage seen in the background that Juan Miguel Company has argued symbolises her fate (2003: 410). This ending differs from the one scripted and shot of a further sequence at the graveyard. Picazo changed his mind about it ('Miguel Picazo' 1964: 48), and ends the film at the station, thereby echoing the ending of *Calle Mayor*, in which Isabel also remains in a provincial station, refusing to board the train and leave her life of frustration,[15] and looking forward to the ending of *La caza*, whose protagonist is likewise figuratively trapped through a freeze-frame shot.

Masculinity

The treatment of masculinity in *La tía Tula* allows Picazo to explore another set of gender-related contradictions. Studies of masculinity in Western Europe and the US cite the post-Second World War period as a time of 'crisis' over male roles, because a military definition of masculinity had to be reconciled with the peacetime situation, and women were seen to have 'taken over' male jobs. Labanyi has noted that in Franco's Spain, 'the enforced return of women to the hearth after the war made such anxieties unnecessary', but that none the less a 'demilitarization' of male roles had to be performed (1995b: 21 n. 11, 12). She has also argued that this transition of roles was played out in late 1940s films (specifically 1945–51), which often contrasted strong heroines with weak heroes, a tendency exemplified by *Agustina de Aragón*, in which Bautista starred. Owing to political unrest and the screening of Neorealist films at the first Italian Week of Cinema in 1951, Labanyi argues that this year 'marked the end of this focus on the family and the feminine, as the development of an oppositional cinema led to a new stress on the political with plot lines consequently focused on the male' (2000: 164–5). In the NCE of the 1960s, plots still tended to focus on the male, for instance *Nueve cartas a Berta* and *La caza*, but it is worth pointing out that this was now to expose and explore male ineffectuality and *angst*.[16] *La tía Tula* bridges the two tendencies of the female-focused 1940s popular cinema and male-focused art cinema of the following decades and reveals the connections between them. On the one hand, like the films analysed by Labanyi, it contrasts a strong female with an ineffectual male protagonist, and on the other, like contemporary NCE films, it depicts a crisis in masculinity. If the way *La tía Tula* shows that these are just two sides of the same coin is obvious, the connections this reveals between popular cinema of the 1940s and auteurist cinema of the 1960s are not.

In *La tía Tula* Ramiro is set up as a counter-point to Tula. Her authority in the domestic realm is opposed to his weakness. This opposition is portrayed through characterisation and plot, which derive from Unamuno, but is underscored by filmic means such as casting and the depiction of the body. While Tula is played by Bautista, one of the most famous national stars, Ramiro is played by the comparatively little-known Argentine actor Carlos Estrada. Thanks to the use of direct sound, Estrada was not dubbed post-synchronisation, and his 'difference' is therefore signalled by the trace of his accent that can be heard on the soundtrack. These actors also represent opposite performance styles, Bautista's, one of overstatement, Estrada's, one of understatement, and these are played off against each other to highlight the male character's weakness. Male disempowerment is also underpinned by the film's negotiation of the male body, which symbolically infantilises the male character.

At the start of the film there seems to be an equivalence between Ramiro and Tula: both are figuratively trapped within the frame, and for both, desire is relegated to off-screen space. For example, a daytime sequence and a night-time sequence allow us to appreciate Ramiro's sense of entrapment in Tula's flat through locating the source of sound in off-screen space. In the first scene, we hear children playing and singing in the street outside, an off-screen space, and then share a point-of-view shot with Ramiro as he gazes longingly at their childhood fun. In the script, the lyrics of their childhood song are spelled out. Although a different piece is sung in the final version of the film, the original one describing the entrapment of nuns in a convent is worth citing as its words project Ramiro's experience of Tula's house of celibacy: 'Ha dado la una. / Cierran los conventos. / Y las pobres monjas / se quedan adentro' (It's one o'clock. / The convents are closing. / And the poor nuns / stay inside) (Hernán et al. 1964: 33). Similarly, in the night sequence we share Ramiro's perspective as he hears drunken revellers return home, a sound that also emanates from an off-screen space, and we again appreciate his longing to join them.

Elsewhere in the film, the experience of entrapment that Tula and Ramiro share is indicated through arrangement within the frame. In a number of interior sequences, Picazo contrasts two focal points within the frame in a long take. For instance, after Tula serves Ramiro lunch, rather than eat with him, she sits behind him and attends to her sewing (Figure 4.2). Ramiro provides one focal point in the frame in the foreground to the right, Tula another in the background to the left. This bipolarity within the frame is

Figure 4.2. Aurora Bautista and Carlos Estrada in *La tía Tula*.
Video Mercury Films.

also noticeable in the bedroom sequence during Ramiro's illness, when Ramiro's presence in the foreground is again contrasted with Tula, as she busies herself changing the bed in the background. A third interior shot, when the family arrive in the village house on holiday, is arranged to contrast Tula sitting in the foreground with Ramiro at a distance behind her in the background, as the family eat fruit. Gubern notes that this bipolar arrangement is also used in the celebrated sequence of Tula's confession (1997: 563). It is furthermore a visual echo of the arrangement within the frame of the husband and wife in a domestic setting of *La gran familia*, a film with the same editor as *La tía Tula*, Del Rey. In the earlier film such an arrangement conveyed harmony; here it represents conflict (Figures 1.4 and 4.2).

The conflict between Tula and Ramiro is also indicated by the differing treatment of the female and male body. As mentioned above, from the start of the film Ramiro is infantilised by Tula: trapped in her web, we watch this male adult descend the developmental scale into childhood. Tula attends to his body as a mother would a baby. For instance, Tula feeds Ramiro's body, and one of the first things we see him do is burp like a baby after a meal (the significance of the burp was intended as it was specified in the script [Hernán et al. 1964: 33]). She also dresses his body, and in one carefully composed sequence she checks what Ramirín is wearing before he leaves the house, then what Ramiro is wearing before he goes out – Picazo ensuring that both man and boy stand in exactly the same place and in exactly the same way so we notice the parallel. Finally, Tula nurses Ramiro's body when he is ill with tonsillitis. This process of infantilisation is reinforced by language, when Tula addresses Ramiro as a child using babyish terms like 'rey' (pet) and playful scolding like '¿qué Ramiro es ése?' (Is Ramiro being a silly-billy?). The lunch sequence (Figure 4.2) is telling in this regard. When Tula serves Ramiro lunch she insists he wear a comically over-sized napkin over his suit, which she has him tuck into his collar so that the viewer cannot miss that it is meant to recall a baby's bib. Notwithstanding this infantilising attire, Ramiro is at his most assertive in this sequence, questioning Tula about why she is avoiding marriage with Emilio. The argument that ensues between the two significantly results in a challenge to Ramiro's manhood. 'Pero soy un hombre' (But I'm a man), he pleads, still wearing the bib, then adds the telling '¿o qué sino?' (or if not, what am I?)

Tula's attempts to de-sex Ramiro's body by infantilising him are doomed. Picazo's most startling illustration of the thesis that excess is the flip-side of repression is his portrayal of the transformation of meek Ramiro into a potent sexual force who attempts to rape Tula and does rape Juanita. But even Ramiro the rapist remains infantilised he is still defined exclusively in terms of his body. The need of an infant to be fed, clothed and nursed transfers to that of a man for sex. It is important that on two occasions Ramiro's body is displayed in *La tía Tula*, as this further indicates that he is defined by it. In an early sequence he strolls down the corridor of the flat in a vest, and Tula draws our attention to his body by asking him to cover it up. In a later sequence, when the family are in the country, Ramiro bathes with the children and we see him in swimming trunks. This contrasts with Tula, who is fully dressed in black as she looks on from the river bank, and even her eyes are covered by sunglasses (see cover illustration). As a male character who is defined by his body, Estrada's Ramiro assumes the role that feminist film critics have argued that women are typically assigned on screen. In *La tía Tula*, we have a dominant female lead and a secondary male character whose role is that which Laura Mulvey famously claimed mainstream narrative cinema gives to women on screen: 'to connote *to-be-looked-at-ness*' (1999: 837).

The most troubling aspect of *La tía Tula* for an audience today is its failure to condemn rape as criminality. An awkward silence surrounds this question in contemporary accounts of the film. Some reviewers even refuse to refer to rape by name, opting instead for euphemisms like 'vampirism'

(Gortari 1964: 692), or 'seduce and make her his own' (*Cine-Asesor* 1964). *La tía Tula* explains that Ramiro's actions are motivated by his treatment by Tula, but fails to condemn them and even seems to suggest they are justified.[17] While we are at least aware of the background of frustration that triggers Ramiro's attempted attack on Tula, his treatment of Juanita is appalling. Little more than a girl herself, she is raped and impregnated by her deceased cousin's husband, then forced to marry him, but her anguish is almost entirely ignored. Antonio Núñez does raise an objection to Ramiro's behaviour in an interview published in *Ínsula* (1964), but his remark reveals a great deal about views of gender in 1960s Spain: why does Ramiro insist on pursuing Tula, he asks Picazo in interview, when he could simply use prostitutes as an 'escape valve' (Núñez 1964)? This comment not only reveals that the reviewer of this prestigious Spanish journal considers brothels necessary (they were legal in Spain until 1956 and their prohibition was never enforced [Hooper 1995: 166]), a view that reflects the double moral standards of the censors of the film, who cut the images of Tula in her underwear, yet left those of the prostitutes Ramiro eyes on the outskirts of the city.[18] More troubling is Núñez's failure to condemn rape itself.

Childhood

If Tula's mothering of Ramiro simultaneously infantilises and criminalises him, what effect does it have on the infants themselves? While *La tía Tula* suggests that adults may behave like children, conversely, Picazo's child characters are prematurely robbed of their innocence and shoulder the burdens of a contradictory adult world. This is highlighted in the pre-credit sequence of the film. As the church bells toll for Rosa's funeral, Picazo records in a tracking shot and long take the approach of a little boy to Ramiro's house, where the wake is taking place. The small child carries an enormous funereal wreath, which both weighs him down, and obscures his face and most of his body from the viewer. Similarly, the children who form part of the narrative of *La tía Tula* are weighed down by the adult world and their individuality is erased by it. Consider, for instance, Juanita, Tula's barely pubescent cousin. It is she who is the target of the excess triggered by Tula's repression as she is raped by Ramiro in place of her aunt. Following this act of abuse, she ceases to be an individual, but becomes trapped in enforced motherhood and marriage. In the final scene of the film it is Tula's anguish we share when she sees off the new family from Guadalajara station because the camera remains on the platform with her. Wife, step-mother and mother-to-be Juanita is hidden away from us in the railway carriage, her face obscured by dark glasses and her body by a voluminous maternity dress.

Even though the repetition of Christian names is common in Spanish families, in the context of *La tía Tula* as a whole, the diminutive names Ramirín and Tulita indicate the future erasure of the children's individuality as they are destined to become versions of their father and aunt. *La tía Tula* indicates that Tula's mothering is suffocating: under her care both Ramiro and Tulita fall ill; Ramirín remains healthy as he does his best to ignore his aunt. Thus she promotes illness rather than growth: her nurturing is symbolic smothering.[19] This depiction of child-rearing allegorises Picazo's own contradictory creative experience.[20] While on the one hand the state, like a nurturing mother, promoted artistic growth through subsidy, on the other it stifled that growth through censorship. In this sense we may see the children as Picazo's on-screen surrogates. Their experiences therefore become doubly representative, of both childhood under Franco and the director's stunted creativity.

Ramirín is of less interest to Picazo than Tulita. The saucy pictures of women in underwear that Tula finds in his school books, and the love letters from his father to his mother that the boy discovers in the backroom trunk, are examples of the standard inquisitiveness of a growing child. What is interesting is that Tula's exaggerated response magnifies their significance. We do not see her confront Ramirín about the pictures directly, but from this point on in the film she ceases to show him affection, lavishing her smothering attention on Tulita instead. Similarly, she snatches the love letters from Ramirín's hands rather than explain their privacy to the boy – we note, of course, that in the next sequence she eagerly reads them herself. There is no evidence in the film that Tula's repressive actions trigger excessive behaviour in Ramirín, and no doubt his frequent absence from her haunted house to play with schoolfriends helps to immunise him against her. However, the sexual material he brings into the house and unearths in the back room redouble Tula's efforts at repression. Hapless Ramiro chooses to propose marriage to Tula on the very day she finds Ramirín's pictures and the letters. The horror with which she rejects his offer is the same horror with which she confronts the pictures and letters, indeed the pictures are lying on the table before them when Ramiro puts the question to her.

If Ramirín is just a screen onto which Tula projects her fear of his father, the treatment of Tulita is of interest in itself. The disturbing sequence of her self-imposed muteness illustrates Tula's (s)mothering of her niece. We learn through Ramirín that his sister has promised to be silent for two hours a day for a month, ostensibly as punishment for shattering the glass of the framed portrait of Gabrielita, but also as training for her future role as an ideal silent woman. In the sequence when the two hours of one day come to an end, we can hardly read her cry '¡Ya puedo hablar!' (I can speak now!) as anything but ironic. As Luis Sánchez Enciso, one of the scriptwriters, explained in interview: 'A Tula se le debería prohibir que educara a la niña' (Tula should be banned from bringing up the girl) (Núñez 1964). It is straightforward to read this scene as an allegory of Picazo's position as a NCE director. If Francoist censorship gagged Spain's artists, its promotion of art cinema through García Escudero's legislation in the 1960s gave directors only an illusory freedom to speak.

The children's dressing-up game illustrates their internalisation of the repressions of the adult world. At the start of the sequence, Tulita is at home from school sick and plays at dressing up on her own. She has rummaged in the forgotten trunk in the back room and found a selection of adult female clothes, which could have belonged to her dead mother, or possibly to her aunt prior to her decision to wear black in mourning for her sister. Decked out with exaggerated symbols of femininity (hat, shawl, ostrich feathers and high heels), Tulita sings a religious song in practice for her first communion to the portrait of the dead cousin Gabrielita that she has taken off the wall and holds up in front of her.[21] Next, Ramirín arrives home and leaves his school books on the kitchen table, in the pages of which Tula discovers his naughty photos of women in underwear. Meanwhile, two *colchoneros* toil on the terrace of the flat, beating the stuffing of Ramiro's mattress. Finally, Ramirín joins in the dressing-up game. He finds his dead uncle Primitivo's priest's hat and his father's love letters to his mother in the trunk; placing the hat on his head, he sets about reading the letters. Rather convoluted on the page, this sequence is dense and layered on the screen also, involving cross-cuts between three different spaces (the back room, the kitchen and the terrace). It is a sequence about the identity formation of children in a repressive society. The image of Ramirín in priestly attire reading the love letters is a straightforward reference to the reconciliation of sex and religion that the boy will confront as he grows. With respect to Tulita, her adult female clothes, together with Ramirín's underwear pictures and her father's love letters, point to her future social role as a wife and mother, and mean that her holy communion looks forward to her marriage not to Christ, but to a man. It is particularly important that all these references to femininity exaggerate female sexuality. Recalling the censored images of Tula's saucy underwear, Tulita dresses in the clothes of a hooker, Ramirín's photos also point to prostitution, while Ramiro's letters speak of the pleasures of the flesh. This indicates that a distorted version of femininity and gender difference arises from a repressive context, like Franco's Spain.[22]

Picazo's sequence is also an ironic commentary on the plot of *La tía Tula*. Tulita sings of the Virgin and conception without sin as the workers beat the mattress, but this does not just register a disjuncture between the worldly and the other-worldly. We know from an earlier sequence that Ramiro cannot sleep on that mattress owing to his sexual frustration, and Tula, refusing to recognise this cause, decides that the solution is to have it beaten to plump it up again.

The detail of the mattress-beating may do more than comment on the plot. Given that it obviously reminds us of a bed, it may be instructive to consider the sequence as a dream scenario, even though in terms of narrative it is not signalled as such. If it is the representation of a dream, we may read it as a nightmarish projection of Tula's fears. Tulita embodies a series of irreconcilable contradictions that govern Tula's character. The child is the fruit of the carnal union of Ramiro and Rosa, yet she sings of conception without sin, and thus projects Tula's inability to reconcile sexuality and maternity. The activity of beating the mattress would underpin this denial of the flesh as it recalls the practice of self-flagellation. According to this interpretation, the clothing, portrait and religious song might all be seen as symbols of the social expectations that also rule Tula's life. The sequence depicts the way the individual must fall into line, a process that is startlingly interrupted by the fact that Tulita falls over. This sequence of a child, ludicrously dressed in adult's clothes that cause her to trip up, holding a portrait of a dead female relative that obscures her vision and also causes her to stumble, and singing a religious song that absorbs her concentration and also contributes to her fall, is one of the most evocative representations in Spanish cinema of the coercion of the individual in a repressive society. As such it may also therefore be interpreted as an allegory of the compromised artist, labouring, like Picazo, under overbearing ideologies.

La tía Tula is a film of contradiction. Its director was funded by the state through the subsidy system, but was also frustrated by the state through censorship, a contradictory creative position allegorised in the film. Its protagonist is the living contradiction of Francoism's gender ideology, for whom 'aunthood', or the equivocal combination of motherhood and virginity, is an entirely logical interpretation of society's expectations. Tula does not rebel against social expectations as we might expect in dissident cinema, the most famous instance of which is the ending of Buñuel's *Viridiana* (1961). Played by an actress continually keeping in check her own excessive performance style, Bautista's Tula embodies repression without outlet. But in this film about repression, excess seeps out of every frame. Outside the home, monotonous provincial life is punctured by the outbursts of hysterical and drunken women. Inside the terrifying family home, which is a microcosm of that society, Tula's repression triggers excess: harmless Ramiro is transformed into a rapist, and innocent Tulita becomes a future Tula, a forerunner of the disturbed children who people Spanish art cinema of the 1970s.

Notes

1. Outside Spain it won best foreign film at Prades (1964) and the critics' prize in New York (1965) (Gubern 1997: 563).
2. In the nostalgic, hagiographic volume published by the Jaén local government (Picazo's birthplace) on the twenty-year anniversary of *La tía Tula*'s release (Iznaola Gómez 2004b), Diego Galán laments that Picazo is a 'wasted auteur' (2004: 113) and Fernando Lara asks why the director made so little of merit after this film (2004: 173).
3. In 1998, he declared 4 minutes and 47 seconds were removed, and described these censored sequences with great poignancy (Castillejo 1998: 138–40; Román Gubern [1981: 212] confirms this figure); in 2004, he stated 6 minutes of the film were cut and lost forever as the negatives were destroyed (Iznaola Gómez 2004a: 34–5).
4. In her blind adherence to ideology, there is scope for an Althusserian reading of Tula as an 'interpellated' subject. See Kinder (1993: 19–20), on applying this theory to oppositional Spanish cinema.
5. See Gavilán Sánchez and Lamarca Rosales (2002: 94). Picazo became a permanent teacher in 1964, resigning, along with Berlanga, in protest against the measures of the new Director-General Alfredo Sánchez Bella in 1969 (Hernández 2003: 320).
6. An earlier version of Unamuno's novella also began with the widowing of Ramiro (Longhurst 1996: 15).
7. Unamuno also declared that he knew of a real case (Longhurst 1996: 13), and in an earlier version of the novella (discussed by Alex Longhurst [1996: 13–18], drawing on Geoffrey Ribbans's work), likewise highlighted environmental factors to explain Tula's attitudes. However, Unamuno aimed to break with nineteenth-century realism, in which time and place are concrete, in favour of abstract settings and a focus on philosophical questions (Longhurst 1996: 52–8), coining the neologism 'nivola' to describe his idiosyncratic approach. Hence in the final version of the text Unamuno eliminates environment to show that 'la actitud anti-masculina de Gertrudis [Tula] le salga de lo hondo del ser y no de ciertos factores condicionantes históricos o ambientales' (Gertrudis's anti-masculine attitude springs from the depths of her

being, and not from certain conditioning historical or environmental factors' [Longhurst 1996: 16]). Picazo's film is in a sense, therefore, an adaptation of the earlier version.

8. Picazo claims that direct sound was used in all but the river sequence and final scene at the station (Julián 2002: 63); Baena states that it was only used in interior sequences (Llinás 1989b: 222).

9. Through this portrait, Picazo is therefore careful to deflect his attack away from contemporary Catholicism. One of the scriptwriters, Hernán, recalls that another contributor, López Yubero, was very devout, and objected to any direct attack against the Church (Castillejo 1998: 131).

10. Enrique Guerner, born Heinrich Gaertner, brought German expressionism to Spanish cinema, and trained the generation of cinematographers that preceded the one who studied at the state Film School, which included Baena.

11. Carmen Martín Gaite's 1978 novel about childhood under Franco also figures the back room as a space of freedom and takes its name from it: *El cuarto de atrás*.

12. Asunción Gómez (2002: 588) points out that *Calle Mayor*'s soundtrack expresses Isabel's emotions. Such a displacement of female emotions from diegetic voice to non-diegetic soundtrack is typical of Hollywood melodrama.

13. A Catholic lay organisation 'dedicated to influencing society in accordance with church teachings' (Grugel and Rees 1997: 130), Acción Católica was most active in the 1960s, but entered into a period of crisis owing to Vatican II (Bellosillo 1986: 11). The film portrays a number of its meetings, but its only social activity that is mentioned is, unsurprisingly, film censorship.

14. This image may no longer be found in the film, but is now part of the iconography of *La tía Tula*, as it is reproduced on the cover of Heredero and Monterde (2003), and in Castillejo (1998: 48).

15. These films both start and end with funerals. Each features an actual coffin in the first sequences (Rosa's in *La tía Tula* and the joke one in *Calle Mayor*) and each a figurative entombment of their female protagonists in their conclusions.

16. A current of films in the early 1970s returned to the opposition of 'heroines without heroes', as I have argued in my reading of Emma Penella's roles in *Fortunata y Jacinta* (Fons 1970) and *La Regenta* (Gonzalo Suárez 1974) (Faulkner 2004: Chapter 4).

17. Susan Martin-Márquez notes that the film of another NCE director, Summers's *Adiós, cigüeña, adiós* (*Goodbye, Stork, Goodbye* 1971), passes rape off 'as intimacy' (1999: 150).

18. This recalls the decision to leave the images of the scantily clad American dancers in the mayor's dream in Berlanga's *¡Bienvenido Mister Marshall!*, but cut the erotic dream of the school mistress. Female sexuality, it seems, was acceptable among prostitutes and foreign women, but not respectable Spanish women.

19. This constitutes the background to both the symbolic revenge visited upon mother figures in Spanish films of the 1970s, like *Pascual Duarte* (Franco

1975) and *Furtivos* (*Poachers*, Borau 1975), and to the psychologically disturbed children that populate other films of that period, like *El espíritu de la
colmena* (Erice 1973) and *Cría cuervos* (*Raise Ravens*, Saura 1975).

20. See Marvin D'Lugo's exploration of 'allegories of authorship' in his mono-
graph on Saura (1991: 9).

21. As in *La ciudad no es para mí* and *Balarrasa* (discussed in Chapter 2), the portrait of a dead female relative haunts future generations by providing authority regarding moral behaviour that cannot be questioned.

22. This sequence influences Saura's treatment of the same subject in *Cría cuervos*
(1975), where the three sisters also dress up and act out adult scenarios, and
Irene cuts out photos of female pop stars and models, which recall Ramirín's
underwear pictures, and pastes them in a scrapbook.

CHAPTER 5

Identity and Nationality in *Nueve cartas a Berta* (*Nine Letters to Berta*, Patino 1965)

Basilio Martín Patino's *Nueve cartas a Berta* of 1965 is widely acknowledged as one of the key works of the NCE. If Camus's *Los farsantes* was made by a producer and technical team of the VCE, and Picazo's *La tía Tula* was largely impervious to the formal experimentation of contemporary New Cinemas, *Nueve cartas a Berta* was, in Casimiro Torreiro's words, 'la película más emblemática del NCE, suerte de manifiesto-compendio de las virtudes y las debilidades del movimiento' (the most emblematic film of the NCE, a sort of manifesto-compendium of the strengths and weaknesses of the movement) (Torreiro 1995b: 318). These 'strengths' were perceived to be first, the film's engagement with an area of Spanish life that was resonant with the experience of certain critics and audiences, and second, its display of cinematic modernity through formal experimentation; they were rewarded with success at the domestic box office (see Introduction), prizes in Spain (including Silver Shell for best first film at San Sebastián, 1966) and the accolade of representing the nation at international film festivals over 1967–8.[1] Progressive, left-wing journals like *Nuestro Cine* and *Cuadernos para el diálogo* championed *Nueve cartas a Berta* at first, as they did the movement as a whole, until its failure became apparent at the end of the decade. Miguel Bilbatúa, for instance, called it a 'valid' and 'necessary' testimony of its time (though he pointed out that it referred to a certain section of Spanish society only, the university population) (1966: 6), and an important film in terms of form (Bilbatúa and Rodríguez Sanz 1966: 10). Bolstered by its commercial success, Carlos Rodríguez Sanz was less reserved: '*Nueve cartas a Berta*, independientemente de su valor intrínseco, es, por su repercusión popular y su profundo valor testimonial, por la actitud responsable ante la sociedad española que de ella se deduce la película clave de los últimos años' (*Nueve cartas a Berta*, quite apart from its intrinsic value, is, owing to its resonance with audiences, its profound testimonial value and the responsible attitude towards Spanish society that can be inferred from it, the key film of recent years) (quoted in Martín Patino 1968, inside cover). The 'weaknesses' of the film indicated in Torreiro's summary would be condemned in *Nuestro Cine* towards the end of the decade (for instance, Llinàs and Marías 1969),[2] but even at the time of its first showing and release, both *Film Ideal*, the journal traditionally hostile to the NCE, and the conservative Francoist press, criticised its flaws. These were seen as its 'chaotic' (Martínez León 1966), or even 'pompous' ('Review of *Nueve cartas a Berta*' 1967) use of film form, which seemed designed deliberately to put off audiences (Martínez León 1966: 343), its defeatist ending (Martialay and Marinero 1966: 377) and its over-illustration of certain theses – with a knowing dig at Patino's organisation of the Salamanca film conference of 1955, José María Palá and Marcelino Villegas compare the director to 'un conferenciante expresándose por medio de dibujos o proyecciones' (a conference speaker expressing himself through drawings and screenings of clips) (1967: 69).

If *Nueve cartas a Berta* had both supporters and detractors in its day, in subsequent criticism it became a victim of its supporters too. Film historians have stressed the naivety of those who placed their faith in García Escudero, and the elitism of those who championed art cinema. The directors themselves experienced the exasperation of having their work rewarded with prizes and promoted abroad on the one hand, yet obstructed through censorship, distribution and exhibition in Spain on the other, and historians have lined up to condemn the cynicism of Francoism's *aperturista* film policy. The films served, in Kathleen Vernon's words, as an 'arm of foreign policy' for the government, because they were aimed at foreign audiences at international film festivals to give an impression of Spain's liberalisation to the outside world (2002: 260; see also Molina-Foix 1977: 18; Kinder 1993: 93; Triana-Toribio 2003: 83). Directors were dubiously implicated in this game of 'international window-dressing' (Torreiro 1995b: 306) because the aesthetic experimentation of their films apparently made them appeal to foreign audiences and ignore domestic ones. (The comparative commercial successes in Spain of both *Nueve cartas a Berta* and *La tía Tula* are cited as exceptions that prove the rule [Caparrós Lera 1983: 48; Triana-Toribio 2003: 82].)

While the contradictions of the regime's policy of promoting, yet obstructing the NCE are a focus of this book, I also maintain that the films are not just documents that illustrate contexts, but artistic responses to those contexts. *Nueve cartas a Berta*, a film that Patino has recently described as shot through with 'limitations and scars' (Torreiro 2003: 312), explores the contradictions of the NCE through the question of nationality. Patino takes the development of identity of a young male protagonist – a standard topic of contemporary New Cinemas – and uses this conceit as a means to interrogate Spanishness. There is a clever match between the conflict over nationality experienced by the protagonist in the film's plot, and the awkward alignment of a traditional Spanish provincial setting with contemporary European film aesthetics in the film's form. These tensions furthermore encode the anxiety over 'the national' experienced by NCE directors both inside and outside Spain. While impetus behind the NCE was nationalistic – Franco's Spain funded an art cinema to rival those of its democratic neighbours – the Francoist state never intended the NCE to be a Spanish national cinema in the sense of a commercially profitable cinema aimed at a domestic market. Whether the films were successful in the home market or not, Spanish directors like Patino experienced the contradiction of being funded by a Spanish government to make films not for Spanish audiences, but foreign ones at film festivals.

Like Picazo, Patino graduated from Film School in 1960, and filled in the years until he made his first film writing commissioned scripts and working in documentaries and advertising. In the interviews that followed the showcasing of his graduation short film *Tarde de domingo* (*Sunday Afternoon* 1960) at San Sebastián he stresses two things that help us understand his approach in *Nueve cartas a Berta*. First, he highlights his refusal to accept any of the numerous commissions offered to him by VCE producers in those years (in 1966 he states there were six offers),[3] declaring stubbornly in 1969: 'haré cine en la medida exacta en que me encuentre a gusto con ello o me sea indispensable para vivir' (I will make films when I feel entirely comfortable with everything, or when it's absolutely essential for me to live) (Maqua and Villegas 1969: 334). The second experience he stresses – and one that explains why he didn't have to take on those commissions for economic survival – is his work in the advertising world (he worked predominantly for the 'Valeriano Pérez' agency [Pérez Millán 2002: 36]), which he claims gave him the practical experience he needed after Film School, and the chance to complete more unusual work than what was offered by the commissions he rejected (Martialay and Marinero 1966: 375).[4] Working on adverts, he claims, also fed his particular interest in montage (Martialay and Marinero 1966: 375; Bilbatúa and Rodríguez Sanz 1966: 9).[5]

It was thus with both this tenacious sense of independence and practical experience that Patino approached *Nueve cartas a Berta*. The first-time director was soon faced with the bemusement, if not downright opposition, of some of his technical crew and cast on the shoot. For instance, he was told that what would become the celebrated travelling shot in the casino, in which the actors stare directly at the camera, would have to be discarded (Bilbatúa and Rodríguez Sanz 1966: 18; Julián 2002: 65). While one of his assistant directors, José Luis García Sánchez, was sympathetic, the other, Ricardo Muñoz Suay, threatened to leave (Julián 2002: 66). Some accounts of the production process reveal a director who was wilfully contrary: 'siempre que oía a alguien del laboratorio decir: "qué parte más mona", veía una necesidad de hacer algo que no fuese "mona". Al músico le obligué a poner unas músicas sincopadas con tamborilazos que están martilleando al espectador' (whenever I heard someone in the laboratory say 'what a pretty part', I felt the need to do something that wasn't 'pretty'. I made the composer include a syncopated score with loud drumbeats that pound on the spectator) (Martialay and Marinero 1966: 381). In a recent interview Patino has recalled that owing to this relationship with his technical crew, the film was made 'en un ambiente . . . de cierta incomprensión' (in an atmosphere . . . of some incomprehension) (Julián 2002: 65), an atmosphere that feeds into the portrayal of the incomprehension of his protagonist in the film itself.

In subsequent criticism, such conflicts between a director and his crew tend to be displayed as the badge of honour of the strident auteur, and possibly for this reason, their description appears rather exaggerated. Apart from Muñoz Suay, who Patino declares belonged to the world of old cinema (Julián 2002: 66), the young director enjoyed the collaboration of Luis Enrique Torán, one of the prominent new Film School-trained cinematographers of the NCE, and Pedro del Rey, the editor responsible for the thoughtful montage of the films discussed in Chapters 1 and 4. Patino may have acquired an unusual level of expertise in the practical aspects of filmmaking through his advertising work, but we must avoid the auteurist trap when we approach his work. *Nueve cartas a Berta* is clearly also dependent on the experience brought by other members of the crew, in particular Torán and Del Rey, and their knowledge of the technical innovations in film stock and camera equipment that underpinned the formal experimentation of all the New Cinemas of the period. Thus the following description of *Nueve cartas a Berta* in interview should be taken as a gesture of Patino's self-presentation as an auteur:

> son intuiciones mías en torno a un trozo de vida, a un muchacho, a unos problemas, a una serie de contradicciones, es un mundo en el que yo me he metido a indagar, en el que me he metido a ver qué había detrás de eso, a comprender una realidad que para mí era difícil. (these are my intuitions about an area of life, a boy, some problems, a series of contradictions, it is a world into which I have dug deep, in which I have become involved to see what lay behind it, to understand a reality that was difficult for me.) (Martialay and Marinero 1966: 377)

In the revised auteurist approach to *Nueve cartas a Berta* I defend here, Patino remains the central source of meaning in the film, in keeping with the emphatic use of the first person in this description, but the contributions of other members of the crew will also be taken into account.

As in previous chapters, I will also argue that the constraints placed on the auteur by the contradictory production context of the NCE enrich the exploration of contradiction in the film. By the end of the decade, Patino would bitterly dismiss the NCE as 'jueguecitos de burguesitos que tienen mala leche' (little games played by little bourgeois directors in a huff) (Maqua and Villegas 1969: 348), but he was none the less aware of his participation in the game when making *Nueva cartas a Berta*: 'Lo mejor para nosotros de esta nueva situación es que se ha constitucionalizado un poco la posibilidad de excepción, de las llamadas rarezas, siempre que se den ciertas condiciones, que se entre un poco en el juego' (The best thing about this new situation for us is that it has institutionalised, up to a point, the possibility of making something out of the ordinary, so-called strange films, as long as certain conditions are met, and one goes along with the game up to a point) (Bilbatúa and Rodríguez Sanz 1966: 9). García Escudero's legislation meant Patino could choose the script for his first film (he had written *Nueve cartas a Berta* as an earlier commission that fell through [Bilbatúa and Rodríguez Sanz 1966: 9]) and he recounts that he was even able to select his own producers (Bilbatúa and Rodríguez Sanz 1966: 10), because 'Special Interest' films like his brought guaranteed financial return through subsidy. However the legislation also meant that the film was censored at both the script and post-production stages,[6] and that the government held up its release for one and a half years before approving its distribution ('¿Crisis en el cine español?' 1967: 14). It is clear that even during the *apertura*, in Franco's Spain films could not be 'institutionalised' that were 'out of the ordinary' and 'strange' – the attempt to do so is a cinema of contradiction.

'Problematising Spanishness': From Dialogue to Monologue

The contradiction explicitly addressed in *Nueve cartas a Berta* concerns the problem of Spanishness. If we turn to the historical context of the film, 'the national' emerges as an urgent concern. In the 1940s, the ideology of Franco's Movimiento Nacional was predicated on a Manichaean opposition of 'Spain' and 'anti-Spain', whereby the latter became a catch-all term for political and religious dissent. Intellectuals and artists like Patino were intensely preoccupied by the hijacking of 'the national' by Francoism. It is important to note, however, that in the 1960s this was no longer the comparatively straightforward case of a dissident artist opposing a repressive regime. In the autarkic period, nationalism was a fundamental tenet of Francoist ideology, which drew on nineteenth-century discourses of nationality and a distorted version of the Generation of 1898 (Labanyi 1989: 35–6, 55–6). But as the regime progressively distanced itself from fascism and overt manifestations of nationalism, the status of 'the national' by the 1960s was less clear. An example of its removal from official discourse was the replacement of the 'National Interest', by the 'Special Interest' award in 1964. But 'the national' did not disappear from public discourse altogether. *Nueve cartas a Berta* shows that the contradictions of the *apertura* are telescoped in this question. This was the era of Fraga's infamous tourist slogan 'España es diferente' (Spain is different), yet also a time when Spain, through the adoption of free market economic practices, sought parity with the democracies of the West. This tension between fetishising Spanish 'difference' on the one hand, yet embracing Western practices on the other, was thrown into relief for many Spaniards by the experiences of tourism inside Spain, and the experiences of emigrant workers, and young students and intellectuals who were able to travel outside Spain.[7]

Nueve cartas a Berta explores the latter experience through its protagonist, Lorenzo Carvajal. Plot is wholly subordinate to characterisation in the film. Thus 'Spanishness is problematised', in José Enrique Monterde's words (1997: 612), through the conflicts concerning identity in the psyche of this adolescent character, played by the type-cast, *angst*-ridden youth of the NCE films, Emilio Gutiérrez Caba, who also stars in *La caza* (Chapter 6).[8] We might first consider *Nueve cartas a Berta* a filmic *Bildungsroman*, but one in which the young male hero shifts not from conformity to rebellion, but the reverse. The film's focus is on the bourgeoisie, thus experience of the outside world, which throws Lorenzo's sense of nationality into question, is not gained by working in tourism, or as an emigrant worker, but rather on a study trip abroad. Lorenzo goes to England and stays with exiled Republican academic José Carballeira,[9] with whose daughter, the eponymous Berta, he becomes romantically involved. The film begins with Lorenzo's return to Salamanca, his family and his law studies at Salamanca University. Berta is contrasted in particular with his Spanish girlfriend (who is never given a Christian name, and referred to as 'la novia' [girlfriend] throughout), though it is rather ironic that in this film about nationality, the role of the quintessentially Spanish girlfriend was actually played by a débuting Cuban actress, Elsa Baeza. *Nueve cartas a Berta* might also be termed a filmic epistolary novel, as it is organised around the nine letters to Berta of the title, each introduced with an intertitle. Berta becomes a code word for outside Spain, and thus for nonconformity, and the film is punctuated by other reminders like the visit to Salamanca of a professor living and working in exile in Harvard, Lorenzo's visit to his French friend Jacques in Madrid and his discovery that Carballeira's old flat in the capital now houses the office of an English-speaking business.

The development of the plot runs parallel to the ways the letters change, so both chart Lorenzo's character arc from tentative dissent to consent. At first the letters chronicle the conflict in Lorenzo's mind between Spain and England, and his rejection of his homeland. 'Es como si todo esto de aquí no tuviera ya sentido' (It's as if everything here doesn't make any sense anymore), he writes to Berta in the first of the nine letters we hear read out loud on the voice-over, and in the third, he asks:

¿Qué sentido tiene el acostumbrarse a vivir así, rutinariamente, sin alicientes, como en el rincón de un planeta parado, conforme a unas normas tan ajenas y viejas que no nos ayudan a vivir mejor, manteniendo y respetando unos intereses en los que no participo, ni me atañen absolutamente? (What's the point of getting used to living like this, in a routine way, with no incentives, as if we were in the corner of a stationary planet, under rules that are so unconnected from us and old that they don't help us to live better, upholding and respecting certain interests that I don't share, that have nothing to do with me?)

These thinly veiled critiques of life in Franco's Spain continue throughout the first two letters, but in the third, the focus shifts and Lorenzo attempts to reconcile Spain and England in his mind. In this third letter he speculates about Berta visiting Salamanca, and in the fifth muses about a life together for them in Spain. From this fifth letter Lorenzo begins to re-engage with his Salamanca life, and subsequently the epistles either become shorter or only a few lines of them are shared with us on the voice-over. This process culminates with the end of the letters at the film's dénouement, in which Lorenzo's marriage to his Spanish girlfriend is intimated and he conforms to life in Spain.

The nature of the communication within the letters changes, as does their content. At first there is a dialogue of sorts between the couple. Berta's letters are never read out loud to us, either by Berta or by Lorenzo, but he makes references to them. In his first letter, for example, he allows us to surmise what her letters contain. He assures her 'también yo estoy deseando volver a abrazarte' (I want to embrace you again too) and also asks '¿Es cierto eso tan bonito que dices de que me echas de menos?' (Is this wonderful thing you say about missing me really true?). Furthermore, in the first section of the film, which covers approximately letters one to five, the most common grammatical form used is the second person. Subsequently, the letters become introspective monologues. The questions previously addressed to the specific grammatical second person Berta become rhetorical questions, and reflections conveyed in the first person predominate. Berta's words are no longer relayed to us through Lorenzo, and his allusions to her become increasingly infrequent. The end of the letters signals Lorenzo's final resigned acceptance of his Salamanca life.

If we consider these parallel developments in the content and the form of the letters together, an existential thesis is clear: Patino posits that acceptance of life in Spain implies the renunciation of the self. *Nueve cartas a Berta* displays the influence of Jean-Paul Sartre, a philosopher whose work was a key source of inspiration for Spanish dissident intelligentsia from the 1950s, in spite of, or indeed because of, the placing of his work on the Index of forbidden books in 1948 – which did not stop his work circulating clandestinely.[10] In the first section of the film, Lorenzo's sense of self is established through dialogue in the letters, and his readiness to question his surroundings and his own role within them is redolent of Sartrean 'being-for-itself'. The process of renunciation of the self begins with Lorenzo's introspection, which is expressed by the transformation of the letters from dialogue into monologue. As the letters become increasingly introspective, Lorenzo gradually retreats from any active engagement with his surroundings in favour of passive acceptance. His seduction by 'bad faith' is exemplified by the empty rhetorical question he poses as he gazes listlessly at the beatific congregation of his uncle's church in the ninth letter: 'Y ¿por qué tengo yo que arreglar el mundo?' (And why must I be the one to put the world to rights?). The process of renunciation culminates with the silencing of the letters, which signals to the viewer that there is no longer any thought or communication on Lorenzo's part at all. We might interpret this as an annihilation of the self in existential terms: Lorenzo succumbs to a longing for the consoling stability, yet ontological stagnation, of 'being-in-itself'.[11] At the end of the film, Gutiérrez Caba's Lorenzo may still be visually present, but, aurally, he is eradicated by the silencing of his voice reading the letters that give the film its title.

As both contemporary commentators and subsequent critics have pointed out, *Nueve cartas a Berta* is indebted less to the Social Novel of the 1950s, than to Luis Martín-Santos's *Tiempo de silencio* (*Time of Silence*) (1961), which broke with its conventions. For example, the opposition poet and publisher Carlos Barral, in whose Biblioteca Formentor series *Tiempo de silencio* first appeared, stated in a note he wrote to Patino that his film was 'la mejor cinta española que he visto nunca. El *Tiempo de silencio* de este cine' (the best Spanish film I've ever seen. The *Time of Silence* of this cinema) (quoted in Bellido López et al. 1996: 115; Pérez Millán 2002: 92, n. 4). While different in plot, Patino's shift away from Neorealism towards greater formal experimentation and exploration of existentialism in the Spanish context in *Nueve cartas a Berta* share ground with Martín-Santos's novel. This debt is acknowledged in the eighth intertitle of the film, which is called 'Tiempo de silencio' (Time of Silence) (Monterde 1997: 612). Patino's choice of the name of his protagonist may also be inspired by Martín-Santos's references in the last lines of *Tiempo de silencio* to St Laurence the martyr (Martín-Santos 1995: 287). Indeed at the end of film and novel alike, the protagonists must suffer in silence the renunciation of ambition and individuality, or metaphorical castration, to use another of Martín-Santos's images (1995: 283). The novel's Pedro finds himself dumbstruck and unable to complain as he journeys to the provinces to take up the humble post of doctor (1995: 279–87), and in the film, Lorenzo's voice-over is also silenced, and he embraces his girlfriend and the conformist life she represents.

Notwithstanding these connections with such an illustrious work of oppositional Spanish letters, the plot and structure of *Nueve cartas a Berta* sketched out thus far might also appear a predictable portrayal of the existential preoccupations of youth typical of contemporary New Wave cinemas. It seems strange that Patino, whose life's work Torreiro sums up as 'Contra los tópicos' (Against clichés) (2003), should choose such a theme. The topic was in fact selected by José Gutiérrez Maesso, who originally commissioned the script, and Patino's treatment of the protagonist seems only perfunctorily to fulfil the expectations of those who funded NCE films with the foreign festival circuit in mind. Furthermore, Gutiérrez Caba's performance betrays a listlessness that goes beyond a convincing portrayal of introverted youth. Gutiérrez Caba has recently recalled Patino's discouraging direction of the actors – whenever they asked him how a scene had turned out he would apparently always reply 'badly' (Julián 2002: 65) – and in contemporary interviews the director stated that the protagonist's role didn't interest him at all: Lorenzo was just a pretext to explore his environment (Bilbatúa and Rodríguez Sanz 1966: 10; Martialay and Marinero 1966: 378).

Thus despite the excessive presence of Lorenzo on the film's sound- and imagetracks, he is in fact a strange absence at its centre. Patino uses a theme in vogue at the time simply as a vehicle to explore the contemporary environment, in particular the contradictions concerning 'the national'. The script even seems knowingly to gesture towards predictability of characterisation when Lorenzo's mother accuses her son of 'haciéndote el existencialista' (playing the existentialist). Lorenzo's simultaneous feelings of attraction and repulsion for Spain, and his fascination with, then rejection of, his experiences outside Spain, are not just the standard emotional vicissitudes of a stereotypical 'angry young man', but convey the conflicts inherent in the tentative opening-up of Spain in the *apertura*, which contradicted the regime's previous rhetoric of isolationism. Further, Lorenzo's equivocal experience of nationality encodes the experience of this NCE director. On the one hand *Nueve cartas a Berta* was condemned in Spain for being too 'foreign'. In a review of the film in the conservative press, for instance, it is considered a work that appeals to 'propagandas venidas de allende las fronteras' (propaganda emanating from beyond our borders) ('Review of *Nueve cartas a Berta*' 1967). On the other, the film was criticised by foreign audiences at film festivals for being too 'Spanish'. 'What is good for Spain,' complained a review for *Variety*, for example, 'is not necessarily fit for foreign consumption; this must be the least universal product of what is coming to be called the "new Spanish cinema." [The picture] demands a much greater knowledge of things Spanish than foreign audiences are likely to have' ('Review of *Nueve cartas a Berta*' 1983). Over the question of 'the national', therefore, Patino, like his protagonist, was entangled in a frustrating paradox.

Formal Disruption: Conflict and Resolution

Conflicts over 'the national' also inform Patino's choices of film form. The literary analysis of the development of the letters I offer above does not do justice to *Nueve cartas a Berta* as cinema. The shift from dialogue to monologue in the letters that announces Lorenzo's embrace of conformity is also conveyed by means of the relationship between the soundtrack and the imagetrack, through which Patino constructs his damning portrayal of contemporary Salamanca. The soundtrack consists of Lorenzo reading his letters to Berta in voice-over, accompanied by Carmelo Bernaola's musical score, and the imagetrack foregrounds Salamanca, Lorenzo's home life and his relationship with his Spanish girlfriend.

Patino uses sound in *Nueve cartas a Berta* to underscore the conflict experienced by Lorenzo on his return from England to Spain and thereby construct a general critique of his Spanish environment. Extra-diegetic music is intentionally intrusive. Bernaola had warned Patino that the combination of the spinet and drum clashed, but the director declared that he was after precisely that effect of cacophony (Martialay and Marinero 1966: 381). The dubbing of the film is also discordant. Its poor quality was pointed out in reviews (Martínez León 1966: 343), but there is a particular problem with Lorenzo's voice. While Patino used Gutiérrez Caba's own

voice for the letters read in voice-over, he did not use it for Lorenzo's dialogue within the diegesis of the film,[12] a decision that the actor has recently
recalled with some resentment, because an actor who did not dub him- or
herself entirely was not eligible for awards: 'Basilio consideró que mi voz
no correspondía a mi imagen, y me dobló de una manera terrible, gratuita'
(Basilio considered that my voice didn't go with my image, and he dubbed
me in a terrible, gratuitous way) (Julián 2002: 81). The voice-over is therefore not only intrusive in itself, it also creates a conflict owing to the
different voices used to dub the protagonist.

Further conflict is created by the opposition of this soundtrack with the
imagetrack. An early example of this opposition comes when Lorenzo and
his girlfriend take a midday stroll around Salamanca's monuments. The
companionship between Lorenzo and his girlfriend displayed on screen
contrasts with the voice-over letter to Berta. After enthusiastically describing the city's sights that we see him visit with his girlfriend, he complains:
'Pero no me sirve de nada venir a verlo yo solo, tan completamente solo,
Berta, mi Berta, estando tú tan lejos' (But it's totally pointless coming to see
it all alone, so utterly alone, Berta, my Berta, because you're so far away).
Juan Antonio Pérez Millán considers that the use of voice-over as a coun-
terpoint to the imagetrack is occasionally excessive (2002: 84), but the
degree of excess always fits with the degree of Lorenzo's rebellion. Thus in
another early sequence, the remarkable disjuncture between what we see
and what we hear conveys the extent of Lorenzo's discontent. As we observe
Lorenzo embrace his Spanish girlfriend, on the voice-over he declares to
Berta: 'Es . . . como si sólo existieras tú' (It's . . . as if only you existed).

Lorenzo's dissatisfaction with, and reluctant participation in, Spanish
life is in fact doubly conveyed in this sequence, first, through this clash
between image- and soundtracks, and second, through the use of freeze-
frames and disruptive editing of that imagetrack. Patino claimed in interview that the intention behind this formal experimentation was to distance
the spectator from Lorenzo's story, disrupting conventional narrative continuity so that 'le duele más, le escuece más' (it hurts them more, stings
them more) (Martialay and Marinero 1966: 381). This may be interpreted
as wilfully perverse (as it was by Martínez León [1966: 343]), but in the
context of the film, it is a coherent component of Patino's strategy to
render Lorenzo's awkward reintegration into Spanish life, and thereby
question the national environment in general. In the early sequence
between Lorenzo and his girlfriend, Patino betrays the influence of both
Soviet montage, which had previously inspired directors like Bardem,[13]
and the playful jump-cuts of Jean Luc Godard's *Breathless* (1959) and
François Truffaut's *The Four Hundred Hits* (1959), by juxtaposing five

shots of the couple from different angles and distances. Far from the formal chaos of which he was accused, this sequence is engineered with absolute precision. There is an exact match between the disruption of continuity of space through the editing of Lorenzo and his girlfriend's embrace, and the disruption of continuity of time through the voice-over that recalls Lorenzo's relationship with Berta. Both of these instances of disruption convey with concision the lack of harmony between Lorenzo and his Spanish girlfriend.

Patino's formal disruptions are intended to convey a profound malaise in contemporary Spain, not just the wavering affection of a law student for his girlfriend. Numerous sequences not directly connected to Lorenzo question this wider environment. The direct stare of the actors in the long tracking shot at the casino that apparently so offended Patino's technical crew effectively disrupts conventional film naturalism to render a familiar community space strange: the actors' impassive gazes make them look like corpses. Similarly, the famous 360° panning shot of the commemorative ceremony of the *alféreces provisionales* taken under cover in the centre of Salamanca's main square runs in direct opposition to the reporting of such events through static long shots on the NO-DO.[14] Patino's slow pan picks out the expressions of disillusionment on the faces of these men, which are hidden from sight in official coverage. Again, on two occasions in the film, Patino interpolates photographic collages of commercial adverts to throw into relief the portrayal of the ancient monuments of Salamanca, and convey the awkward co-existence of tradition and the contemporary embrace of consumer capitalism in 1960s Spain.

Prior knowledge of non-Spanish cinemas may reveal the influences that informed these images,[15] but it is not necessary to appreciate the disruption conveyed in these sequences. Patino's aim is not to show off his fluency in the language of contemporary foreign cinemas, but to find a way to render the familiar environment of Salamanca unfamiliar. In *La tía Tula*, Picazo achieves this by portraying provincial life through a haunted house. In *Nueve cartas a Berta*, Patino takes one of Spain's most famous provincial cities, but problematises the viewer's recognition of its well-known streets, river and monuments through formal disruption at every level. On the soundtrack, this is achieved through an intrusive, irritating musical score and conflicts in dubbing between Lorenzo's voice in dialogue and voice-over, and on the imagetrack, through freeze-frames, slow motion and rapid montage, as well as the particular instances of long takes and 360° tracking shots discussed. Álvaro del Amo noted in his prefatory essay to the 1968 published script of the film that *Nueve cartas a Berta*, 'Cinematográficamente, niega la sólida coherencia de la vida provinciana, privándola de sentido' (In cinematic terms, negates the solid coherence of provincial life, robbing it of significance) (Amo 1968: 26). I would suggest that the critique extends beyond provincial life to national life, as Lorenzo's failure to reintegrate in Spain following his trip indicates an equivocal experience of nationality.

It is therefore coherent in terms of form that Patino conveys Lorenzo's ultimate resignation and acceptance of conformity through the alignment of image- and soundtracks in the final sequences. This begins with the harmonisation of diegetic and non-diegetic sound. Lorenzo's gradual acceptance of paternal authority is conveyed in a late sequence in which he returns to Salamanca and walks home with his father. His father's words of advice, which constitute diegetic sound, are echoed with only slight modification on the non-diegetic voice-over of Lorenzo reading a letter to Berta:

> *Padre*: Tú dedícate bien a tu carrera, que es lo práctico, lo que tiene que hacer cada uno es trabajar honradamente.
> *Lorenzo*: Mi padre me ha venido aconsejando que me dedique bien a mi carrera, que es lo práctico, que lo que tiene que hacer cada quisqui es trabajar honradamente.
> (*Father*: You just devote yourself to your degree, that's the practical thing to do, what we all have to do is work honourably.
> *Lorenzo*: My father has been advising me just to devote myself to my degree, that's the practical thing to do, what everyone has to do is work honourably.)

This alignment between diegetic and non-diegetic sound is repeated when Lorenzo echoes his mother's comment about the family's new television in a letter: '¡Fíjate qué lujo para nosotros!' (Just think what a luxury this is for us!) she exclaims, and he writes 'No sabes el acontecimiento y el lujo que esto representa para ellos' (You don't know what a big event and luxury this is for them). The alignment between diegetic and non-diegetic sound also looks forward to the synthesis between image- and soundtracks, which communicates Lorenzo's acceptance of life in Spain.[16] In the final sequence of the film, the voice-over is silenced, and Lorenzo's conformity is conveyed by his absolute occupation of diegetic space, that is to say, his occupation of diegetic space in terms of both image and sound.

Perverse Metaphors

Patino also explores contradiction in *Nueve cartas a Berta* by enriching the imagetrack through metaphors, and these often reverse conventional associations. The film is a city portrait of Salamanca, and in the context of the 1950s and 1960s, when Patino himself knew the city as a young student,

Salamanca was a double-sided, or contradictory, national metaphor. This is indicated by Patino's own recollection of his feelings about the city when he made the film: 'poco a poco nos fuimos convenciendo de que había otras posibilidades en aquella Salamanca congelada, insufrible, que había otras perspectivas, otras visiones. . . . Era una ciudad terrible, pero al mismo tiempo con un gran encanto' (we became gradually convinced that there were other possibilities in that static, insufferable Salamanca, that there were other views, other visions. . . . It was a terrible city, but at the same time it had a great charm) (Julián 2002: 17, 64). On the one hand, the ancient city symbolises Spain's venerable past through its monuments and architecture, and is thus associated with conservatism, and the contemporary political expression of that conservatism, Francoism. On the other, Salamanca is a cipher of tentative dissent: its university was a forum to express political discontent in the early 1950s (Grugel and Rees 1997: 144); and it hosted the Conversations of Salamanca of 1955, which Patino organised as director of the university film club. The characterisation of Lorenzo's two university professors encodes these differing attitudes. The older academic in charge of the lecture by the visiting professor seems closed to new ideas (he is uninterested in his colleague's recommendation of a new book on *La Celestina* by Carballeira), whereas the younger one is apparently more in tune with the students, offering Lorenzo support when he is taken ill at the university.

In *Nueve cartas a Berta* Patino does not reclaim Salamanca as a space of dissent, but rather echoes these contradictions. The city's architecture is portrayed in the film's *mise en scène* as 'a great charm' when Lorenzo strolls through the streets and contemplates the monuments that had witnessed the great events of the Spanish Golden Age, yet simultaneously the city seems 'terrible' as the bright sunlight reflected off the monuments blinds the viewer, a bleached effect created by Torán's filming on sensitive film stock – a technique that Luis Cuadrado was also to use in *La caza*. The medieval-style drawings that form the background to each intertitle (these are actually Alfredo Alcaín's contemporary illustrations [Pérez Millán 2002: 83]) have a similarly equivocal effect, intrusively reminding us throughout the film of the presence of the city's venerable yet antiquated past.

At the end of the film, Lorenzo and his girlfriend embrace on the bank of the River Tormes and the camera then pans to the Salamanca cityscape. Although the couple are located in a bucolic *locus amoenus* outside the city, the pan to the cityscape indicates that, through his decision to conform, Lorenzo will now be imprisoned in the city.[17] Following the pan there is a fade to a medium shot of a stone statue of an angel, over which the end credits role. There are at least two literary intertexts present here. Just as in Rafael Sánchez Ferlosio's *El Jarama* (1956) the river continues to flow at the end of novel as it did at the beginning, despite the intervening narrative events (1967: 7, 364–5), so Lorenzo's conformity in *Nueve cartas a Berta* is conveyed figuratively as his going with the flow of the river and accepting life in the Castilian city. This living death is also indicated through the metaphor of petrification, as the credits of the film roll to the final image of the stone statue.[18] Lorenzo's fate thus again recalls that of Martín-Santos's Pedro in *Tiempo de silencio*, whose name is etymologically linked to stone matter by its Greek root 'petra' (Labanyi 1989: 54).

I have argued that *Nueve cartas a Berta* is formally coherent throughout, in the way that the relationship between the image- and soundtracks changes in line with the evolution of Lorenzo's character arc. Although the city of Salamanca is an equivocal metaphor, my argument that we may read the river and the statue of the last scene as symbols of conformity and petrification retrospectively suggests transparency in the film at the level of metaphor. Closer examination of symbol in *Nueve cartas a Berta*, however, reveals that the use of other key tropes is often perverse, although always aligned with Lorenzo's shift from rebellion to conformity. With respect to the treatment of movement and light, two abstract categories of obvious relevance to the visual and kinetic medium of film, Patino reverses conventions. Standard associations are apparent in the treatment of other characters. For instance, freeze-frames, or lack of movement, convey stasis and stagnation when they portray Lorenzo's mother, father or grandmother (Pérez Millán 2002: 88). However, when they depict Lorenzo, these shots suggest the energy and dynamism of his thoughts, as in the sequences where he resists the entrapment of Salamanca and his girlfriend by thinking about Berta. Consequently, the use of an apparently liberating mobile camera to shoot Lorenzo's return home through Salamanca's streets with his father at the end of the film is perverse.[19] Here, the dynamic cinematography in fact conveys Lorenzo's entrapment, stasis and stagnation. This is a contradictory reversal of the standard association of movement, but is entirely logical given the use of the metaphor of movement in Lorenzo's characterisation in the film as a whole; a static camera indicates mental dynamism, a dynamic camera, mental stasis.

Similarly, light, especially sunlight, is not a source of enlightenment or illumination but one of obfuscation in *Nueve cartas a Berta*.[20] We may compare the three tours of Salamanca's monuments that feature in the film, two by day and one by night, to explore this point. In the first, Lorenzo wanders around the city alone, and in the second takes a stroll with his girlfriend (Figure 5.1). In both, Torán's use of overexposed stock

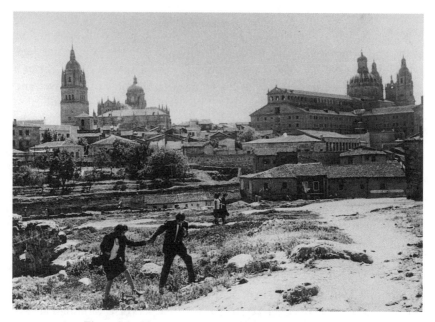

Figure 5.1. *Nueve cartas a Berta*. La linterna mágica, P.C.

renders the bright sunlight blinding, suggesting the characters' listlessness and frustration. In the third, Lorenzo and his fellow students' nocturnal tour of the monuments with the Harvard professor brings knowledge. Lorenzo discovers, for instance, further information about Carballeira. Patino had persuaded the city authorities to floodlight emblematic monuments like the university, the Old Cathedral, the Casa de las Conchas (House of Shells) and the main square (Julián 2003: 67) (Figure 5.2), and Torán's sensitive film stock captured the architectural detail of the buildings, despite the dark (Torán 1989: 114). Had the monuments formed a gloomy background that loomed behind the characters, the impact of the sequence would have been diminished. The intellectual light cast by the Harvard professor, and the capturing of the illuminated details of the monuments on the imagetrack, are crucial to the implication of the film: that while sunlight blinds the eyes and dulls the senses, darkness connotes enlightenment.

It is useful to consider the Spanish fascist anthem, 'Cara al sol' (Face to the Sun) in this context, which Patino was later to use at the start of his *Canciones para después de una guerra* (*Songs for after a War*).[21] Patino's treatment of light in *Nueve cartas a Berta* draws on the association of sun and fascism, made clear by the title of the anthem, which is also its first line. When Lorenzo tells Berta twice in his first letter that 'valoré

Figure 5.2. *Nueve cartas a Berta*. La linterna mágica, P.C.

demasiado ese sol' (I overrated this sun), we may infer that this is a significant questioning of the dictatorship, not just a throw-away comment on the weather. In the context of fascist ideology that idealised the healthy male body, it is perhaps to be expected that Patino also reverses standard connotations of health and illness. In *Nueve cartas a Berta*, Lorenzo's illness indicates his rebellion, while his restoration to health at the end of the film signifies his resignation and conformity. It is noteworthy that one of Lorenzo's excruciatingly reactionary uncles is a chemist, but his pharmacy has no cure for Lorenzo's ailment, nor for his mother's nerves. Instead, Lorenzo is 'cured' by a stay in the countryside during Holy Week with his other uncle, the ultra-conservative village priest who is immune from the changes introduced by Vatican II.

Finally, Patino reverses the trope of the seasons in *Nueve cartas a Berta*. Through the conversation between Lorenzo and his girlfriend in the final sequence our attention is drawn to the fact that it is spring: 'Ya oscurece más tarde' (It gets dark later now) comments Lorenzo's girlfriend, to which he replies, 'es que está llegando la primavera' (that's because spring is on its way).[22] Here, rather than the standard associations of new life and new hope, spring connotes fall and inertia. The sequence thus also subverts another line of the fascist anthem: 'volverá a reír la primavera' (spring will smile again).[23]

In *Nueve cartas a Berta*, Patino adopts one of the standard themes of the contemporary European New Cinemas, discontented youth, and uses it as a vehicle to explore conflicts over 'the national' that are particular to Spain. Lorenzo's existential crisis, during which he values then questions Spain by turns, allows Patino to explore the wider question of Spain's contradictory attempts to liberalise relations with the outside world during the *apertura*. Film form is harnessed in *Nueve cartas a Berta* to represent this fitful evolution of Lorenzo's character arc. Thus the relationship between sound- and imagetracks, the portrayal of the city and the treatment of metaphor evolve in accordance with Lorenzo's psychological state. Through both alliance and conflict with his technical teams, *Nueve cartas a Berta* displays Patino's remarkable command of film form, which is deployed to create a particularly dense, occasionally perverse, sometimes irritating, but always entirely coherent filmic world in which Lorenzo's experience of rebellion and conformity, symbolic of the national question, unfolds.

Notes

1. For details of prizes and festivals in which *Nueve cartas a Berta* represented Spain, see Bellido López et al. (1996: 228).
2. See José Enrique Monterde's survey (2003) of the rise and fall of the NCE in *Nuestro Cine* during the 1960s.
3. See 'Interview with Patino' (1961: 14); Martialay and Marinero (1966: 376); Bilbatúa and Rodríguez Sanz (1966: 9); Maqua and Villegas (1969: 334).
4. The experience may also have given him the chance to become familiar with new equipment, like the macrokilar camera, which was first introduced in Spain for making adverts (Bilbatúa et al. 1966: 9).
5. An extract from Patino's entrance examination for a teaching post at the Film School entitled 'Hacia un nuevo concepto de montaje' (Towards a New Concept of Montage) was published in *Film Ideal* (Martín Patino 1964).
6. Three intertitles were removed from the script, 'La guerra' (The War), 'La posguerra' (After the War) and 'Los aires de la paz' (The Appearance of Peace), certain scenes and phrases were cut from the finished film, and the censors insisted that intertitles were added at the start of the picture to explain that Berta was not Lorenzo's Spanish girlfriend. The commemorative ceremony of the association of *alféreces provisionales* was a particularly controversial scene, and was only passed when Patino produced a letter of support from a representative of the association (Monterde 1997: 613). (The *alféreces provisionales* were ex-soldiers who fought for Franco, and made up the officers in his army. Most returned to civilian life after the war, and the 'hermandad' [association] was formed in 1958.)

7. Barry Jordan (1995: 248), notes that Joaquín Ruiz Giménez, Minister of Education from 1951 to 1957, increased the number of travel grants awarded to university students. The NCE directors experienced both work and travel abroad. Prior to beginning at Film School, Patino had travelled to England and Italy (Julián 2002: 16), and Julio Diamante spent his summers working on building sites in Paris in order to watch screenings at the Cinémathèque Française (Colorado 2003: 264). After joining the Film School, directors would travel together to European film festivals. See the account of such trips in Julián (2002: 50) and Bellido López et al. (1996: 28).

8. Although Gutiérrez Caba shot *Nueve cartas a Berta* before *La caza*, Patino's film was released after Saura's.

9. On the question of exile in the film, see López (2005: 86–8, 91–2).

10. See Jordan (1990), in particular the sub-section 'Sartre and *Engagement*' (1990: 85–101), which charts the impact of Sartre's work following the 1950 translation into Spanish of *Qu'est-ce que la littérature?* (1948).

11. On 'being-for-itself' and 'being-in-itself', see Sartre (1981). On 'bad faith', see in particular his Part I, Chapter 2.

12. My thanks to José Luis Ortiz, who suggested to me that Lorenzo's dialogue was dubbed by Simón Ramírez.

13. However, the film also encodes a critique of Soviet cinema through the parody of Jacques, who is aligned with Buñuel's most committed film *Tierra sin pan* (*Land without Bread*) (1932) through his juxtaposition with a poster. Jacques jokes that his Russian girlfriend looks like a peasant character from a social realist film.

14. Thanks to the weight and size of the new Arriflex cameras, Patino's camera-man (the director doesn't recall if it was Torán or Fernando Arribas) shot the sequence without the knowledge of the crowd. Apparently, Patino and other members of the crew created diversions to distract attention away from the camera as it filmed (Pérez Millán 2002: 89–90). Román Gubern traces this shot back to the Champs Élysées crowd scene in *Breathless* (Castro de Paz 2003: 422).

15. Critics have highlighted further influences, including Pier Paolo Pasolini, Bernardo Bertolucci, Marco Bellocchio (Monterde 1997: 612), Theo Angelopoulos (Castro de Paz 2003: 422) and Michelangelo Antonioni (Torreiro 2003: 316).

16. Helena López observes that Lorenzo's acceptance of conformity coincides with 'the acclimatisation of the régime to the international economy' (2005: 87). The coincidence of conformity and consumerism is confirmed when Lorenzo arrives home to discover his family has purchased the television set.

17. In *El buen amor* (*Good Love* 1963), Francisco Regueiro similarly imprisons his young couple in the venerable architecture of another ancient Castilian city, Toledo (Galán 2003: 385).

18. In *Tarde de domingo*, the entrapment of the female protagonist is similarly indicated by her juxtaposition with a lifeless doll.

19. See Francia (2002: 116) for an account of the difficulties with this shot, which reveals Patino's insistence on its importance. The sequence was filmed from a car boot, a photograph of which features on the cover of Bellido López et al. (1996).

20. In Saura's *La caza*, sunlight is also figured as a source of oppression, a point emphasised by the use of high-contrast film stock (Stone 2002: 65). In the final freeze-frame of Saura's film, however, in which Enrique is caught as he flees from the theatre of violence, stasis does seem to convey entrapment.

21. Made in 1971, this film was not released until 1977, owing to problems with censorship. Quotations of the anthem are taken from the soundtrack of this film.

22. The film was shot as spring advanced, from 12 April to 22 May 1965 (Francia 2002: 118).

23. A failure to read these metaphors 'perversely' may explain why some progressive contemporary critics condemned the ending of the film for celebrating resignation and failure (Pérez Millán 2002: 90), or for being too ambiguous and for not taking sides (Patino, quoted in Julián 2002: 77).

CHAPTER 6

Ageing and Coming of Age in *La caza* (*The Hunt*, Saura 1965)

Such has been the critical acclaim enjoyed by *La caza* over the forty years since its release that its origins in the NCE are sometimes overlooked. The film is both typical and atypical of the movement. Carlos Saura was slightly older than its other directors, many of whom he taught at the Film School where he had a post from 1957 to 1964, and he had already completed three shorts, a medium-length documentary (*Cuenca* 1958) and two feature-length films, when García Escudero's new protectionist measures enabled him to make *La caza*. While his second film, *Llanto por un bandido* (1963), had flopped, his first, *Los golfos* (1959), which represented Spain at Cannes in 1960, had established him as the leading Spanish auteur to follow Bardem and Berlanga (San Miguel 1962a: 7). A combination of this previous experience, his partnership with such a tenacious producer as Elías Querejeta, plus good old-fashioned talent, meant that, unlike many of its other directors, Saura was immune to the collapse of the NCE, and has continued to make auteurist cinema uninterrupted to this day.

In terms of production, distribution and exhibition, *La caza* was typical of the NCE. It was simultaneously supported through the 'Special Interest' subsidy, yet stifled through censorship (although the censors' changes have now become one of the legendary examples of how their interventions sometimes opened up, rather than closed down, a film's meaning).[1] It had a mixed reception from contemporary specialist journals (as expected, *Nuestro cine* championed the film, which it featured twice on its front page [Monterde 2003: 113 n. 28], but *Film Ideal* questioned it [Sánchez Vidal 1988: 44]),[2] and while limited exhibition and distribution were blamed for the relatively small impact of the film on Spanish audiences at the time of its release (Monleón 1967: 61), *La caza* caused a stir at foreign film festivals, such as Berlin (where it was awarded the Silver Bear), New York, London and Acapulco, although it had been rejected by Cannes (Gómez 2003: 364; Sánchez Vidal 1988: 44).

Auteur studies of Saura's work are concerned with the development of the director's creative vision, but this chapter argues that much can be gained from restoring *La caza* to the context of 1960s Spain. Like the other

NCE films examined in this book, Saura's picture exposes and condemns the contradictions of the decade. In particular, I will read *La caza* against the two connected questions raised in my chapter title: the ageing of both the dictator and the dictatorship by 1965, the year that followed the anniversary celebrations of '25 años de paz' (25 Years of Peace); and the coming of age of a new generation of Spaniards born after the Civil War that brought that dictatorship to power. Saura's film denounces the contradiction of a government headed by an increasingly frail Franco and supported by a generation now on the far side of middle age, which was dependent for its duration on an ill-informed and immature youth. *La caza*, therefore, revisits through tragedy the question of ageing explored in *La gran familia* through comedy (Chapter 1). These apparently opposing NCE and VCE films not only address the same question, but do so through the performances of popular cinema stars – José Isbert in the earlier film, and Alfredo Mayo, Ismael Merlo and José María Prada in the later one.

The production context of Saura's earlier *Llanto por un bandido* is typical of the contradictions between creative aspiration and actual practice that characterise the other NCE films studied in this book. Stung by the disastrous experience and outcome of making a low-budget epic ('a hand-held arriflex and five metres of tracks' [quoted in Hopewell 1986: 71]), Saura approached *La caza* with absolute single-mindedness. It was the 'producto de un momento de violencia, de rabia personal' (product of a moment of violence, of personal fury) (Gómez 2003: 362) he states in his most recent interview, a comment that reveals his anger at both the specific experience of making *Llanto por un bandido*, and general experience of living under Francoism. Saura's intentions will therefore be central to the interpretation of *La caza* offered here, but even in the work of this fiercely defensive auteur, the contributions of actors and technical teams will also be considered. For instance, although *La caza* may be the result of Saura's determination and Querejeta's shrewd dealing with the authorities, it owes a considerable debt to Luis Cuadrado, arguably Spain's top art cinematographer of all time. Cuadrado was as tenacious as Saura – having finished at the Film School within three years, he stayed for seven, apparently to ensure he had mastered every aspect of his art (Torán 1989: 115). His collaboration with the director, with whom he also worked on *Stress es tres, tres* (*Stress is Three, Three* 1968), was by all accounts cooperative. For instance, it was Saura, himself an expert in photography, who suggested they use the macrokilar lens that made the extreme close-ups of the film possible (Bilbatúa et al. 1966: 9), and both director and cinematographer had to join forces to win what Cuadrado called 'la guerra con el laboratorio' (the war with the laboratories) (Bilbatúa et al. 1966: 10). As was the case with cinematographer Juan Julio Baena and *Los golfos* (Llinàs 1989b: 216–17), the laboratory technicians were at first reluctant to work with the extreme contrasts of light and dark on the film stock, but finally agreed (though with *Los golfos*, this came only after the suggestion that Baena be sacked! [Llinàs 1989b: 216]). Saura's personal vision in *La caza* has been immortalised in a frequently cited comment by fellow Spanish auteur Manuel Gutiérrez Aragón, who declared that it 'dio la vuelta al cine que se hacía en España. En cuanto a tener un lenguaje aseado, para mí hay un cine español de antes de *La caza* y otro después' (turned Spanish cinema upside-down. In terms of a well-worked language, there is a cinema before *La caza* and a different one after it) (Torres 1992: 28).[3] That 'well-worked language' was the fruit of Saura's collaboration with Cuadrado.

If Gutiérrez Aragón considered Saura's third feature a watershed in the history of Spanish cinema, its merit has not always been undisputed. In an early indication of his contribution to the film, Mayo, one of the main acting leads, recognised its potential before the shoot,[4] but a dozen producers rejected the project until it was taken on by Querejeta, the Basque producer who exploited the state subsidy system with brilliant effect, and with whom Saura was to work in creative tandem in twelve further features over the following sixteen years.[5] *La caza* has enjoyed more consistent acclaim in later years, and has been praised by both practitioners of, and commentators on, Spanish cinema, especially those concerned with its auteurist traditions.

Over four decades, scholarly understanding of the importance of *La caza*, and of the nature of its 'well-worked language', has evolved. Critical responses are parables for their own times, as they shift in focus from emphasising the film's political import in accounts written during, and immediately following, the dictatorship, to wider concerns in recent years. Thus Manuel Villegas López, who published the first Spanish book on the NCE in 1967, would stress the indirect political critique encrypted in *La caza*, in a style of expression that is itself indirect and encrypted – the result, no doubt, of the time of writing. He describes the film variously as a 'máscara. Todo está detrás' (mask. Everything is behind it), a 'fórmula [que] es preciso desarrollar para llegar a su verdadero y concreto significado' (formula [that] needs to be worked out to get to the true and secret meaning) (1967: 83), a 'kábala' (cabala), a 'jeróglífico, cada uno de [sus elementos] significa una cosa y todos juntos, otra' (hieroglyphic, each of its components means one thing, but together they mean another) (1967: 85) and finally, 'Lo que se verá, si se puede, está más allá de lo que se ve: es el secreto del film' (What one will see, if one can, is beyond what one sees: it is the secret of the film) (1967: 86). This emphasis on the film's 'secret' critique remained central to analyses well into the 1980s. Even though the regime was over and the dictator dead, the fight against Francoism on the ideological front continued on the pages of film criticism. These accounts of *La caza* tended to focus on its evasion of censorship. In particular, the rabbit hunt was understood as a metaphor for the Spanish Civil War; consequently the self-destruction of the rabbit hunters/war victors at the end of the film looked forward to the inevitable collapse of the dictatorship established by that conflict (see Hopewell 1986: 71–6; Higginbotham 1988: 79; Kinder 1993: 160; Torreiro 1995b: 320; Monegal 1998: 203–8).

In 1988, Agustín Sánchez Vidal suggested that political readings of the film were tied to the time of its reception:

> Si en su día la construcción arquetípica de los personajes y el sentido parabólico de la película imponían por encima de cualquier otra consideración una lectura política, la perspectiva actual libera a *La caza* de esas servidumbres coyunturales. (If in its day archetypal characterisation and the parable meaning of the film imposed a political reading at the expense of all other considerations, today's perspective liberates *La caza* from that time of slavery.) (1988: 48)

Further lines of enquiry have included the film's exploration of private property (Pérez Rubio 1997: 609); the pictorial antecedents of Saura's hunting imagery (Wood 1999); its analysis of illness (Wood 2000) and use of film form (Heredero 2003; Zunzunegui 2003).

This chapter is also a product of its own time, as it draws on this previous scholarship, reacts to a recent emphasis in Spanish film criticism on questions of gender and masculinity, and applies new theoretical insights, such as Gilles Deleuze's concepts of the 'movement-image' (1997) and the 'time-image' (1994) in cinema (first published in 1983 and 1985), and Judith Butler's work (1993) on the materiality of the body.[6] First, it argues that the two rabbit hunt sequences, rather than conspicuous metaphors, are a force of violent interruption in the narrative that prevents the viewer's facile involvement with a straightforward – if shocking – plot, and predictable – if critical – characterisation. This main narrative, not the hunt sequences, encodes critique, and its analysis will reveal the wider nature of Saura's satire of 1960s Spain. This is most profound in the treatment of ageing, a question that has received only passing critical attention thus far (D'Lugo 1997: 44).[7] Finally, this chapter offers a new reading of film form in *La caza* that draws on Deleuze and Butler, and lays particular stress on the significance of the landscape and body shots of the siesta sequence halfway through the film.

Violent Interruptions: The Rabbit Hunt

La caza is the portrayal of a day out hunting. At first we assume that this is an occasion for three old friends to be reunited and to introduce a young relative to the supposed pleasures of the chase. This fictional narrative is interrupted by two sequences of hunting, which, given their accuracy of detail and objective narration, belong to the documentary genre.[8] The first hunt takes place in the morning, and is carried out by the four armed men using a dog as a retriever; and the second, in the afternoon, involves the introduction of ferrets in the warrens to flush the rabbits out. On a first viewing of *La caza*, these images cause the greatest emotional impact. Despite the fact that they make up only 6 of the 83 minutes of running time, the profound impression they make on the viewer surely explains why the rabbit hunt has become so central to the interpretation of the film. Despite the unsettling directness of these images of the unstaged rabbit slaughter, which at times become almost unwatchable, in critical accounts, the hunt has none the less been inscribed in the poetic register of 'indirection' (Monegal 1998: 203) and understood as a metaphor for the violence and killing of the Civil War. For instance, Antonio Monegal interprets the hunt sequences as an example of

> the rhetorical devices that, in spite of being incorporated into the narrative and participating in its development, generate a discourse that is not ruled by narrative economy . . .. We may identify those devices as figural operations, equivalent to metaphor and metonymy, which, when combined, make up the allegorical texture of the film. (1998: 204)

While I also consider the hunt sequences to operate outside 'narrative economy', the point I contend here is the extent to which they are 'figural' or 'allegorical'. Rob Stone has recently argued that the images of cruelty to animals in films like *La caza*, *Furtivos* (Borau 1975) and *Pascual Duarte* (Franco 1975) appeal to us on such a visceral level that we should be shocked by the reality of the slaughter, and not dilute this response by considering it intellectually. He argues that we must

> observe the indisputable reality of these incidents rather than the narrative-bound symbolism of the slaughter. . . . Audiences should therefore not dismiss the slaughter onscreen as a device or an artistic conceit when they are faced with real pain and real killing. (2004: 76, 80)

The images of the rabbit slaughter in *La caza* are so direct that they must be seen for what they are, rather than as indirect metaphors. We should therefore acknowledge that their role is to deal us 'a smack up the side of the head' (Stone 2004: 81): they violently interrupt the narrative and shake us out of our viewing complacency.

Saura's own statements about his intentions in making the film also cast doubt on the hunt-as-metaphor interpretation. In a 1969 interview, he stated that originally the idea behind *La caza* had indeed been to make a film about the Civil War. The setting was to be a hunting ground and old Civil War battlefield he discovered during the shoot of *Llanto por un bandido* (1963), and the hunting party was to be split between two camps, two men in one, three in the other, clearly to evoke the two opposing sides in the conflict (Torres and Molina-Foix 2003: 8). Although the setting was retained, the split-party idea was scrapped:

> we took out the allusions to the Spanish Civil War . . .. The basic idea had evolved quite a bit. Of course, there was a Spanish Civil War, but we wanted a broader meaning. . . . We deliberately took out the allusions because that seemed to [*sic*] easy to us. (Torres and Molina-Foix 2003: 10)

The hunt/war metaphor is 'too easy'. The documentary hunt sequences interrupt: their function is to jolt us out of our involvement with the narrative and force us to maintain a critical distance from the film, a Brechtian process common to much of the NCE (see Chapters 3 and 5). For, without these interruptions, and other key moments of self-consciousness and de-naturalisation that I discuss in the final section of this chapter, *La caza* is a conventional narrative, with coherent characterisation and a linear plot, which progresses, with increasing inevitability, to its tragic dénouement.

'25 años de paz' (25 Years of Peace), 25 years older

Saura's 'broader meaning' emerges from the narrative of *La caza*, rather than the hunt sequences. The film is a critical study of ageing. The development of this theme encodes Saura's critique of Franco's Spain, as it probes current tensions surrounding the age of the dictator and the first generation of Franco loyalists, and the regime's failure to garner the support of middle-class youth, upon which it depended for its survival. The official celebration of the dictatorship's longevity, the '25 años de paz', was a massive attempt to disavow both the decline of those who were ageing and the discontent of those coming of age. These two preoccupations are visible beneath the surface of the film commissioned for the celebrations, José Luis Sáenz de Heredia's *Franco, ese hombre* (1964). In the final section of this chapter, I will analyse film form in *La caza* to explore ageing in the wider context of the representation of the body.

We know that the idea for this film came to Saura during the shoot of *Llanto por un bandido* in 1963, and that *La caza* itself was shot in 1965: the project was therefore in preparation throughout 1964. The year in which the 'the basic idea evolved' was the year of the '25 años de paz', and while *La caza* is no mechanical representation of events in this period, current causes of anxiety informed its own critical concerns. '25 años de paz' was a propaganda slogan coined by Fraga, the recently appointed Minister for Information (who was also responsible for the infamous 'España es diferente' [Spain is Different] tourist catchphrase). Fraga masterminded the nationwide celebrations: there were exhibitions, prizes and extensive press coverage, as well as *Franco, ese hombre*, Sáenz de Heredia's biopic (Preston 1993: 714–15). 'The anniversary revels', Paul Preston recounts in his biography of the Caudillo, 'confirmed Franco's belief in his own immense popularity' (1993: 714). They may also be seen as an attempt to disguise the disquiet felt in official circles over the continued viability of a leader who seized power in a very different, and long past, era.[9] The economic and social changes of the *apertura* might be rhetorically spun as part of a planned development of Francoism (Preston 1993: 706), but the material manifestation of its anachronism was the physical presence of the dictator. Franco's ageing could not be hidden: he turned seventy in 1962, and his visible decline, accelerated by the onset of Parkinson's disease (an illness never officially acknowledged [Preston 1993: 729]), became increasingly obvious.

The second cause of concern, the other side of the coin of old age, was youth, or coming of age. The regime was always aware that its survival depended on attracting the loyalty of new generations, as the establishment of the Falangist youth organisations in the 1940s made clear. While the failure to win the support of working-class youth, represented in the characters of Saura's *Los golfos* (1959), or Jesús Fernández Santos's *Llegar a más* (1963), might be expected, and thus comparatively tolerable, the opposition of the middle-class children of the victors of the Civil War was not. These young people made up the student population, and disturbances and demonstrations at Spain's universities from the 1950s onwards were a thorn in the side of the regime.[10] Dissident cinema recorded this discontent: Bardem's *Muerte de un ciclista* (1955), for instance, included a brief, but important, sequence showing student riots (most of it was censored), and Patino's *Nueve cartas a Berta* (1965) (Chapter 5) offered a detailed exposé of an *angst*-ridden student.

The context of the '25 años de paz' also explains the role of the Civil War in *La caza*. Throughout the dictatorship, this conflict was perpetually present in the public sphere, through the media coverage of commemorative events such as the annual military parades of 18 July and 1 April, and the opening of the 'Valle de los caídos' (Valley of the Fallen) in 1959.[11] While there was an apparent shift away from the language of triumphalism by the 1960s, as younger ministers became involved in writing Franco's speeches,[12] this was just rhetorical spin. Constant affirmations of 'peace' in Fraga's '25 años de paz' celebrations were, of course, a constant reminder of the war. This obsession with the war of 1936–9 also underlined the differences between young and old in the 1960s. This is a textbook case of generational conflict exacerbated by war and its aftermath, whereby the clash between young and old is intensified as it is one between a group that has fought in a war and a group that has not.

Ageing and coming of age, key sources of anxiety to Francoism in the 1960s, are probed in *La caza* through a critique of masculinity. Saura overturns in this film the kind of homosociality described and prescribed by the consensual Francoist cinema of the 1940s. It has been noted that casting Mayo intertextually evokes the actor's former embodiment of the 'galán' (idol) of Francoism in films such as *Raza* (Sáenz de Heredia 1941), *¡Harka!* (Arévalo 1941) and *¡A mí la legión!* (*Raise the Legion!*, Orduña 1942) (D'Lugo 1991: 57; Sánchez Vidal 1988: 48 n. 24). Santos Zunzunegui has pointed out (2003: 417) the similar function of Ismael Merlo, who plays José, and José María Prada, who takes the role of Luis, the third member of the trio. The point here is not to repeat the truism that male characterisation in consensual Francoist cinema heroicises,[13] and dissident cinema de-heroicises, but rather to stress that casting these particular actors in *La caza* foregrounds their ages and their ageing. Marvin D'Lugo states that the choice of Mayo, who plays Paco, is 'a shattering statement of the passage of time and the transformation of a bygone mythic hero into a venal and narcissistic old man' (1991: 57), and the same might be said of Merlo and Prada. In 1965, the year Franco was seventy-three, these actors were in fact only fifty-four, forty-seven and forty respectively. But just as Cuadrado's monochrome photography avoided the middling tones of grey in favour of the startling extremes of black and white (Sánchez Vidal 1988: 48), so the narrative avoids the middle ground: these middle-aged men are portrayed as old. Furthermore, although the actor Emilio Gutiérrez Caba, who plays Paco's brother-in-law Enrique, was twenty-three in 1965, in a parallel gesture of exaggerating extremes, he is infantilised in the film.

Narrative and cinematography were crucial to emphasising age, but so was performance style. If we are willing to accept that actors in the VCE could subversively undercut the conservatism otherwise presented by a film (see, for instance, my reading of José Isbert's role in *La gran familia*,

Chapter 1), then we may allow for the possibility of actors contributing in a similar way to the NCE. Aurora Bautista (discussed in Chapter 4) or Mayo, who had previously starred in the popular Spanish cinema of the 1940s, cannot simply be dismissed as passive participants in art films, whose material presence is manipulated by the director to evoke their earlier films. While it would be possible for the performance of an actor to introduce an element of conservatism in an otherwise subversive film, in fact Bautista of *La tía Tula* and the cast of *La caza* share the directors' oppositional vision. The participation of Mayo in the early stages of the *La caza* project, for instance, indicates his involvement with, or at least knowledge of, the creative development of the work. Saura is to be credited for shrewd casting in *La caza* (as César Santos Fontenla pointed out in *Nuestro Cine* [1966c: 17]), but a balance must be struck when apportioning creative responsibility for performances. In an interview of 1974, Saura stated with respect to directing actors that 'durante las primeras semanas estudio a los actores, qué es lo que me pueden aportar, etc., y les dejo una cierta libertad para ver hacia donde derivan' (in the first weeks I study the actors, consider what use they can be to me, etc., and I give them a certain amount of freedom to see in which directions they drift) (Castro 1974: 395). None the less, when interviewed in 1988, the proud auteur would play down any actor's contribution: 'the actors . . . do only what the director allows. The director must openly answer for their ideas, the actors not' (Zeul 2003: 113). The overall vision of the critique of ageing in the film is Saura's, and no doubt he instructed the cast not to act their age, but old age. Still, the strutting arrogance of Mayo's Paco, the stooping bitterness of Merlo's José, the sulking moods of Prada's Luis, combined with the actors' own awareness of their previous roles, also play an important part in *La caza*'s narrative of ageing.

The ageing, anxiety about ageing and defiance of ageing exhibited by these three old friends are evident throughout the narrative. In the opening sequence, Saura is perhaps over-keen to establish character and context – a result, no doubt, of shooting in sequence. The relationship between the men is immediately explained: they are old army pals, reunited for a day's hunting. 'Después de tanto tiempo' (After such a long time), José comments as he puts his arm round Paco in a repeated gesture of forced comradeship, 'otra vez juntos' (we're together again). He then reminisces about a fourth old friend who, we later learn, has committed suicide: 'si llega a venir Arturo, los cuatro de siempre. Pobre Arturo' (if Arturo were here, it would be the four of old times. Poor Arturo). The intention behind this exchange is to evoke, from the outset, the men's former youthful and chummy selves to contrast them with their present situation. We soon appreciate that their friendship is now a sham, as all three are motivated by self-interest. José has organised the outing as a pretext to ask Paco for a loan, Luis has come along to keep in with his current boss, though he is keen to find a new one, and Paco just wants to take some exercise. Nor are family ties disinterested: Paco has invited along his brother-in-law Enrique because, through him, he has gained access to his father-in-law's jeep.

Saura brings the theme of ageing to the fore through Paco and José, the two older men played by the two older actors. They initially represent two different approaches to ageing, but prove to be mirror-images of one another. José is the obsessive. He claims he is ill, complains of stomach pains and periodically takes pills. The illness is unspecified, but José's characterisation as an ageing ex-soldier is underscored when he admits to Paco: 'tengo dolores desde que me dieron el tiro' (it's hurt ever since I was shot). During a break before lunch, Enrique takes a photograph of José as he crouches over a pool to wash. He rips it up then glowers jealously at Paco's comparatively statuesque physique, while reproaching himself for being old and letting himself go. 'Parecí [en la foto] a un viejo de estos que toman el sol en una esquina' ([In that photo] I looked like one of those old men you see sitting in the sun on a corner), he scolds himself in voice-over, 'tengo que llevar cuidado. Es natural. Después de tanto tiempo sin hacer ejercicio. En cambio, él sigue igual. No le importa nada' (I must be careful. It's not surprising. It's been such a long time since I've done any exercise. However, he's just the same. Nothing bothers him). Paco is the narcissist. He takes pride in his well-preserved body, and his character anticipates that of Julián in Saura's next feature, *Peppermint frappé* (1967), in his interest in exercise and cosmetics: while Enrique applies lip salve, Paco is the only character to use suntan cream. In voice-over we learn of his fascist intolerance of the physical imperfections of the weak and the lame. However, just as his confidence driving the jeep at the beginning of the film is undercut by José's revelation of his former, lowly position as a truck-driver, so his anxiety about ageing is revealed at the end of the film. In the sequence that immediately precedes his murder by José, we see him examine his wrinkles in the drinks-box mirror, then pull at his temples to smooth out the crow's feet. Like José, then, he rejects the reality of his ageing and acts out the equivalent of tearing up the unflattering photograph by altering his appearance before the mirror.

Cinematic form is used so that the whole film may be likened to an unflattering photograph of ageing men. Critics have previously noted the way camera-work, lighting and overexposure of the film stock depict the oppressive environment of the old Civil War battlefields (Figure 6.1), but those cinematic resources are also harnessed in order cruelly to expose the

Figure 6.1. *La caza*. Elías Querejeta, P.C.

ageing and suffering of the body. Cuadrado trains his camera on those bodies in starkly lit medium shots, dehumanising long shots and cruelly detailed close-ups, which pick out their scars and wrinkles. Cuadrado didn't usually use the sun as a source of light when shooting outdoors, but in *La caza* all the lighting was natural owing to the key role played by the sun in the plot (Llinàs 1989: 245). (The sun is also crucial in the portrayal of hard agricultural work in Saura's earlier documentary, shot by Baena and Antonio Álvarez, *Cuenca* [1958].) In *La caza* the men's ageing bodies sweat and burn under the scorching Castilian summer sun (Figure 6.2) and Saura reminds us in interview that no artificial resources were needed to evoke this heat: the sweat and panting were genuine and experienced by the whole crew during the arduous four-week August shoot.[14] As in *Nueve cartas a Berta* (Chapter 5), figuring the Spanish sun as an enemy was also an indirect attack on Spanish fascism, as audiences would link it to the title and first line of the anthem 'Cara al sol' (Face to the Sun) (Oms 1981: 30).

Figure 6.2 Alfredo Mayo in *La caza*. Elías Querejeta, P.C.

The equivalence between José and Paco is conveyed through their portrayal using the same cinematic resources. Saura also exploits the potential offered by frames and mirrors to reinforce this similarity. The enclosure of the two characters within a single frame becomes a visual leitmotif in *La caza*, which echoes the credit sequence in which the camera slowly zooms towards two caged ferrets. In the café at the start of the film, for instance, the four men sit together at the bar, but, in medium shot, and through a long take, the camera tracks from side to side to ensure that only two characters occupy the frame at any one time. Again, when Paco drives from the café to the hunting ground, he and José, who sit in the front seats, are linked by *mise en scène*. In a long shot, we see the two men through the car windscreen as it approaches, and the windscreen partition simultaneously divides and unites them. They are trapped by the frame of the windscreen within the frame of the cinema screen in a visual refrain of the two ferrets of the credit sequence, which share a cage that also contains a divide. There follows an exchange between José and Juan's mother that reinforces the similarity between the hunters and ferrets, introduces the tension that governs the film and looks forward to its violent end: '[los hurones] se pasan el día gruñendo y removiéndose sin parar . . .. Están como locos, y alguno se va a escapar' ([the ferrets] spend the day growling and endlessly moving around . . .. They're sort of mad, and one of them is going to escape).[15] Ferrets are 'notoriously vicious and ferocious creatures', Gwynne Edwards notes, 'and the pair in the cage are kept in separate compartments to prevent them tearing each other apart' (1995: 73), but his reading only draws a parallel between the combative animals and the two sides of the Civil War conflict. Through cinematography, editing and *mise en scène*, the caged ferrets image resonates throughout the film's portrait of Paco and José, conveying the similarities and rivalries between these two ageing male characters.

Mirrors are also used to link them. For instance, as the group prepares for the hunt, we see José open the drinks-box to check its contents in the left side of the frame. Paco is positioned in the right of the frame facing his friend, and between them is the large mirror set in the lid of the drinks-box. The image of José in the mirror matches the image of Paco located behind it and implies that the two characters are mirror-images of one another. This mirror-image conceit is used again to indicate equivalence when the two men argue after Paco refuses José's request for a loan. Both characters stare at the camera straight on in close-up, as if the camera itself were a mirror, and the images of the two men's faces are cross-cut ten times. Diegetically, we understand that the characters are staring at one another, thus the sequence implies that each character contemplates not his mirror-image, but the face of the other.

Rather than mirror-images, the other two older male characters in the film – Luis, part of the original military foursome, and Juan, the exploited, impoverished gamekeeper who looks after José's land played by Fernando Sánchez Pollack – are projections of José and Paco's fears of ageing. Luis's weakness and clumsiness are caused by alcoholism, but when he falls off a donkey in a rare moment of horse-play early in the film, José does not tease him about his inadequate manhood, which one might expect in a context where the ability to dominate animals would be considered a marker of masculinity.[16] He reproaches him instead for his ageing: 'eres más joven que yo y estás completamente acabado' (you're younger than I am and you're completely finished). Likewise, Juan functions as a manifestation of this fear of ageing. The script specifies that 'tendrá cincuenta años, pero parece más viejo. Los rasgos de su cara son secos y recios. Tiene la piel surcada de arrugas, reticulada y renegrida del sol y de la intemperie' (he is about fifty years old, but looks older. His facial features are pronounced and shrivelled. His skin is furrowed by wrinkles, crunched up and blackened by the sun and the elements) (Saura and Fons 1965: 36), a description that Sánchez Pollack's physique. Juan also projects Paco's fear of physical disability: 'no soporto los tullidos' (I can't stand cripples), he complains, 'me dan escalofríos. Prefiero morirme antes de quedarme cojo o manco. Además, dan mala suerte' (they give me the creeps. I'd rather die than be lame or lose an arm. Also, they bring bad luck). Finally, the absent Arturo casts a shadow over Paco and José's lives, as his suicide signals their own fear of death.

Through this exploration of ageing and anxiety over ageing, Saura exposes what official discourse attempted to disguise in the '25 años de paz' celebrations: the decline of a dictator and a dictatorship that had outlived its time. *Franco, ese hombre* may be seen as an attempt to disguise this anachronism. The title promises an insight into the life of Franco the 'man', but the demonstrative adjective 'ese' indicates its respectful distance: he is 'ese' (that), not 'este' (this), man. Only the start and end of the 96-minute film show the Franco of 1964; the biography is mainly a predictable, triumphalist romp through Spanish history of the twentieth century. It is telling that Franco's youth is emphasised, his early promotions stressed by the voice-over narrator with reminders such as 'una vez más se repite la constante de ser el más joven en este empleo' (once again the ever-present theme of his being the youngest in this job is repeated). This is an attempt to link him to the youthful soldiers of the military parade at the beginning of the film, who are described as 'hombres jóvenes – los hijos y nietos de los que, bajo el mando de este mismo Caudillo, conquistaron el porvenir de España' (young men – the sons and grandsons of those who, under the command of this same Caudillo, conquered the future of Spain). The film culminates with an interview with the revered figure himself, whose pre-prepared monologue features familiar references to the Civil War as a 'Cruzada' (Crusade), and Spain's high mission as 'la reserva espiritual de Europa' (the spiritual reserve of Europe), and addresses the young once again with a plea that they should recognise that 'el progreso de la patria se alcanza con las aportaciones de las sucesivas generaciones' (the progress of the country is achieved through the contributions of subsequent generations). No matter how deferential the interviewer, or sympathetic the lighting, camera angle and distance, the dictator now appears an out-of-touch old man.

Saura's film includes a fascinating reference to a similar attempt to disguise old age through manipulating representation. Enrique's snapshot of the hunting party with the spoils of the morning's rabbit hunt has become representative of the whole film; the still is reproduced as an illustration in published commentaries (D'Lugo 1991: 62; Sánchez Vidal 1988: 40) and it is one of the three chosen for Saura's official website, over which the director presumably has authorial control.[17] This photograph is a reference to masculinist hunting and military iconography. It recalls portraits of Franco himself, and may even directly refer to the images of the dictator posing with fish and game caught in the pursuit of his favourite hobbies in the credits and at minute 90 of *Franco, ese hombre*. Its general purpose, as Guy Wood has pointed out, is to caricature the kind of hunting images that abounded in the period:

> este fotograma . . . es una genial parodia de las 'proezas' constatadas por la iconografía cinegética 'oficial' y encierra un fin propicatorio [*sic*] mucho más sutil. Tenía que haber calado muy hondo en la psique de los espectadores a mediados de los sesenta, público que habría visto y estaría harto de ver poses casi idénticas e igualmente vanas del Jefe del Estado y sus sicofantes después de sus cacerias [*sic*] en los NO-DO o en la prensa, imágenes con que la maquinaria propagandística franquista intentaba la captura ideológica masiva del pueblo. (this still . . . is a brilliant parody of the 'exploits' paraded in 'official' hunting iconography and has a far more subtle propitiatory purpose. It must have had a very deep impact on the psyche of spectators in the mid-1960s, an audience that who would have seen and been fed up of seeing almost identical and equally vain poses of the Head of State and his sycophants after their hunting expeditions in the NO-DO and the press, images with which the Francoist propaganda machine tried ideologically to imprison the people on a massive scale.) (1999: 363–4)

The parody is carried out in *La caza* by exposing the artifice of the shot. The four men strike pompous poses – particularly Paco, who puffs out his chest and straightens his back to gain a few inches in height.[18] But their exhaustion and hotness, made visible through the sweat beaded on their brows and soaking through their shirts, debunk the triumphalist visual rhetoric to suggest that this photograph is just a cover for the crisis of masculinity and ageing beneath.

La caza exaggerates age in order to critique ageing. On the one hand, the middle-aged actors portray old age, and on the other, twenty-three-year-old Gutiérrez Caba's Enrique acts like a child. Middle age, old age and fear of old age mark a new departure for Saura in his third feature, but these are preoccupations to which he returns, for instance in Antonio's anxieties about age in *Carmen* (1983), and the experience of old age in *Goya en Burdeos* (*Goya in Bordeaux* 1999). Adolescence, or coming of age, was an interest explored in Saura's first film, *Los golfos* (1959), although this is carried out in a manner more in keeping with the 'angry young man' theme of contemporary New Wave cinemas (Delgado 1999: 41–2). Saura's infantilisation of Enrique, the young man of *La caza*, in fact looks forward to his exploration of adults behaving as children later in his work. In *Stress es tres, tres* (1968), for instance, he explores, in his words, the world of 'tres adultos que se portan como adolescentes' (three adults who behave like teenagers) (quoted in Sánchez Vidal 1988: 60); *La madriguera* (*The Warren* 1969) also investigates the consequences of childhood games played out in an adult context; and both *Stress es tres, tres* and *Peppermint frappé* investigate 'el problema . . . del sexo inmaduro en el mundo de pretendida adultez profesional' (the problem . . . of an immature attitude to sex in a world of supposed professional maturity) (Sánchez Vidal 1988: 60).

Enrique works with Paco and his father, and he is characterised as a child of the winners. We learn over the course of the film that his father owns land, a factory and the jeep, and that he has lent Enrique his German gun, which implies that he participated, along with Luis, in the Blue Division. The portrayal of Enrique's relations with the older group of men in *La caza* is typical of generational conflict: the other men had fought in the war and Enrique had not. But this is not just a case of what is rather fondly evoked as 'Loca juventud' (Crazy Youth) in the title of one of the pop songs (by Huerta Navarro) played on the men's flashy new radio. This conflict is pushed to extremes by emphasising the old age of the middle-aged men, and infantilising Enrique, the youth.

At the start of the film Enrique commands no interest – in terms of cinematography he never occupies the frame alone, attracts no close-ups or point-of-view shots, and his face is actually obscured in our first view of him by the vizor of his cap. At first he uses the polite second-person 'usted' form to address the older men, and throughout the film is referred to by Luis as 'muchacho' (boy) and by Paco with the diminutive 'Quique'. There is a visual and acoustic parallel between Paco periodically slapping Enrique on the back and calling him 'Quique', and José patting his dog and cooing its name, 'Cuca'. D'Lugo has emphasised the growing importance of Enrique's role as the viewer's figure of identification, or 'on-screen observer', later in the film (1991: 60–6). The first point-of-view shot is Paco's, the second is José's, as he observes a couple arrive in the café, then most belong to Enrique. But these point-of-view shots indicate the inquisitiveness of a child, rather than a masterful control of the gaze. For instance, when Enrique first picks up the gun and we share his point-of-view as he scans the landscape through the sight, we hear him make the sound '¡pío, pío!' (bang, bang!) as if he were playing a childhood game.

Saura and Angelino Fons's script specifies that Enrique has a 'rostro . . . algo aniñado' (slightly childish face) (1965: 4) and make his clothes a point of interest too: he is to wear a jacket that is too small (1965: 4), like a child who has outgrown his clothes. In the film as it stands, the tight jacket has been replaced by a pair of extra-short shorts that similarly infantilise him. Saura emphasises this point when the camera tilts down after the scene at the village bakery to take in two small boys wearing identical short trousers. Here we see a man dressed as a child, just as, in terms of characterisation, we have a child in an adult's body. Saura is wrong, or forgetful, when he says in an interview of 1996 of his *La prima Angélica* (*Cousin Angélica* 1973) that 'it is the first time in cinema that an adult adopts, let's say, the form of a child and acts like a child' (Castro 2003: 129). The adult Enrique dressed as a child in *La caza* is an example of what we may term generational trans-vestism, of which there are other instances in the NCE. For instance, in Picazo's *La tía Tula* (1964) (Chapter 4), the adult Ramiro wears a bib, simi-larly indicating his emasculation and infantilisation.

Through its focus on the extremes of age, *La caza* circles around a void, which becomes an absence that is always present: manhood in its prime. Significantly, this was Saura's time of life: he shot the film in 1965 when he was thirty-three. This is a state for which the older men are nostalgic and which the younger man cannot reach. This absence points to the void at the heart of Franco's patriarchy. If the ageing and fear of ageing of the three war comrades signal the decrepitude of a regime in its twenty-sixth year and a dictator in his seventy-third, the infantilising treatment of youth indicates a new generation ill-equipped to bring about change and assume adult responsibility.

'Idle Periods': Time, Space, Body

La caza is therefore metaphorical cinema as it criticises the regime indi-rectly through its narrative. But an analysis of the narrative alone, like the excessive focus on the rabbit hunt sequences, still leads to only a partial interpretation of the film. The reading of *La caza* carried out thus far has shown that Saura uses a conventional film narrative of coherent character-isation and linear plot to expose and critique anxieties about ageing that characterised 1960s Spain. This is violently interrupted by the hunt sequences, which establish an important critical distance between the viewer and the narrative. But the progress of the plot is also arrested through 'idle periods', a term used by Deleuze to describe pauses in a film that are not justified in narrative terms.[19] Like the rabbit hunt sequences, these also interrupt the fictional narrative, but unlike those hunt sequences, which reach the viewer through the gut because they launch an assault on our emotions, these idle periods reach the viewer through the mind because they question our knowledge of time, space and the body. There are a number of de-naturalising moments in *La caza*, which function as minor interruptions to the conventional narrative: the two instances where characters speak directly to the camera; the montage sequence when the guns are loaded, which is edited so that the men appear to point the guns at each other; the midday snapshot of the four men with their hunting trophies and the freeze-frame shot of Enrique at the end of the picture. I will focus here on the unsettling pause that takes place half-way through the narrative – actually 54 minutes into the 83-minute film – the siesta sequence.

This sequence may at first seem justified diegetically, as it is culturally: the two older men take a nap after lunch on a hot day. We might consider it in relation to the film's characterisation. Paco and José's siesta is an indicator of class and age – the downtrodden Juan must work, we presume, not sleep, and the younger Enrique and Luis don't bother with a snooze. It is a nice detail of context that in the early 1960s Franco himself began to depend on a daily nap (Preston 1993: 700). The siesta sequence of *La caza* therefore debunks, succinctly and effectively, the rhetoric of virile masculinity that reaches its climax in Saura's portrayal of the snapshot of the hunters/warriors with their spoils. In a Western cultural context in which the reclining, sleeping or dead human form is overwhelmingly figured as female, as Elisabeth Bronfen has demonstrated in *Over Her Dead Body* (1993), the focus on these dozing old men, like grotesque 'sleeping beauties', is particularly startling. Saura draws our attention to preceding traditions of the gendering of the passive human form by juxtaposing his slow pan over the two men's bodies from left to right in the siesta sequence with a point-of-view shot of Enrique's fetishising gaze drifting, this time from right to left, across the similarly reclining body of a blonde model in one his girlie magazines.[20] Thus Saura parodies his ex-soldier hunters not only by depicting them in a period of inactivity – which is remarkable in itself in a film about ex-soldiers on a rabbit hunt – but also by portraying them using the fetishising conventions of pornography. The passive, sleeping bodies of Paco and José reveal their weakness and ageing, and the stillness of their forms looks forward to their ultimate inertia, at the end of the film, in death.

During the siesta sequence we are afforded an insight into Paco's and José's dreams through voice-over, which also confirms the characterisation of the two men constructed thus far in the film. Paco's reverie contains a dream within a dream. His son recounts his nightmare of being killed by dogs,[21] to which his father responds with a condescending lament about the younger generations, and then a comparison between his son's upbringing and his own: 'les enseñan cuatro cosas. No hacen nada en todo el día y sueñan con perros. Si se hubiera criado como yo . . .' (They hardly teach them anything. They do nothing all day and then they dream about dogs. If he'd been brought up like me . . .). José's dream, meanwhile, reveals his anxiety over his emotional and physical failings. His separation from his wife is evoked through an argument with her, and his failing body is alluded to through her accusation: 'te has envenenado: tienes la piel vieja y seca' (you've poisoned yourself: your skin is old and dry).

However, the siesta sequence in *La caza* is unsettling in ways that transcend its role within the narrative. Its experimental filmic depiction wrenches it from the register of the everyday – the nap after lunch to aid digestion and avoid the sun – and from its place in the story – the necessary period of rest during a hot day out hunting. No special effects or change of location here (the budget of two million pesetas[22] would have permitted neither): using exactly the same actors and location, experimentation occurs by reversing the relation between plot development and its filmic portrayal. In other words, while in the narrative sections film form advances plot and underpins characterisation, in the siesta sequence narrative is suspended and form is all. It is one example of a number of formally disruptive moments highlighted by Carlos Heredero in his study of the aesthetics of the NCE, 'cuya inclusión se desentiende de los nexos espaciales y causales hasta escapar de toda referencialidad o vinculación representacional, hasta convertirse en meros iconos de cerrada función expresiva' (the inclusion of which bring about a detachment from spatial and causal bounds to the point of escaping all modes of reference or representational connections and of becoming pure icons with a restricted expressive function) (2003: 152).[23] The experimental formal presentation of the siesta sequence is not, therefore, used only to create an oneiric atmosphere, as Sánchez Vidal suggests (1988: 48), because the dreams are linked to narrative and characterisation, and they only form part of the second shot. The formal representation of this 'idle period' is rather to transcend narrative and challenge the viewer's perception of time, space and the body.

Manuel Villegas López argued that in sequences such as this:

El tiempo es una imagen y la imagen no tiene tiempo. Se ha pasado del propósito de narrar al propósito de expresar, y es la expresión y no la narración lo que da su profunda y definitiva unidad al film. (Time is an image and the image has no time. There has been a move away from the desire to narrate to the desire to express, and it is expression not narration that gives the film a profound and definitive unity.) (1967: 66)

This observation anticipates Deleuze's work on the 'time-image', as Heredero has pointed out (2003: 141). Deleuze's account of the shift from the 'movement-image' to the 'time-image' offers a way of thinking through the implications of the switch between narrative and experimental sections of *La caza*. Sánchez Vidal's observation that the film is 'un relato lineal y de corte realista, "a la americana"' (a linear, realist story told 'in an American way') (1988: 46) – which echoes M. Marinero's observation that it drew on the American thriller (1967: 145) – may be developed if we consider the narrative sections of *La caza* as cinema of the 'movement-image', which corresponds in Deleuze's work to 'classical' film, or pre-Second World War American cinema, particularly the Hollywood genre film. In the 'movement-image' sections of *La caza* time and space are subordinate to action: the plot unfolds through linear succession in the present tense, and space becomes the specific place of the hunting ground and old Civil War battlefield owned by José. Consequently, the characters are bound by the action of the plot, and we appreciate their ageing through the plot, even if it is exaggerated and reinforced by its filmic portrayal.

Deleuze contends that a crisis in the 'movement-image' occurred in post-Second World War cinema because the nature of experience in this period so radically altered that a brand-new mode of cinematic expression was necessary to represent it (1997: 210–11). This is the 'time-image', by which Deleuze means post-war 'modern' film, such as Neorealism and the French New Wave (Spanish cinema is not mentioned), in which time and space are no longer subordinate to action. Time, in this type of cinema, may thus transcend the tyranny of the present and space may become indeterminate and strange. Characters are no longer bound by action, so ageing, in the siesta sequence of *La caza*, is conveyed uniquely through film form. This sequence of *La caza* might be considered a 'time-image', though it is important to stress that this sequence lies embedded in a film of 'movement-images'. Saura's *La caza* shows that both classic, narrative 'movement-image' cinema, and modern, experimental 'time-image' cinema are capable of portraying and critiquing a modern world.[24]

If we examine the two sequences at the opening and end of the film that concern the relationship between character and space, the difference between the 'movement-image' and 'time-image', and Saura's use of both, are clear. In the first, we see Paco driving the jeep along a highway through the Castilian plain. The narrative begins when he drives into the foreground of the camera's range; therefore, this specific jeep is singled out for us as the subject of the film from the anonymous vehicles that pass along the road. The jeep continues to approach the camera, there is a hidden cut, then, in medium shot, we see Paco park and get out of the car. A tracking shot, still at medium distance, follows him as he walks away from the car to look at the view, while he polishes the lenses of his sunglasses. We then share the first point-of-view shot of the film with him as he surveys the skyline. In medium shot we see his eyes move from left to right, then Saura cuts to an eye-line match point-of-view shot that scans the landscape in the same direction.[25] This is a good example of how, in the 'movement-image', space is transformed into a specific place in relation to plot. Through the point-of-view shot, this indeterminate space, crossed by an unspecified highway, becomes the specific place where the day's hunting will occur. Moreover, Paco's visual ownership of that place through subjective cinematography introduces the conflict with José that will drive the plot forward, for José is the legal owner of that same place.

The final shot of the film focuses on the same landscape. Enrique has run away from the theatre of violence up the valley side. But no controlling point-of-view shot is offered here. Rather, he is trapped in the frame surrounded by the landscape, as his panting continues on the soundtrack for a lengthy 10 seconds. Critics have previously interpreted this image allegorically: either in a negative sense, whereby Enrique stands for the young generation trapped by the hatred and violence of the older one (Kinder 1993: 165; Wood 1999: 369); or a positive one, according to which Enrique represents a generation that has succeeded in running away from these murderous rivalries of the former (Millar 1975: 236).[26] But if we consider it as a 'time-image', its meaning is more profound. The shot indicates man trapped by time: both the vertiginous rush from past to future (the panting on the soundtrack) and the terrifying stasis of the present (the freeze-frame).

The siesta sequence lasts 2 minutes and consists of two extreme long takes, one of 44 seconds and one of 73. In the first, Cuadrado's camera slowly sweeps from left to right and moves down, in extreme long shot, across the arid landscape of the Castilian valley from a point high up the valley side. This space is not linked to the narrative as in the 'movement-image' because this shot is not, as D'Lugo claims (1991: 65), the point-of-view of one of the characters. There is a cut to an extreme close-up of the radio, which is the starting point of another pan, again from left to right, along the sleeping forms of Paco and José in continued extreme close-up.[27] There is a jarring contrast between these two shots in terms of proximity to subject – extreme long shot cuts to extreme close-up – yet similarity in terms of camera movement and length of take. At the end of the pan over the men's bodies, the camera rests on José's right eye, which cuts horizontally across the screen, because he is lying down and the camera is upright. His eye opens and through a point-of-view shot we share his view of Enrique in the distance; there follows the point-of-view shot where Enrique spies on the double-page spread of the magazine model. These two point-of-view shots mark the end of the siesta sequence and a return to the narrative. On the soundtrack, during the first shot, the faint sound of the music the group were listening to on the radio is gradually drowned out by the monotonous clicking of the cicadas. This forms a soundbridge to the second shot. The cicadas are audible in the background as we hear the voices of Paco and his son in the first dream. These voices fade out to the clicking sound, then we finally hear the voices of José and his estranged wife in the second dream.

Unlike Deleuze's cinema of the 'movement-image', there is no action motivated by the narrative here, nor is there movement in terms of plot. Although the camera moves physically, it is not for the sake of narrative. In the 'movement-image', movement usually occurs, in any case, through montage (Deleuze 1997: 29). The 'time-image' opens up time through tracking shots and depth-of-field (Deleuze draws examples from Alain Resnais and Luchino Visconti for the former, and Orson Welles for the latter [1994: 39]), and for both of these shots the long take is necessary.[28] Deleuze (whose writing on cinema can be at once evasive and engaging, frustrating and fascinating) is characteristically vague on the exact nature of the treatment of time in the 'time-image'; however, its fragmentation, or stratification, is key. His use of the term 'crystal-image' is more helpful, as it indicates this textured temporal quality: 'What the crystal reveals or makes visible is the hidden ground of time, that is, the differentiation into two flows, that of presents which pass and that of pasts which are preserved' (Deleuze 1994: 98). Jacques Aumont, who quotes this passage, summarises this as 'temporal collage' (1997: 183).

The notions of the 'crystal-image', in Deleuze's terminology, or 'temporal collage', in Aumont's, throw light on Saura's treatment of time in the two long takes of the siesta sequence. We are no longer in the present tense of the narrative sections of the film. The extremely long takes emphasise the passage of time, making it both expand into synchronous 'presents which pass', and contract into diachronic 'pasts which are preserved'. In the first shot, the slowness of movement on the imagetrack, and the monotonous rhythm of the cicadas on the soundtrack, expand time to the point that it stands still. Long takes, intense heat and the drone of the insects are similarly used in Peter Weir's *Picnic at Hanging Rock* (1975) (a film not mentioned by Deleuze). In both Saura's and Weir's films, the landscape takes on a hypnotic, static quality, which points to the timelessness of the physical environment, whose monumentality, compared to man's ephemerality, seems overwhelming. On the other hand, that same shot contracts time, and the landscape becomes, in Santos Zunzunegui's

words, a 'lugar de sedimentación del pasado' (place where the past is sed-
imented) (2003: 416). With the heightened sensitivity to the image that the
long take brings about, this shot becomes a 'temporal collage'. We see not
only the human time of the twentieth century, when the valley witnessed
the Civil War, and left its trace in the form of bunkers (as Zunzunegui
points out [2003: 416]) but also geological time, when the rock developed
into its present formation, and a river, now no more than a stagnant pool,
carved out the valley itself.

The second shot, which is both similar, through camera movement,
length of take and the sound of the cicadas, yet different, through the distance between the viewer and the object viewed, also performs this con-
traction of time. In the 'movement-image', the body is most often
represented in action, and its movement is paralleled by the progressive
succession of shots in montage. This is reversed here. The body is static
and the camera slowly moves in a long take. Just as the landscape reveals
the strata of time in the first shot, so the body acts as an index of time in
the second. Though referring to the cinema of Antonioni, the following
passage from *The Time-Image* evokes with accuracy this sequence: 'The
body is no longer exactly what moves; subject of movement or the instrument of action [as it is in the 'movement-image'], it becomes rather the
developer [*révélateur*] of time, it shows time through its tiredness and
waiting' (Deleuze 1994: xi). The two bodies presented to us by Saura in
this second shot thus 'reveal' or 'develop' time through their agedness:
each wrinkle encodes passing human time, like each fold of the rocks in the
landscape indicates geological time. The scar on Mayo's upper left arm
recalls the bunkers we see on the hillside. We presume it is a war wound,
like the one José complains of, so the scar, like the bunkers, is the trace that
remains in space of a human event in time.

In this second shot, the human body fills the frame through excessive
close-up just as the landscape fills it through excessive distance in the first,
and the slow, tracking movement is the same in each. Here, Saura is experi-
menting with the equalising role of the screen as frame. Deleuze, writing
at this point on the 'movement-image', observes that

> the screen, as the frame of frames, gives a common standard of measurement to
> things which do not have one – long shots of countryside and close-ups of the face,
> an astronomical system and a single drop of water – parts which do not have the same
> denominator of distance, relief or light. (Deleuze 1997: 14–15)

But these effects of 'Gulliverisation' and 'Lilliputisation', to quote Philippe
Dubois (Aumont 1997: 103), are more than just a curiosity of the cinematic
medium. For, if emphasised, their impact on the viewer may be profoundly

unsettling. Saura exaggerates scale in the siesta sequence shots and shows that, in Deleuze's words, 'the cinema can, with impunity, bring us close to things or take us away from them and revolve around them, it suppresses both the anchoring of the subject and the horizon of the world' (1997: 57).

Following Deleuze, we may conclude that the siesta sequence is unsettling because it disrupts time and space, and thus questions the viewer's extra-cinematic knowledge and expectation of each acquired through his or her own perception of 'the horizon of the world'. Time no longer unfolds in a linear manner in the present tense, but is fractured and evokes present and past simultaneously. Space is no longer a specific place explained by the plot, and our relationship to it is no longer stabilised through the point-of-view shots of a protagonist. Finally, our location within space is also disrupted by the radical shifts of extreme distance to extreme proximity. All these elements 'suppress', in Deleuze's words, 'the anchoring' of the viewing subject.

That Saura chooses to portray the human body in extreme close-up is of course especially significant. The over-proximity of this shot renders the body unsettling: simultaneously familiar, yet strange, in the manner of the Freudian *Unheimlich*. This shot denies the humanist urge, satisfied by narrative cinema, to link the human form on screen to character and make it a vehicle for narrative. In the siesta sequence, the portrayal of Paco and José by Mayo and Merlo is incidental. Neither actor nor character counts, only the materiality of their bodies – robbed of their individuality through over-proximity – matters. Butler's insights into the materiality of the body in *Bodies that Matter* (1993) are therefore instructive here, although our concern is with age rather than sex. Butler draws a distinction between the material 'facts' about a body that are 'primary and irrefutable' – for 'bodies live and die; eat and sleep; feel pain, pleasure; endure illness and violence' – and the affirmation of those 'facts' within discourse: 'their irrefutability in no way implies what it might mean to affirm them and through what discursive means' (1993: xi). Thus, Butler proceeds to show that 'sexual difference [is materialised] in the service of the heterosexual imperative'. In other words, the sexed body is made to 'matter' or made 'intelligible' through its location within the hegemonical discourse of heterosexuality. Discourse, therefore, has 'the power . . . to enact what it names' (1993: 187). If we consider *La caza* within Butler's framework, the body in question is not so much one that signifies sexual difference, as one that signifies ageing. The ideological matrix that gives those bodies meaning, or makes them 'matter', is Francoism. Its discourses of triumphalism and patriarchy are crucial to characterisation in the narrative sections of the film. Paco's beliefs, for instance, lead to his sense of self-worth, and those beliefs hinge on a fascist exaltation of the healthy, male body. Even though, as I discuss above, the narrative itself offers a critique of those discourses, especially through the similarities revealed between Paco and José, the siesta sequence takes the critique further. It wrests those bodies from the discursive constructs that give them meaning, from the constructs that both signify them and give them significance. For example, within the narrative, war wounds are a marker of virile heroism and military glory, but in the new 'arrangements' thrown up by the 'time-image' they are just scars. In the non-narrative siesta sequence these bodies are laid bare, as it were, before us: scarred, weak, suffering and ageing.

The radical equivalence between body and landscape implied through these two shots also deserves comment.[29] In 1958, Saura described his intention to create such a parallel. The passage reveals the consistency between Saura's vision and its realisation seven years on:

> Intentaría un cine brutal, primitivo en sus personajes, un cine para rodar en la Serranía de Cuenca, en Castilla, en los Monegros, en los pueblos de Guadalajara, Teruel . . . allí donde el hombre y la tierra se identifican formando un todo. Seguramente sería un cine no conformista – aquí estaría lo aragonés – directo, sencillo de forma y muy real. Real en la valoración de las pequeñas superficies: la piel, el tejido, la tierra, las gotas de sudor . . . (I would try to make a brutal cinema, with primitive characterisation, a cinema to be shot in the mountains of Cuenca, in Castile, in Los Monegros, in the villages of Guadalajara, Teruel . . . those places where man and land are inter-connected and form a whole. No doubt it would be a non-conformist cinema – that would be what was Aragonese about it – direct, simple in form and very real. Real in the way small surfaces would be valued: skin, textiles, earth, beads of sweat . . .) (Sánchez Vidal 1988: 24)

The list with which this quotation ends reminds us of the levelling effect achieved through the two shots. In formal terms – and, as I have argued, in the siesta sequence, form is all – body and land are equal. This levelling effect has quite startling implications: the landscape is personified, and the human body is, simultaneously, reified. While the former may be an anthropomorphic gesture familiar to us from poetry,[30] the latter has a terrifying effect of objectification. The human form becomes no more than inert matter, and Job's 'All flesh shall perish together, and man shall turn again unto dust' (34: 15), is enacted through the living body before our eyes.[31]

This chapter is divided into three sections, which correspond to the three distinct elements of *La caza*. This division is intended to highlight the important differences and changes in the film between the narrative and non-narrative sections, but it may also suggest that *La caza* is fragmentary.

On the one hand, the tripartite structure of this chapter may be challenged by affirming that coherence is maintained in the film through the strong linear narrative (we know the men are on a day out hunting rabbits when we see the hunt sequences) and continuity of space and actors (we know Paco and José have a siesta after lunch at the camp). On the other, we may defend this structure by proposing that the disjointed nature of the film is precisely the point. The violent interruptions of the narrative caused by the hunt sequences reinforce the viewer's distance from that narrative, and encourage his or her scrutiny of its critique of 1960s Spain. Through this narrative, *La caza* launches an assault on fading Francoism by probing the questions of ageing and coming of age, and to ignore this context is to betray the period in which the film was made. However, Saura's feature also moves beyond politics to question the viewer and his or her experience of self and world in a particularly profound way. In the siesta sequence, the 'unanchoring' (to use Deleuze's term) of the viewing subject through experimentation with time, space and the representation of the body, brings about a violent interruption to the narrative as the hunt sequences do, though in a very different way. Here the violence is not experienced at the level of emotion – we physically wince as we hear the rabbits squeal and see them die in the documentary footage of a real hunt – but at the level of perception – the excessive distance and proximity of the landscape and body in the siesta sequence, and the disturbing parallel implied between the two, disrupt our knowledge of time and space. The film therefore scrutinises our emotional experience of violence, our conceptual experience of ageing and our perceptual experience of our environment through the body and the co-ordinates of time and space. The latter, in particular, is dependent on Saura and Cuadrado's use of film form in *La caza*, the importance of which is implied by Gutiérrez Aragón's reference to its 'well-worked language'.

Notes

1. The sexually suggestive original title *La caza de conejos* (*The Rabbit Hunt*) was shortened, and the words 'guerra civil' (Civil War) were replaced by 'guerra', changes that rendered the film's meaning more open.
2. M. Marinero's review in *Film Ideal* is entirely laudatory, however, citing the director's 'maturity' and the 'exceptional' nature of the film (1967: 145).
3. I take this translation from Hopewell (1986: 72).
4. In recent interviews, Saura has been keen to emphasise Mayo's contribution to these early stages of the project, which cannot be acknowledged in the film's credits (Julián 2002: 68; Gómez 2003: 363).

5. In the interview included on the DVD version of the film, released as part of the *El País* 'Un País de Cine' collection in March 2003, Saura mentions that ten or eleven producers rejected it. Querejeta mastered the system of the double-script: one was presented to the censors and the original one was shot anyway. He got away with it as the films made with Saura enjoyed such prestige abroad: 'no sooner would a serious problem come up than we would mobilise our contacts in France and Germany so that they would protest . . .. That often helped to free a film blocked by a censor. Nothing scared the Francoist regime more that what was said of it outside Spain' (Saura, quoted in Hopewell 1986: 134–5, 256–7 n. 5).

6. My thanks to Chris Perriam, who suggested I look at Deleuze and Peter Weir, and to Julián Gutiérrez-Albilla, who pointed out the relevance of Butler's study to my work. On gender and masculinity in Spanish cinema, see, for example, Perriam (2003).

7. There are other studies of ageing in the NCE, like Manuel Summer's documentary of bygone heroes, *Juguetes rotos* (*Broken Toys* 1966).

8. Guy Wood notes, with reference to Miguel Delibes's *El libro de caza menor*, that the level of detail in the hunt sequences reveals Saura's knowledge of hunting (1999: 371 n. 10).

9. Fraga writes in his memoirs of Franco's evident ageing when he saw him deliver the speech that marked the end of the '25 años de paz' celebrations (Preston 1993: 715).

10. *La caza* was made in the year that the student union (SEU) was abolished (Grugel and Rees 1997: 92–3).

11. This grotesque fascist mausoleum, constructed by Republican prisoners of war and resting place of both José Antonio Primo de Rivera (the founder of the Spanish fascist party) and now Franco, looms over the city of Madrid from the mountains in the north-west. The future of this monument is under discussion in Spain today.

12. See Preston's example of Fraga and Laureano López Rodó's interventions on Franco's end of year broadcast on 30 December 1962 (1993: 706).

13. In any case, recent readings of these films reveal that their gender dynamics are more complex than hitherto supposed. On *Raza*, see Triana-Toribio (2000) and Martin-Márquez (1999: 89–96); on *¡Harka!*, Evans (1995: 218–19).

14. Interview, *La caza*, 'Un País de Cine' DVD.

15. At script stage, the image of the caged ferrets was to be the final sequence of the film (Saura and Fons 1965: 152).

16. Saura's *Los golfos* dramatised this. As María Delgado notes, '[Juan's] domination of the bull offers an expression of disciplined masculinity' (1999, 43).

17. See http://www.clubcultura.com/clubcine/clubcineastas/saura/peli-caza. htm. Consulted 24 March 2004.

18. The script specifies that Paco should walk with a straightened back, 'para disimular el vientre' (to hide his stomach) (1965: 2).

19. Deleuze notes regarding such a pause in Vittorio De Sica's *Bicycle Thief* (1948): 'there is no longer a vector or line of the universe that extends and links up events . . . the rain can always interrupt or deflect the search fortuitously . . .. The Italian rain becomes the sign of idle periods and of possible interruption' (Deleuze 1997: 212). In *La caza*, Spanish midday sun plays a similar role to Italian rain.

20. Zunzunegui has pointed out that Saura's treatment of femininity in *La caza* looks forward to his exploration of eroticism in his immediately subsequent filmography (2003: 415).

21. Like Rita, who dreams of a big, black bull entering her bedroom to figure Jaime's quasi-rape of the nun in *Viridiana* (Buñuel 1961), so in *La caza* a child's dream encodes adult actions, for Paco will be killed, not by dogs, but by José.

22. Saura, interview, *La caza*, 'Un País de Cine' DVD.

23. Heredero also interprets the skinning of the rabbit and the burning of the mannequin as disruptive (2003: 152), but their comparative brevity and clear function within the narrative (Juan and Carmen are preparing the paella; Luis and Enrique are building a fire) make them less significant than the siesta sequence.

24. The application of the concepts of the 'movement-image' and 'time-image' to this film would seem to expose the rudimentary nature of Deleuze's division. As Donato Totaro points out, the 'polarity of action-image/American and time-image/European is not that clear cut' (1999: 7). Directors who belong to the period of the 'movement-image', like Max Ophüls and Orson Welles, are celebrated as great cineastes of the 'time-image' (Totaro 1999: 7). Moreover, key notions, such as the opposition of indeterminate space versus specific place and the 'idle period', are actually discussed in both realms. Indeterminate 'any-space-whatevers', for instance, are included as a dimension of the 'movement-image' (Deleuze 1997: Chapter 7), as are 'idle periods'. Cinema of the 'movement-image', Deleuze notes, values 'episodes outside the action, or in idle periods between actions' (1997: 205).

25. This point-of-view shot initially encourages us to identify with Paco: he is the active agent of the narrative because he drives the jeep, and the active controller of the gaze, through subjective cinematography, and his association with the gaze is reinforced by the detail of him polishing his sunglasses. However, the film recounts the diminution of his narrative agency and of his control of the gaze. We are encouraged to identify with Antonio at the start of *Carmen* (1983) in exactly the same way, through a point-of-view shot and an eye-line match as he surveys the dancers in the pre-credit sequence. Antonio, like Paco, loses narrative agency and control of the gaze and his ageing is likewise exposed.

26. 'Only the young man is spared the onus of the past', writes Peter Besas (1985: 120), a point D'Lugo refutes when he argues that in the last shot, Enrique has lost his 'innocence' and must acknowledge 'the history he had previously

refused to identify as his own' (1991: 66). In the script, Enrique ends up symbolically trapped – he catches his foot in one of the animal traps as he runs away – and injured – when he finally gets the trap off he is left limping, which signals his future exploitation like the lame Juan (Saura and Fons 1965: 149).

27. These extremes of distance and proximity were made possible by using a macrokilar lens. Normally associated with advertising in the period, this lens, in Cuadrado's words, 'permitía enfocar desde diez centímetros hasta infinito, pasando por todas las distancias intermedias' (made it possible to focus from ten centimetres to infinity, with all the distances in between) (Bilbatúa et al. 1966: 9).

28. Totaro notes that the 'time-image is not necessarily a cinema governed by long takes – though it can be – but a broader, philosophical separation from movement-image. However, much of what Deleuze says about depth-of-field . . . relates explicitly to the long take' (1999: 8).

29. Zunzunegui points out the difference between these shots in terms of distance (the title of his study is 'Mirada distante, mirada lejana' [Distant Gaze, Faraway Gaze]), and similarity in terms of movement (2003: 417). Length of take and the soundbridge also imply a parallel. He does not explore, however, the effects of these similarities.

30. Consider, for instance, the equivalence implied between female body and land in Pablo Neruda's love poetry (e.g. poem 1 of *Veinte poemas de amor y una canción desesperada* [1996: 9]), or the experience of landscape through the poet's body in Antonio Machado's *Campos de Castilla* (e.g. 'A orillas de Duero', lines 2–11 [1999: 151]).

31. This equivalence between landscape and body may have contributed to Guillermo Carnero's 'Castilla' (1979: 80–1), published in 1967, the year after the film's release – though in correspondence with the author the poet doubts there was any influence. 'No sé hasta dónde se extiende mi cuerpo . . . Tampoco sé hasta dónde se extiende la tierra' (I don't know where my body extends . . . Neither do I know to where the land extends) (lines 1 and 6) evoke the experimentation with scale and length of take in the two shots of the siesta sequence, which also render land and body endless. The shift of focus from extension to entrapment between walls in the second part of the poem also brings to mind the freeze-frame ending of *La caza*. Just as the poet recalls Castile's military past (21–6), Enrique, overwhelmed by a more recent conflict, flees up the valley side to be entrapped by the four walls of the frame. For Carnero, this entrapment indicates future nightmares by the repeated line 'Me han despertado' (I have been awoken) (21 and 24), or living death by the description of 'estos muros lisos como una tumba' (31) (these walls as smooth as a tomb) (translations from Walters 2002: 81–2).

Conclusion: Overlaps

A Cinema of Contradiction seeks to interpret, not survey, Spanish film of the 1960s. Thus while the two examples selected in Part I show that popular cinema of this period may sustain contestatory readings, we must be equally attentive to the construction of conservative discourses in such films. Likewise, the examples of the NCE I analyse in Part II cannot chronicle the evolution of an entire movement, though my selection of four films is intended to show both its diversity, and its shared responses to contradiction.

The key difference between the VCE and the NCE highlighted in this book is that of single and plural authorship. In popular cinema, the voices of producers, directors, actors, scriptwriters, cinematographers, editors, composers and costume designers may clash in creative cacophony, and these clashes sometimes prove propitious in exposing the very ideological contradictions that the conservative contents of the films intended to conceal. Thus in *La gran familia*, producer, director and assistant director may focus on the film's jolly parents and cute kids in order to celebrate large families, but José Isbert seems to follow the same acting directions as the children, becoming a comic but troubling man-child who questions the patriarchal order he is meant to represent. Likewise, editing and cinematography in the urban prologue of *La ciudad no es para mí* casts doubt on its otherwise reactionary ruralism, and Luchy's appearance in its epilogue also contradicts the condemnation of female sexuality recommended elsewhere in the film.

In the NCE too there are both intended and unintended outcomes. On the one hand, these singly-authored films successfully condemn the contradictions of *aperturista* Spain, as was the intention of their auteurist directors. In my examples, directors focus in particular on disparities of wealth (*Los farsantes*), excessive sexual behaviour as a consequence of repression (*La tía Tula*), the attraction and repulsion of national identity (*Nueve cartas a Berta*) and the ineffectuality of both the old and young (*La caza*). But on the other, the NCE itself laboured under contradictions, and the films are shot through with the tensions of this ironic situation. Considering these films as contradictory in terms of both their subject matter and their production contexts leads to a new reading of the NCE as a cinema of critique that operates on a number of levels. *Los farsantes* appears to condemn the popular entertainment on which the film was paradoxically dependent through its VCE producer Ignacio Iquino, but the film also harnesses popular entertainment's appeal to emotional audience identification to effect its political critique. Similarly, the stifling repression of *La tía Tula* may encode the limited creative freedom about which Picazo bitterly complained, but this atmosphere also effectively conveys the stasis of 1960s provincial life. Again, Patino's awkward relations with his cast and crew in *Nueve cartas a Berta* enrich the film's portrayal of Lorenzo's experience of miscomprehension in contemporary Salamanca. Saura's *La caza* has acquired such a mythical status as a work of dissent that it is difficult to peel back the layers of adoration and return it to its context. Although it suffered censorship too, its talented director and plucky producer ensured that this would be one of the few films to break free from the NCE and become part of the much admired pantheon of Spanish auteurist work.

If the conclusion that the NCE came of age with *La caza* is anticipated by the admiring attention already lavished on Saura the auteur, the relations between the VCE and the NCE revealed by this book are not. A consideration of production contexts shows that NCE films like *Los farsantes* were made only thanks to the practical backing of the VCE. Furthermore, the juxtaposition of Parts I and II of this book reveals other overlaps between these two cinemas. For example, the stunning originality of Saura's film has rightly captured critics' attention, but *La caza* could not exist without the VCE. The exploration of male bonding in a military context in Saura's film gains its meaning through its dialogue with the popular cinema, not only through recasting its actors, but also by rerunning its plots. In a fascinating interview with Saura in 1988, Mechthild Zeul suggested to the director that *La caza* was similar to the VCE film of military male comradeship, which similarly features a trio of chums, *Botón de ancla* (*Brass Button* Torrado, 1948) (a remake of which was released in 1961 [*Botón de ancla* Lluch]). This observation is rejected outright by Saura, whose laughter at the idea is recorded in the interview transcription (Zeul 2003: 108), and who states of the comparison that 'Such things give me great anxiety' (Zeul 2003: 109). When Zeul persists, the director's denial of the influence of popular film borders on excess: 'my films are the *total* opposite of those of the 1940s'; 'We didn't consider the films of [Saénz de Heredia or Rafael Gil, etc.] *at all*' (Zeul 2003: 111, 113; emphasis added). I suggest that Saura's laughter and denials try to mask the interdependency between the NCE and the VCE that Zeul uncovers.

The migration of actors between the VCE and the NCE gave a face to this interdependency. Recasting might be dismissed as a matter of crass commercialism – NCE directors cast VCE actors in a bid for audiences – or practical expediency – NCE directors cast VCE actors as there were few to choose from. Critics have tended to argue that NCE directors cast actors like Bautista and Mayo in films such as *La tía Tula* and *La caza* to play roles that were the opposite of their previous parts in popular film. But star studies have taught us that it is no longer sufficient to consider all actors passive objects manipulated by an auteur, and that some may be creative agents in their own right. In *La tía Tula* and *La caza*, these actors' simultaneous evocation and repression of their previous roles are especially effective. This is not to discount Picazo and Saura's thoughtful selection and direction of their cast, but to suggest a more balanced view of recasting as an example of the fruitful cross-fertilisation between popular and art cinemas.

The two parts of this study also reveal the shared conceptual terrain of the NCE and the VCE. To be mentioned in the same line as Fernando Palacios would be risible to Saura, but none the less the juxtaposition of *La gran familia* and *La caza* in this book reveals a shared critique of the ageing dictator, which is carried out through the casting of popular male stars of a similar age. Likewise, both *La ciudad* and *Nueve cartas a Berta* record the allure of the Spanish capital, even though this goes against the critique of Madrid in the first film, and forms part of the condemnation of the provinces in the second. Similarly, the view of the family presented in both *La gran familia* and *La tía Tula* exploits long takes and a static camera to indicate the suffocation of domestic life.

This example of editing and cinematography points to a final area of overlap: technical teams. The specific example of Pedro del Rey's editing in both *La gran familia* and *La tía Tula* indicates a domestic industry where crews and casts were shared between popular films and art alternatives. It is hoped that this analysis will lead to further work on cross-over figures, like Juan Julio Baena, the celebrated cinematographer of the auteurist *Los golfos* and *La tía Tula*, who also worked on the popular cinema of Pedro Lazaga, Luis Lucia and León Klimovsky. The comparisons of the VCE and the NCE offered in this book subject the divisions between popular and art cinemas erected by critics, directors and politicians to scrutiny. What emerges is a picture of Spanish film of the 1960s that is much less tidy, but one that is all the more interesting for its messiness.

Filmography

La gran familia (*The Great Family*, 1962)

Director:	Fernando Palacios
Producer:	Pedro Masó
Production Company:	Pedro Masó P.C.
Scriptwriters:	Pedro Masó; Rafael J. Salvia; Antonio Vich
Director of Photography:	Juan Mariné
Music:	Adolfo Waitzman
Décor:	Antonio Simont
Editor:	Pedro del Rey
Principal Actors:	María José Alfonso (La enamorada); Alberto Closas (Carlos, the father); José Isbert (the grandpa); José Luis López Vázquez (Juan, the godfather); Pedro Mari Sánchez (El petardista); Amparo Soler Leal (Mercedes, the mother)
Running Time:	104 minutes
Release Date:	21 December 1962 (Madrid)

Los farsantes (*Frauds*, 1963)

Director:	Mario Camus
Producer:	Ignacio F. Iquino
Production Company:	I.F.I. España S.A.
Scriptwriters:	Mario Camus; Daniel Sueiro
Director of Photography:	Salvador Torres Garriga
Music:	Enrique Escobar
Décor:	Andres Vallvé
Editor:	Ramón Quadreny
Principal Actors:	Luis Ciges (Justo); Amapola García (Milagros); Fernando León (Rogelio); Angel Lombarte (Avilés); Margarita Lozano (Tina); José Montez (Currito);

	Consuelo de Nieva (Pura); José María Oviés (Don Pancho); Luis Torner (Vicente); Víctor Valverde (Lucio)
Running Time:	82 minutes
Release Date:	Autumn 1963 (Barcelona)

La tía Tula (*Aunt Tula*, 1964)

Director:	Miguel Picazo
Producers:	Ramiro Bermúdez de Castro; Juan Miguel Lamet; José López Moreno; Nino Quevedo
Production Companies:	Eco Films; Surco Films
Scriptwriters:	José Miguel Hernán; Manuel López Yubero; Miguel Picazo; Luis Sánchez Enciso
Director of Photography:	Juan Julio Baena
Music:	Antonio Pérez Olea
Décor:	Luis Argüello
Editor:	Pedro del Rey
Principal Actors:	Aurora Bautista (Tula); Mari Loli Cobo (Tulita); Carlos Estrada (Ramiro); Carlos Sánchez Jiménez (Ramirín)
Running Time:	109 minutes
Release Date:	2 September 1964 (Madrid)

La ciudad no es para mí (*The City's Not For Me*, 1965)

Director:	Pedro Lazaga
Producer:	Pedro Masó
Production Company:	Pedro Masó P.C.
Scriptwriters:	Vicente Coello; Pedro Masó
Director of Photography:	Juan Mariné
Music:	Antón García Abril; 'Los Shakers' (songs)
Décor:	Antonio Simont
Editor:	Alfonso Santacana
Principal Actors:	Doris Coll (Luchy/Luciana); Eduardo Fajardo (Agustín 'Gusti'); Alfredo Landa (Jerónimo); Paco Martínez Soria (Tío Agustín); Gracita Morales (Filomena)
Running Time:	96 minutes
Release Date:	14 March 1966 (Madrid)

Nueve cartas a Berta (*Nine Letters to Berta* 1965)

Director:	Basilio Martín Patino
Producer:	Ramiro Bermúdez de Castro
Production Companies:	Eco Films; Transcontinental Films Española
Scriptwriter:	Basilio Martín Patino
Director of Photography:	Luis Enrique Torán
Music:	Carmelo A. Bernaola
Décor:	Pablo Gago
Editor:	Pedro del Rey
Principal Actors:	Elsa Baeza (la novia); Emilio Gutiérrez Caba (Lorenzo); Mari Carrillo (mother); Antonio Casas (father); Yelena Samarina (Trini); Iván Tubau (Jacques)
Running Time:	95 minutes
Release Dates:	27 February 1967 (Madrid); 21 April 1967 (Barcelona)

La caza (The Hunt, 1965)

Director:	Carlos Saura
Producer:	Elías Querejeta
Production Company:	Elías Querejeta P.C.
Scriptwriters:	Angelino Fons; Carlos Saura
Director of Photography:	Luis Cuadrado
Music:	Luis de Pablo
Décor:	Carlos Ochoa
Editor:	Pablo del Amo
Principal Actors:	Emilio Gutiérrez Caba (Enrique); Alfredo Mayo (Paco); Ismael Merlo (José); José María Prada (Luis); Fernando Sánchez Pollack (Juan)
Running Time:	83 minutes
Release Date:	28 November 1966 (Madrid)

Bibliography

Aguilar, C. and J. Genover (1996), *Las estrellas de nuestro cine*, Madrid: Alianza.

Alberich, F. (2002), *Antonio Drove: la razón del sueño*, Madrid: 32 Festival de Cine de Alcalá de Henares; Comunidad de Madrid; Ayuntamiento de Alcalá de Henares; Fundación Colegio del Rey.

Álvarez Junco, J. (1995), 'Rural and Urban Popular Cultures', in Graham and Labanyi (eds) (1995b), pp. 82–90.

Amo, Á. del (1968), 'A partir de estas nueve cartas', prefatory essay to script, Martín Patino (1968), pp. 13–28.

—— (1975), *Comedia cinematográfica española*, Madrid: Cuadernos para el diálogo.

Amorós, C. (1986), 'Algunos aspectos de la evolución ideológica del feminismo en España', in Borreguero et al. (1986), pp. 41–54.

Angulo, J. (2003a), 'Antxón Eceiza: el cine de la raigambre', in Heredero and Monterde (eds) (2003), pp. 271–85.

—— (2003b), 'Los antecedentes (1951–1962): el cine español de los años cincuenta', in Heredero and Monterde (2003), pp. 29–52.

Arocena, C. (2003), '*El próximo otoño* (Antxón Eceiza, 1963): sentimientos y realismo crítico', in Heredero and Monterde (eds) (2003), pp. 393–6.

Aumont, J. (1997), *The Image*, trans. C. Pajackowska, London: British Film Institute.

Barbachano, C. J. (1966), '*El rostro del asesino*, *La ciudad no es para mí*, *Un vampiro para dos*, de Pedro Lazaga', *Film Ideal*, 194, 430.

Bellido López, A., in collaboration with J. Arranz Parra, A. Bellido Ramos and P. Núñez Sabín (1996), *Basilio Martín Patino: un soplo de libertad*, Valencia: Filmoteca Generalitat Valenciana; Generalitat Valenciana, Consellería de Cultura, Educació i Ciència.

Bellosillo, P. (1986), 'La mujer española dentro de la Iglesia', in Borreguero et al. (eds) (1986), pp. 109–26.

Benayoun, R. (1968), 'The King is Naked', in Graham (ed.) (1968), pp. 157–80.

Besas, P. (1985), *Behind the Spanish Lens: Spanish Cinema under Fascism and Democracy*, Denver, CO: Arden.

—— (1997), 'The Financial Structure of Spanish Cinema', in Kinder (ed.) (1997a), pp. 241–59.

Bilbatúa, M. (1966), '*Nueve cartas a Berta*', *Nuestro Cine*, 52, 6–7.

Bilbatúa, M., J. L. Egea, C. Rodríguez, A. del Amo and J. Royo, (1966), 'El operador: Luis Cuadrado', interview with L. Cuadrado, *Nuestro Cine*, 51, 8–10.

Bilbatúa, M. and C. Rodríguez Sanz (1966), 'Conversación con Basilio Martín Patino', interview with B. Martín Patino, *Nuestro Cine*, 52, 8–21.

Borreguero, C., E. Catena, C. de la Gandara and M. Salas (eds) (1986), *La mujer española: de la transición a la modernidad (1960–1980)*, Madrid: Tecnos.

Bourdieu, P. (1999), *Distinction: A Social Critique of the Judgement of Taste*, trans. R. Nice, London: Routledge.

Braudy, L. and M. Cohen (eds) (1999), *Film Theory and Criticism: Introductory Readings*, Oxford: Oxford University Press.

Bronfen, E. (1993), *Over her Dead Body: Death, Femininity and the Aesthetic*, Manchester: Manchester University Press.

Brooksbank Jones, A. (1997), *Women in Contemporary Spain*, Manchester: Manchester University Press.

Buceta, R., 1964, '*La tía Tula*', *Film Ideal*, 148, 480–1.

Butler, J. (1993), *Bodies that Matter: On the Discursive Limits of 'Sex'*, New York: Routledge.

Camus, M. and D. Sueiro (1963), *Los farsantes*, script, unpublished typed copy held at the Biblioteca Nacional, Spain.

Caparrós Lera, J. M. (1983), *El cine español bajo el régimen de Franco*, Barcelona: Publicacions i edicions de la Universitat de Barcelona.

Carnero, G. (1979), *Ensayo de una teoría de la visión (Poesía 1966–1977)*, Pamplona: Peralta.

Castillejo, J. (1998), *Las películas de Aurora Bautista*, Valencia: Fundació municipal de cine.

Castro, A. (1974), *El cine español en el banquillo*, Valencia: Fernando Torres.

—— (2003), 'Interview: Carlos Saura', trans. L. M. Willem, in Willem (ed.) (2003), pp. 115–43.

Castro de Paz, J. L. (2003), '*Nueve cartas a Berta* (Basilio Martín Patino, 1965): sin remedios, sin facturas . . .', in Heredero and Monterde (eds) (2003), pp. 419–22.

Cine-Asesor (1962), '*La gran familia*', n. p.

—— (1964), '*La tía Tula*', n. p.

—— (1966), '*La ciudad no es para mí*', n. p.

Clouzot, C. (1966), 'The Young Turks of Spain', *Sight and Sound*, 35, 2, pp. 68–9, 103.

Cobos, J. and G. Sebastián de Erice (1963), 'El director y su película: Mario Camus', *Film Ideal*, 134, 745–7.

Coca Hernando, R. (1998), 'Towards a New Image of Women under Franco: The Role of Sección Femenina', *International Journal of Iberian Studies*, 11, 5–13.

Colorado, L. F. (2003), 'Julio Diamante: las huellas del compromiso', interview with J. Diamante, in Heredero and Monterde (eds) (2003), pp. 261–8.

Company, J. M. (2003), '*La tía Tula* (Miguel Picazo, 1964): un alma llena de cuerpo', in Heredero and Monterde (eds) (2003), pp. 407–10.

Cooper, N. (1976), 'The Church: From Crusade to Christianity', in Preston (ed.) (1976), pp. 48–81.

'¿Crisis en el cine español?' (1967), includes interview with J. M. Lamet, *Nuestro Cine*, 62, 9–20.

Crisp, C. (1993), *The Classic French Cinema, 1930–1960*, Bloomington and Indianapolis: Indiana University Press.

Deleuze, G. (1994), *Cinema 2: The Time-Image*, trans. H. Tomlinson and R. Galeta, London: Athlone.

—— (1997), *Cinema 1: The Movement-Image*, trans. H. Tomlinson and B. Habberjam, London: Athlone.

Delgado, M. (1999), 'Saura's *Los golfos* (1959; Released 1962): Heralding a New Cinema for the 1960s', in Evans (ed.) (1999), pp. 38–54.

D'Lugo, M. (1991), *The Films of Carlos Saura: The Practice of Seeing*, Princeton, NJ: Princeton University Press.

—— (1997), *Guide to the Cinema of Spain*, Westford, CT: Greenwood Press.

Dyer, R. and G. Vincendeau (eds) (1992), *Popular European Cinema*, London: Routledge.

Edwards, G. (1995), *Indecent Exposures: Buñuel, Saura, Erice and Almodóvar*, London: Marion Boyars.

Egea, J. L. (1963), '*La gran familia*', *Nuestro Cine*, 16, 59.

Erice, V. (1962), 'Festival internacional de Cannes, 15', *Nuestro Cine*, 11, 15–39.

Evans, P. W. (1995), 'Cifesa: Cinema and Authoritarian Aesthetics', in Graham and Labanyi (eds) (1995b), 215–22.

—— (ed.) (1999), *Spanish Cinema: The Auteurist Tradition*, Oxford: Oxford University Press.

—— (2000), 'Cheaper by the Dozen: *La gran familia*, Francoism and Spanish Family Comedy', in Holmes and Smith (eds) (2000), 77–88.

Ezcurra, J., J. M. Forqué, J. M. García Escudero, L. Martín and J. Monleón (1961), 'Cine y realidad española', *Nuestro Cine*, 3, 15–19, 63.

Faulkner, S. (2004), *Literary Adaptations in Spanish Cinema*, London: Támesis-Boydell & Brewer.

—— (2006), 'Nostalgia and the Middlebrow: Spanish Ruralist Cinema and Mario Camus's *The Holy Innocents* (*Los santos inocentes*, 1984)', in Fowler and Helfield (eds) (2006).

Fernández Santos, A. (1967), 'Encuesta sobre el Nuevo Cine Español', *Nuestro Cine*, 60, 16–21.

'Festival de San Sebastián' (1967), *Cahiers du cinéma*, 193, 12–13.

Fontenla, C. S. (1966a), *Cine español en la encrucijada*, Madrid: Editorial Ciencia Nueva.

—— (1966b), '*La busca* de Angelino Fons', *Nuestro Cine*, 55, 6–9.

—— (1966c), 'Tiempo de violencia: *La caza* de Carlos Saura', *Nuestro Cine*, 51, 12–17.

—— (1986), '1962–1967', in Torres (ed.) (1986), pp. 172–99.

Fowler, C. and G. Helfield (eds) (forthcoming), *Representing the Rural in the Cinema*, Detroit: Wayne State University Press.

Francia, I. (2002), *Salamanca de cine*, Salamanca: Caja Duero; Salamanca 2002, Ciudad Europea de la Cultura.

Frugone, J. C. (1984), *Mario Camus: oficio de gente humilde*, Valladolid: Semana de Cine de Valladolid.

Galán, D. (1983), '*La ciudad no es para mí*, reivindicación del subdesarrollo', *El País*, 7 May 1983.

—— (2003), '*El buen amor* (Francisco Regueiro, 1963): Destellos de modernidad', in Heredero and Monterde (eds) (2003), pp. 385–7.

—— (2004), 'Un autor desperdiciado' in Iznaola Gómez (ed.) (2004b), pp. 113–14.

García de Dueñas, J. (2003), 'A la deriva por el Cabo de Buena Esperanza: travesías por unos cursos de la EOC', in Heredero and Monterde (eds) (2003), pp. 79–102.

García Escudero, J. M. (1962), *Cine español*, Madrid: Rialp.

—— (1967), *Una política para el cine español*, Madrid: Editora Nacional.

—— (1970), *Vamos a hablar de cine*, Madrid: Salvat; Alianza.

—— (1978), *La primera apertura: diario de un director general*, Barcelona: Planeta.

—— (1995), 'Las políticas del cine español', in Pérez Millán (ed.) (1995), pp. 13–23.

García Fernández, E. C. (1985), *Historia ilustrada del cine español*, Madrid: Planeta.

García Hortelano, J. (1961), 'Alrededor del realismo', *Nuestro Cine*, 1, 6–7.

Gavilán Sánchez, J. A. and M. Lamarca Rosales (2002), *Conversaciones con cineastas españoles*, Córdoba: Universidad de Córdoba.

Gies, D. T. (ed.) (2002), *Modern Spanish Culture*, Cambridge: Cambridge University Press.

Gómez, A. (2002), 'La representación de la mujer en el cine español de los años 40 y 50: del cine bélico al neorrealismo', *Bulletin of Spanish Studies*, 79, 575–89.

Gómez, C. (2003), 'Carlos Saura: la pasión de explorar nuevos caminos', in Heredero and Monterde (eds) (2003), pp. 354–67.

Gómez Mesa, L. (1966), 'Crónica breve de un festival: Berlin 66', *Film Ideal*, 193, 393–401.

Gómez-Sierra, E. (2004), ' "Palaces of Seeds": From an Experience of Local Cinemas in Post-War Madrid to a Suggested Approach to Film Audiences', in Lázaro Reboll and Willis (eds) (2004b), pp. 92–112.

Gortari, C. (1964), '*La tía Tula* por Miguel Picazo', *Film Ideal*, 154, 691–2.

Gracia Pascual, J. (2002), *Paco Martínez Soria: actor con mayúsculas*, Tarazona: Excelentísimo Ayuntamiento de Tarazona.

Graham, H. (1995a), 'Gender and the State: Women in the 1940s', Graham and Labanyi (eds) (1995b), pp. 182–95.

—— (1995b), 'Popular Culture in the "Years of Hunger" ', in Graham and Labanyi (eds) (1995b), pp. 237–45.

Graham, H. and J. Labanyi (1995a), 'Culture and Modernity: The Case of Spain', in Graham and Labanyi (eds) (1995b), pp. 1–19.

—— (eds) (1995b), *Spanish Cultural Studies: An Introduction. The Struggle for Modernity*, Oxford: Oxford University Press.

Graham, H. and A. Sánchez (1995), 'The Politics of 1992', in Graham and Labanyi (eds) (1995b), pp. 406–18.

Graham, P. (ed.) (1968), *The New Wave. Critical Landmarks*, London: Secker & Warburg; British Film Institute.

Grugel, J. and T. Rees (1997), *Franco's Spain*, London: Arnold.

Gubern, R. (1963), '¿Qué es el realismo cinematográfico?', *Nuestro Cine*, 19, 4–13.

—— (1981), *La censura: función política y ordenamiento jurídico bajo el franquismo (1936–1975)*, Barcelona: Ediciones península.

—— (1997), '*La tía Tula*', in Pérez Perucha (ed.) (1997), pp. 561–3.

—— (ed.) (2000), *Un siglo de cine español*, Madrid: Academia de las Artes y las Ciencias Cinematográficas de España.

Gubern, R., J. E. Monterde, J. Pérez Perucha, E. Riambau and C. Torreiro (1995), *Historia del cine español*, Madrid: Cátedra.

Hansen, H. (2001), 'Painted Women: Framing Portraits in *Film Noir* and the Gothic Women's Film in the 1940s', PhD Diss., Southampton University.

Haro Tecglen, E. (2004), 'Viejo cine español', *El País*, 13 January 2004, www.elpais.es, consulted on 13 February 2005.

Heredero, C. F. (1993), *Las huellas del tiempo: cine español 1951–1961*, Valencia: Filmoteca de la Generalitat Valenciana.

—— (ed.) (2002), *La imprenta dinámica: literatura española en el cine español*, Madrid: Academia de las Artes y las Ciencias Cinematográficas de España.

—— (2003), 'En la estela de la modernidad: entre el Neorrealismo y la *Nouvelle Vague*', in Heredero and Monterde (eds) (2003), pp. 137–62.

Heredero, C. F. and J. E. Monterde (eds) (2003), *Los 'nuevos cines' en España: ilusiones y desencantos de los años sesenta*, Valencia: Festival Internacional de Cine de Gijón; Institut Valencià de Cinematografía Ricardo Muñoz Suay; Centro Galego de Artes da Imaxe; Junta de Andalucía, Consejería de Cultura; Filmoteca de Andalucía; Filmoteca Española.

Hernán, J. M., M. López Yubero, M. Picazo and L. Sánchez Enciso (1964), 'La tía Tula: Adaptación de la novela de Don Miguel de Unamuno', script, *Nuestro Cine*, 25, 30–47 and *Nuestro Cine*, 26, 43–57.

Hernández, J. (2003), 'Miguel Picazo: el reverso de la España idealizada', interview with M. Picazo, in Heredero and Monterde (eds) (2003), pp. 318–31.

Hernández Ruiz, J. (1997), '*La gran familia*', in Pérez Perucha (ed.) (1997), pp. 515–17.

Higginbotham, V. (1988), *Spanish Film under Franco*, Austin, TX: University of Texas Press.

Holmes, D. and A. Smith (eds) (2000), *100 Years of European Cinema: Entertainment or Ideology?*, Manchester: Manchester University Press.

Hooper, J. (1995), *The New Spaniards*, London: Penguin.

Hopewell, J. (1986), *Out of the Past: Spanish Cinema after Franco*, London: British Film Institute.

'Interview with Patino' (1961), *Film Ideal*, 85, 14–15.

Iznaola Gómez, E. (2004a), 'Entrevista', interview with M. Picazo, in Iznaola Gómez (ed.) (2004b), pp. 19–58.

—— (ed.) (2004b), *Miguel Picazo: un cineasta jiennense*, Jaen: Diputación Provincial de Jaen.

Jordan, B. (1990), *Writing and Politics in Franco's Spain*, London: Routledge.

—— (1995), 'The Emergence of a Dissident Intelligentsia' in Graham and Labanyi (eds) (1995b), pp. 245–55.

Julián, Ó. de (2002) *'De Salamanca a ninguna parte'. Diálogos sobre el Nuevo Cine Español*, Salamanca: Junta de Castilla y León, Consejería de Educación y Cultura.

Kaes, A. (1997), 'The New German Cinema', in Nowell-Smith (ed.) (1997b), pp. 614–27.

Kinder, M. (1993), *Blood Cinema: The Reconstruction of National Identity in Spain*, Berkeley, CA: University of California Press.

—— (ed.) (1997a), *Refiguring Spain: Cinema / Media / Representation*, Durham, NC: Duke University Press.

—— (1997b), 'Spain after Franco', in Nowell-Smith (ed.) (1997b), 596–603.

Labanyi, J. (1989), *Myth and History in the Contemporary Spanish Novel*, Cambridge: Cambridge University Press.

—— (1995a), 'Literary Experiment and Diversification', in Graham and Labanyi (eds) (1995b), pp. 295–9.

—— (1995b), 'Masculinity and the Family in Crisis: Reading Unamuno through *Film Noir* (Serrano de Osma's 1946 Adaptation of *Abel Sánchez*)', *Romance Studies*, 26, 7–21.

—— (1997), 'Race, Gender and Disavowal in Spanish Cinema of the Early Franco Period: The Missionary Film and the Folkloric Musical', *Screen*, 38, 215–31.

—— (1999), 'Gramsci and Spanish Cultural Studies', *Paragraph*, 22, 1, 95–113.

—— (2000), 'Feminizing the Nation: Women, Subordination and Subversion in Post-Civil War Spanish Cinema', in Sieglohr (ed.) (2000), 163–84.

Lara, F. (2004), '¿Por qué?', in Iznaola Gómez (ed.) (2004b), 173–5.

Larraz, E. (2003), 'L'esthétique néoréaliste dans le cinéma espagnol des années soixante: *Los farsantes* (1963) de Mario Camus', in Larraz and Lavaud-Fage (eds) (2003), 247–62. Web version consulted at http://www.u-bourgogne.fr/index/front_office/index_co.php?site_id=106&rid=629&cidori=977&cid=11 10&uid=79 on 5 April 2005. Web pagination cited in text.

Larraz, E. and E. Lavaud-Fage (eds) (2003), *Esthétique et idéologie au XXième siècle*, Dijon: Université de Bourgogne.

Lázaro Reboll, A. and A. Willis (2004a), 'Introduction: Film Studies, Spanish Cinema and Questions of the Popular', in Lázaro Reboll and Willis (eds) (2004b), pp. 1–23.

—— (eds) (2004b), *Spanish Popular Cinema*, Manchester: Manchester University Press.

Llinàs, F. (ed.) (1989a), *Directores de fotografía del cine español*, Madrid: Filmoteca Española.

—— (1989b), 'Entrevista con Juan Julio Baena', interview with J. J. Baena, in Llinàs (ed.) (1989a), pp. 212–27.

Llinàs F. and M. Marías (1969), '*Del amor y otras soledades* de Basilio Martín Patino: en la encrucijada del "Nuevo Cine Español" ', *Nuestro Cine*, 90, 64–9.

Longhurst, C. A. (1996), 'Introducción', in Unamuno (1996), pp. 11–58.

López, H. (2005), 'Exile, Cinema, Fantasy: Imagining the Democratic Nation', *Journal of Spanish Cultural Studies*, 6, 1, 79–99.

Lozano, F. A. (1965), *La ciudad no es para mí*, Madrid: Escelicer.

Lyon, J. (1983), *The Theatre of Valle-Inclán*, Cambridge: Cambridge University Press.

Machado, A. (1999), *Poesías completas: Soledades / Galerías / Campos de Castilla*, ed. M. Alvar, Madrid: Espasa Calpe.

Maqua, J. and M. Villegas (1969), 'Conversación con Basilio M. Patino', interview with B. Martín Patino, *Film Ideal*, 217–218–219, 331–48.

Marinero, M. (1967), '*La caza* de Carlos Saura', *Film Ideal*, 205–206–207, 145–7.

Marsh, S. (2002), 'Comedy and the Weakening of the State: An Ideological Approach to Spanish Popular Cinema 1942–1964', PhD Diss., London University.

—— (2003), 'The *Pueblo* Travestied in Fernán Gómez's *El extraño viaje* (1964)', *Hispanic Research Journal*, 4, 2, 133–49.

—— (2004), 'Populism, the National-Politic and the Politics of Luis García Berlanga', in Lázaro Reboll and Willis (eds) (2004b), pp. 113–28.

Martialay, F. and R. Buceta (1964), 'Miguel Picazo dice', interview with M. Picazo, *Film Ideal*, 148, 482–7.

Martialay, F. and M. Marinero (1966), 'Palabras con Basilio Martín Patino', interview with B. Martín Patino, *Film Ideal*, 193, 373–81.

Martin-Márquez, S. (1999), *Feminist Discourse in Spanish Cinema: Sight Unseen*, Oxford: Oxford University Press.

Martín Patino, B. (1964), 'Hacia un nuevo concepto de montaje', *Film Ideal*, 152, 621–9.

—— (1968), *Nueve cartas a Berta*, script, Madrid: Ciencia Nueva.

Martín-Santos, L. (1995), *Tiempo de silencio*, Barcelona: Seix Barral.

Martínez Aguinagalde, F. (1989), *Cine y literatura en Mario Camus*, Bilbao: Universidad del País Vasco.

Martínez León, J. (1966), '*Nueve cartas a Berta*, de Basilio Martín Patino', *Film Ideal*, 192, 343–4.

Martínez Tomás, A. (1967), 'El pobre cine "joven" ', reprinted in *Nuestro Cine*, 60, 6.

Méndez-Leite, Fernando (1969), review of *Esa mujer* by M. Camus, *Film Ideal*, 213, 99–103.

'Miguel Picazo, después de *La tía Tula*', interview with M. Picazo (1964), *Nuestro Cine*, 31, 42–8.

Millar, S. (1975), '*La caza (The Hunt)*', *Monthly Film Bulletin*, 42, 502, 235–6.

Molina-Foix, V. (1977), *New Cinema in Spain*, London: British Film Institute.

—— (2003), 'Nuevo cine español, joven cine español', in Heredero and Monterde (eds) (2003), pp. 474–7.

Monegal, A. (1998), 'Images of War: Hunting the Metaphor', in Talens and Zunzunegui (eds) (1998), pp. 203–15.

Monleón, J. (1966), 'El nuevo cine español en Venecia: *La busca*', *Nuestro Cine*, 56, 8–9.

—— (1967), '*La caza* de Carlos Saura', *Nuestro Cine*, 58, 61–3.

Monleón, J. and J. L. Egea (1965), 'Entrevista con Mario Camus', interview with M. Camus, *Nuestro Cine*, 39, 9–19.

Monterde, J. E. (1993), *Veinte años de cine español: un cine bajo la paradoja. 1973–1992*, Barcelona: Paidós.

—— (1997), '*Nueve cartas a Berta*', in Pérez Perucha (ed.) (1997), pp. 610–13.

—— (2003), 'La recepción del "nuevo cine" ', in Heredero and Monterde (eds) (2003), pp. 103–19.

Monterde, J. E. and E. Riambau (eds) (1995), *Historia general de cine. Vol XI: nuevos cines (años 60)*, Madrid: Cátedra.

Mulvey, L. (1999), 'Visual Pleasure and Narrative Cinema', in Braudy and Cohen (eds) (1999), pp. 833–44.

Muñoz, D. (2004), 'El cine que se hace hoy en España no me gusta', interview with C. Saura, *La Vanguardia*, 3 September 2004, 31.

Neruda, P. (1996), *Veinte poemas de amor y una canción desesperada*, Barcelona: Seix Barral.

Nowell-Smith, G. (1997a), 'Art Cinema', in Nowell-Smith (ed.) (1997b), pp. 567–75.

—— (ed.) (1997b), *The Oxford History of World Cinema: The Definitive History of Cinema Worldwide*, Oxford: Oxford University Press.

'Nuevo Cine Español a la vista' (1960), Editorial, *Film Ideal*, 61, 3.

Núñez, A. (1964), 'Unamuno al cine (Miguel Picazo y *La tía Tula*)', interview with M. Picazo and L. Sánchez Enciso, *Ínsula*, 216–17, 7.

Oms, M. (1981), *Carlos Saura*, Paris: Edilio.

Palá, J. M. (1966), 'Pedro Lazaga', *Film Ideal*, 169, 363.

Palá, J. M. and M. Villegas (1967), 'Nuevo Cine Español visto desde fuera', *Film Ideal*, 205–206–207, 65–80.

Paolini G. and C. J. Paolini (eds) (1999), *La Chispa 99: Selected Proceedings*, New Orleans: Louisiana Conference on Hispanic Languages and Literatures, Tulane University.

Pavlović, T. (2003), *Despotic Bodies and Transgressive Bodies: Spanish Culture from Francisco Franco to Jesús Franco*, Albany, NY: State University of New York Press.

Payne, S. G. (1984), *Spanish Catholicism: An Historical Overview*, Madison, WI: University of Wisconsin Press.

—— (1987), *The Franco Regime 1936–1975*, Madison, WI: University of Wisconsin Press.

Pérez Merinero, C. and D. Pérez Merinero (1973), *Cine español: algunos materiales por derribo*, Madrid: Cuadernos para el diálogo.

Pérez Millán, J. A. (ed.) (1995), *El cine español, desde Salamanca (1955/1995)*, Salamanca: Junta de Castilla y León.

—— (2002), *La memoria de los sentimientos: Basilio Martín Patino y su obra audiovisual*, Valladolid: 47 Semana Internacional de Cine.

Pérez Perucha, J. (ed.) (1997), *Antología crítica del cine español 1906–1995: flor en la sombra*, Madrid: Cátedra; Filmoteca Española.

Pérez Rubio, P. (1997), '*La caza*', in Pérez Perucha (ed.) (1997), pp. 607–9.

Perriam, C. (ed.) (1999), *Paragraph*, 22, 1.

—— (2003), *Stars and Masculinities in Spanish Cinema*, Oxford: Oxford University Press.

Pozo Arenas, S. (1984), *La industria del cine en España: legislación y aspectos económicos (1986–1970)*, Barcelona: Edicions Universitat de Barcelona.

Preston, P. (ed.) (1976), *Spain in Crisis: The Evolution and Decline of the Franco Régime*, Hassocks: Harvester.

—— (1993), *Franco: A Biography*, London: Fontana-HarperCollins.

—— (1996), *A Concise History of the Spanish Civil War*, London: Fontana-HarperCollins.

Redondo, R. G. (1964), 'Cine joven español, parada y fonda', *Film Ideal*, 154, 683–5.

'Review of *La caza*' (1983), copy of review originally published in *Variety*, 6 July 1966, *Variety Film Reviews 1964–1967*, vol. 11, New York: Garland, n. p.

'Review of *La tía Tula*' (1983), copy of review originally published in *Variety*, 28 April 1965, *Variety Film Reviews 1964–1967*, vol. 11, New York: Garland, n. p.

'Review of *Nueve cartas a Berta*' (1967), copy of review originally published in *Pueblo* n. d., *Nuestro Cine*, 60, 7.

'Review of *Nueve cartas a Berta*' (1983), copy of review originally published in *Variety*, 2 August 1965, *Variety Film Reviews 1964–1967*, vol. 11, New York: Garland, n. p.

Riambau, E. (1995), 'Un modelo industrial ortopédico' in Monterde and Riambau (eds) (1995), pp. 69–94.

Riambau, E. and C. Torreiro (1999), *La Escuela de Barcelona: el cine de la 'gauche divine'*, Barcelona: Anagrama.

Richardson, N. (2000), ' "*Paleto* Cinema" and the Triumph of Consumer Culture in Spain: The Case of Pedro Lazaga's *La ciudad no es para mí*', *Arizona Journal of Hispanic Cultural Studies*, 4, 61–75.

—— (2002), *Postmodern Paletos: Immigration, Democracy, and Globalization in Spanish Narrative and Film, 1950–2000*, Lewisburg, PA: Bucknell University Press.

Río Carratalá, J. A. (1997), *Lo sainetesco en el cine español*, Alicante: Universidad de Alicante.

Riquer i Permanyer, B. de (1995), 'Social and Economic Change in a Climate of Political Immobilism', in Graham and Labanyi (eds) (1995b), pp. 259–71.

Rodero, J. A. (1981), *Aquel 'Nuevo Cine Español' de los 60: espíritu, estética, obra y generación de un movimiento*, Valladolid: 26 Semana Internacional de Cine de Valladolid.

Rodríguez Merchán, E. (2003), '*Young Sánchez* (Mario Camus, 1963): la fisicidad de los sentidos', in Heredero and Monterde (eds) (2003), pp. 397–401.

San Miguel, S. (1962a), 'El cine español y su nueva etapa', *Nuestro Cine*, 15, 2–7.

—— (1962b), 'Posibilidades de un realismo cinematográfico español', *Nuestro Cine*, 12, 1–5.

'San Sebastián' (1964), *Cahiers du cinéma*, 160, 65.

Sánchez Biosca, V. (1989), 'Fotografía y puesta en escena en el film español de los años 1940–50', in Llinàs (ed.) (1989a), pp. 57–91.

Sánchez Ferlosio, R. (1967), *El Jarama*, Barcelona: Ediciones Destino.

Sánchez Noriega, J. L. (1998), *Mario Camus*, Madrid: Cátedra.

—— (2003), 'Mario Camus: la generación de la conversación', in Heredero and Monterde (eds) (2003), pp. 249–59.

Sánchez Vidal, A. (1988), *El cine de Carlos Saura*, Zaragoza: Caja de Ahorros de la Inmaculada.

Sartre, J.-P. (1981), *Being and Nothingness: An Essay on Phenomenological Ontology*, trans. H. E. Barnes, London: Methuen.

Saura, C. (2003), 'Para una autocrítica', in Heredero and Monterde (eds) (2003), pp. 457–8.

—— (2004), 'Imágenes que permanecen', in Iznaola Gómez (ed.) (2004b), pp. 203–5.

Saura, C. and A. Fons (1965), *La caza de conejo*, script, unpublished typed copy held in the Biblioteca Nacional, Spain.

Schubert, A. (1990), *A Social History of Modern Spain*, London: Unwin Hyman.

Schwartz, R. (1976), *Spain's New Wave Novelists 1950–1974*, Metuchen: Scarecrow.

—— (1986), *Spanish Film Directors*, Metuchen: Scarecrow.

—— (1991), *The Great Spanish Films: 1950–1990*, Metuchen: Scarecrow.

Sieburth, S. (1994), *Inventing High and Low: Literature, Mass Culture and Uneven Modernity in Spain*, Durham, NC: Duke University Press.

—— (2002), 'What Does It Mean to Study Modern Spanish Culture?', in Gies (ed.) (2002), pp. 11–20.

Sieglohr, U. (ed.) (2000), *Heroines without Heroes: Reconstructing Female and National Identities in European Cinema 1945–51*, London: Cassell.

Smith, P. J. (1994), *Desire Unlimited: The Cinema of Pedro of Almodóvar*, London: Verso.

—— (1998), 'Homosexuality, Regionalism, and Mass Culture: Eloy de la Iglesia's Cinema of Transition', in Talens and Zunzunegui (eds) (1998), pp. 216–51.

Stone, R. (2002), *Spanish Cinema*, Harlow: Longman.

—— (2004), 'Animals were Harmed during the Making of this Film: A Cruel Reality in Hispanic Cinema', *Studies in Hispanic Cinemas*, 1, 2, 75–84.

Sueiro, D. (1988), *Cuentos completos*, Madrid: Alianza.

Talens, J. and S. Zunzunegui (eds) (1998), *Modes of Representation in Spanish Cinema*, Minneapolis: Minneapolis University Press.

Torán, L. E. (1989), 'Nuevo Cine Español: tiempo de renovación', in Llinàs (ed.) (1989a), pp. 93–117.

Torreiro, C. (1995a), 'El estado asistencial', in Monterde and Riambau (eds) (1995), pp. 41–68.

—— (1995b), '¿Una dictadura liberal? (1962–1969)', in Gubern et al. (1995), pp. 295–340.

—— (2000), 'Entre la esperanza y el fracaso: nuevo(s) cine(s) en la España de los 60', in Gubern (ed.) (2000), pp. 151–61.

—— 2003, 'Basilio Martín Patino: contra los tópicos', interview with B. Martín Patino, in Heredero and Monterde (eds) (2003), pp. 303–17.

Torres, A. M. (1973), Cine español, años sesenta, Barcelona: Anagrama.

—— (1992), Conversaciones con Manuel Gutiérrez Aragón, Madrid: Fundamentos.

—— (1997), El cine español en 119 películas, Madrid: Alianza editorial.

—— (ed.) (1986), Spanish Cinema 1896–1983, Madrid: Editora Nacional.

Torres, A. M. and V. Molina-Foix (2003), 'From Black Spain to Silver Bears: Part One', interview with C. Saura, trans. L. M. Willem, in Willem (ed.) (2003), pp. 3–16.

Totaro, D. 1999, 'Gilles Deleuze's Bergsonian Film Project', www.horschamp.qc. ca/9903/offscreen_essays/deleuze1.html and www.horschamp.qc.ca/9903/ offscreen_essays/deleuze2.html. Consulted on 20 August 2004.

Tranche, R. R. and V. Sánchez Biosca (2002), NO-DO: el tiempo y la memoria, Madrid: Cátedra; Filmoteca Española.

Triana-Toribio, N. (2000), 'Ana Mariscal: Franco's Disavowed Star', in Sieglohr (ed.) (2000), pp. 185–95.

—— (2003), Spanish National Cinema, London: Routledge.

Unamuno, M. de (1996), La tía Tula, ed. C. A. Longhurst, Madrid: Cátedra.

Valis, N. (2002), The Culture of Cursilería: Bad Taste, Kitsch and Class in Modern Spain, Durham, NC: Duke University Press.

Vázquez Montalbán, M. (2003), Crónica sentimental de España, Barcelona: Random House.

Vernon, K. (2002), 'Culture and Cinema to 1975', in Gies (ed.) (2002), pp. 248–66.

Vilarós, T. (1998), El mono del desencanto: una crítica cultural de la transición española (1973–1993), Madrid: Siglo veintiuno.

Villegas López, M. (1967), Nuevo cine español, San Sebastián: 25 Festival Internacional del Cine.

—— (1991), Aquel llamado Nuevo Cine Español: obras completas de Manuel Villegas López, Madrid: Ediciones JC.

Walters, D. G. (2002), The Cambridge Introduction to Spanish Poetry, Cambridge: Cambridge University Press.

Willem, L. M. (ed.) (2003), Carlos Saura: Interviews, Mississippi: University Press of Mississippi.

Wilson, D. (1966), 'San Sebastián', Sight and Sound, 34, 4, 172–3.

Wood, G. (1999), 'La inspiración prehistórica de La caza de Carlos Saura', in Paolini and Paolini (eds) (1999), pp. 359–73.

—— (2000), 'Stásis y peste en *La caza* de Carlos Saura', *Cine-Lit*, 4, 155–64.

Zatlin, P. (2002), 'Theater and Culture, 1936–1996', in Gies (ed.) (2002), pp. 222–36.

Zeul, M. (2003), 'Continuity, Rupture, Remembering: The Spanish Cinema during Franco's Time', interview with C. Saura, trans. V. Chamberlin, in Willem (ed.) (2003), pp. 103–14.

Zuzunegui, S. (2002a), 'Críticos al borde de un ataque de nervios: "realismo" y "realismos" en el cine español', in Heredero (ed.) (2002), pp. 471–83.

—— (2002b), 'De cuerpo presente: en torno a las raíces literarias del "Nuevo Cine Español"', in Heredero (ed.) (2002), pp. 103–16.

—— (2003), '*La caza* (Carlos Saura, 1965): mirada distante, mirada lejana', in Heredero and Monterde (eds) (2003), pp. 415–18.

Index